AMERICANIZATION STUDIES

THIS IS A PAPERBOUND EDITION OF
VOLUME 3 OF THE AMERICANIZATION STUDIES,
A 10-VOLUME SET PUBLISHED AS NO. 125 IN THE
PATTERSON SMITH SERIES IN
CRIMINOLOGY, LAW ENFORCEMENT, AND SOCIAL PROBLEMS

A listing of publications in the SERIES *will be found at rear of volume*

OLD WORLD TRAITS TRANSPLANTED

AMERICANIZATION STUDIES
THE ACCULTURATION OF IMMIGRANT GROUPS
INTO AMERICAN SOCIETY

WILLIAM S. BERNARD, EDITOR

VOLUME 1
GENERAL INTRODUCTION BY WILLIAM S. BERNARD

SCHOOLING OF THE IMMIGRANT
BY FRANK V. THOMPSON
New Introduction by Clarence Senior

VOLUME 2
AMERICA VIA THE NEIGHBORHOOD
BY JOHN DANIELS
New Introduction by Florence G. Cassidy

VOLUME 3
OLD WORLD TRAITS TRANSPLANTED
BY WILLIAM I. THOMAS
New Introduction by Donald R. Young

VOLUME 4
A STAKE IN THE LAND
BY PETER A. SPEEK
New Introduction by Rabel J. Burdge & Everett M. Rogers

VOLUME 5
IMMIGRANT HEALTH AND THE COMMUNITY
BY MICHAEL M. DAVIS, JR.
New Introduction by Raymond E. O'Dowd

VOLUME 6
NEW HOMES FOR OLD
BY SOPHONISBA P. BRECKINRIDGE
New Introduction by William S. Bernard

VOLUME 7
THE IMMIGRANT PRESS AND ITS CONTROL
BY ROBERT E. PARK
New Introduction by Read Lewis

VOLUME 8
AMERICANS BY CHOICE
BY JOHN PALMER GAVIT
New Introduction by William S. Bernard

VOLUME 9
THE IMMIGRANT'S DAY IN COURT
BY KATE HOLLADAY CLAGHORN
New Introduction by Ann S. Petluck

VOLUME 10
ADJUSTING IMMIGRANT AND INDUSTRY
BY WILLIAM M. LEISERSON
New Introduction by Gerd Korman

OLD WORLD TRAITS
TRANSPLANTED

BY
WILLIAM ISAAC THOMAS
TOGETHER WITH
ROBERT E. PARK AND HERBERT A. MILLER

REPRINTED WITH INTRODUCTION BY
DONALD R. YOUNG
AND INDEX

MONTCLAIR, NEW JERSEY
PATTERSON SMITH

Copyright 1921 by Harper & Brothers
Republished 1971 by special arrangement with
The Carnegie Corporation by
Patterson Smith Publishing Corporation
Montclair, New Jersey 07042
New material copyright © 1971 by
Patterson Smith Publishing Corporation
First paperback edition 1975

INTERNATIONAL STANDARD BOOK NUMBER: 0-87585-905-4
LIBRARY OF CONGRESS CATALOG CARD NUMBER: 74-37237

INTRODUCTION TO THE REPUBLISHED EDITION

By Donald R. Young

Old World Traits Transplanted, when first published in 1921, carried only the names of Robert E. Park and Herbert A. Miller as authors. It was, however, immediately obvious, at least to sociological colleagues of the listed authors, that there must have been a third and easily identifiable major participant in its writing. Both Park and Miller were distinguished contributors to the scholarly literature on racial and ethnic problems and could have been expected by themselves to produce a volume on the assimilation of immigrants. Yet, the style of the book, its theoretical analysis, and the selection of illustrative immigrant material were not what could have been anticipated on the basis of the previous writings of either man. Rather, the book was just what would have been expected from a sociologist colleague and friend of theirs, William Isaac Thomas.

Not until 1951 was Thomas definitely and publicly given credit for being the main author of *Old World Traits Transplanted.* In that year Chapter IX was reprinted in *Social Behavior and Personality: Contributions of W. I. Thomas to Theory and Social Research,* edited by Edmund H. Volkart and published by the Social Science Research Council. Volkart, in his commentary on the reprinted chapter, quotes the following

INTRODUCTION TO THE REPUBLISHED EDITION

extract from a letter to E. W. Burgess by Allen T. Burns, Director of the Studies in Methods of Americanization supported by funds furnished by the Carnegie Corporation of New York:

> The volume, *Old World Traits Transplanted,* of the Americanization Studies was written primarily by W. I. Thomas though at the time it was considered by all concerned best to have it appear under the authorship of Park and Miller who also worked on the volume. I am very glad that Professor Thomas is to receive credit for his invaluable contribution. [P. 259]

A quotation from the "Biographical Note" in the Volkart volume ends any mystery about why the prime author was not listed as such:

> The association of W. I. Thomas with the Department of Sociology at the University of Chicago continued unbroken until 1918, shortly after he was arrested on a charge involving allegations of violation of the Mann Act and of an act forbidding false registration at hotels. Although the charge was thrown out of court, the extensive publicizing of the arrest, particularly in the Chicago press, resulted in the termination of his appointment at the University. [P. 323]

The obvious inference is that the sponsors of the Studies in Methods of Americanization were as sensitive as the University of Chicago concerning possible adverse reactions if Thomas's name were carried on the title page.[1]

The book here reprinted should be read, as should

---

[1] For a brief biography of Thomas which includes an account of the incident, see Morris Janowitz, *W. I. Thomas on Social Organization and Social Personality* (Chicago: The University of Chicago Press, 1966), pp. xiv ff.

INTRODUCTION TO THE REPUBLISHED EDITION

all the volumes in the series of which it is a part, with cognizance of the great pressures exerted on immigrants promptly to become "Americanized" during and right after World War I. The concept of Americanization then prevalent demanded the giving up of all "alien" values and patterns of behavior in favor of some undefined and undefinable "American way of life." This was to be accomplished, should immigrants be slow and reluctant to do so, by a variety of compulsions, such as limitation of public and private employment and other forms of discrimination. Those who held the opposing opinion that effective immigrant assimilation needed to be an entirely voluntary process, who realized that immigrant cultural traits were of essential value in the difficult period of adaptation to a new milieu, and who saw the advantages of some degree of cultural pluralism for the nation as well as for the immigrant, were widely regarded as impractical "do-gooders" if not as un-American troublemakers. *Old World Traits Transplanted* served as a powerful refutation of the then common demand for prompt and total extinction, by compulsion when necessary, of immigrant heritages from the country of birth.

The understanding of social change was the lifelong concern of Thomas and his collaborators, as it is of all social scientists. The thesis of their book is that such understanding requires detailed knowledge of the interrelationships of the social personalities of individuals and of the social organizations in which they participate. The former are treated as "attitudes"; the latter are viewed as "organized values." "The set of attitudes and values, which we call the immigrant's heritage, are the expression in ideas and action of his apperception mass. 'Heritages' differ because the races and nationalities concerned have developed different apperception masses; and they have developed different apperception masses because, owing to historical circumstances, they have defined the situation in different ways" (pp. 267–68). Emphasis on the origin and significance of the varying heritages of immigrants brings to mind the increasing social science interest in cross-cultural research as a corrective for the limitations of more traditional single-culture studies. Insistence that the study of social change requires integrated attention both to "organized values" and to "attitudes" is an early example of the growing fusion of much of sociology and social psychology, as in studies of the interrelations of personality and culture.

The half-century old analysis of immigrant assimilation and its practical implications is as valid today as when published. The book as a whole, however, may seem naive in terms of modern research methods. It should not be read as a research effort, for that is not what it was intended to be. The data in it consist mostly of extracts from published and manuscript immigrant autobiographies and autobiographical fragments, from immigrant letters, from foreign-language newspapers, from court and other available records, from government reports, and from books by and about immigrants. They are primarily human documents, offered with no statistical or other overt attempt to establish their representative quality. They are not included as proof of the generalizations offered, but as concrete, interesting and persuasive illustrations

INTRODUCTION TO THE REPUBLISHED EDITION

selected to give life to theoretical abstractions and generalized practical suggestions. The validity of the abstractions and suggestions is allowed to rest mainly on the earlier work of Thomas and his collaborators, especially on the massive study reported in *The Polish Peasant in Europe and America*.[2]

Similarly, the theoretical conceptualization and terminology of *Old World Traits Transplanted* may seem old-fashioned. The statement that "a poem, a folk dance, a church, a school, a coin, is a value, and the appreciation of any one of these objects is an attitude" (p. 3) is so inclusive as to be practically useless to the modern sociologist or social psychologist. Discussion of immigrant motivation under the headings of desire for new experience, security, response, and recognition, is antiquarian in contrast with current motivational theory and research. Critics of these well-known "four fundamental wishes," however, may be reminded that their author, Thomas, regarded them as no more than relatively arbitrary categories convenient for exposition, a purpose for which they and a variety of modifications still find use. Stress on the importance of the subjective "definition of the situation" currently is much more in favor. In reading throughout the book it can be profitable in gaining perspective concerning the development of social analysis and theory to give thought to the use fifty years ago not only of the terms "attitude," "value," "fundamental wishes," and "definition of the situation," but also of such other concepts as "role," "primary group," "assimilation," "status," and "cul-

[2] W. I. Thomas and Florian Znaniecki, *The Polish Peasant in Europe and America*, 5 vols. (Boston: Richard G. Badger, 1918–1920).

INTRODUCTION TO THE REPUBLISHED EDITION

ture." The more refined use of social science concepts today has grown out of such early necessarily rough-and-ready—as now seen—innovating conceptualizations.

The purpose and particular contribution of *Old World Traits Translated* were the development of practical guiding principles for the mutual adaptation of the values and attitudes of immigrants and also those of the older population elements on the basis of previously published social science findings. The work is an early example of applied sociology and social psychology, of what currently is sometimes termed "policy science." The title of the final chapter, "Reconciliation of the Heritages," makes the purpose plain.

A fundamental and unassailable assumption of the authors is that the American democratic creed requires that immigrants become "a working part in our system of life, ideal and political, as well as economic" (p. 264) if the basic character of American culture not be lost. That this is less difficult than frequently claimed is supported by the observation in the opening chapter that studies of the various peoples of the world show that "the nature of man is everywhere essentially the same and tends to express itsel everywhere in similar sentiments and institutions. On the other hand, the different races and nationalities differ widely in the details of their conception and practice of life, and even their behavior in connection with general ideals which they hold in common is often curiously and startlingly different" (p. 2). The guiding principles offered are grounded on this quoted fundamental conviction.

INTRODUCTION TO THE REPUBLISHED EDITION

Old World Traits Transplanted gives two main practical principles as basic for effective immigrant assimilation—principles which were a direct challenge to predominating formal Americanization programs then sponsored and operated by federal, state, and local governments and under private auspices, as in some industries and private welfare agencies. One principle is that "a wise policy of assimilation, like a wise educational policy, does not seek to destroy the attitudes and memories that are there, but to build on them. There is a current opinion in America, of the 'ordering and forbidding' type, demanding from the immigrant a quick and complete Americanization through the suppression and repudiation of all the signs that distinguish him from us" (pp. 280-81). Quick destruction of the immigrant's original heritage was rejected as unwise both because it would destroy the firmest foundation for adaptation to new circumstances and because it denied valuable potential cultural immigrant contributions to American civilization.

The second challenging principle is that distinctive immigrant organizations, even those of a nationalistic nature and including nationalistic foreign-language newspapers, were influential and necessary contributors rather than obstacles to assimilation. "The present immigrant organizations represent a separateness of the immigrant groups from America, but these organizations exist precisely because they enable the immigrants to overcome this separateness. They are signs, not of the perpetuation of immigrant groups here, but of their assimilation. We know no type of immigrant organization which is able to live without

INTRODUCTION TO THE REPUBLISHED EDITION

some feature related to the needs of the immigrant in America" (pp. 306-07).

Although the now current term "cultural pluralism" is not to be found in the book, it strongly supports a pluralistic policy by its convincing argument for forbearance rather than suppression of cultural differences and its emphasis on the necessity for taking advantage of such differences in the assimilative process. Yet, it is recognized that immigrant groups and their original heritages cannot survive indefinitely. Assimilation is "as inevitable as it is desirable; it is impossible for the immigrants we receive to remain permanently in separate groups. . . . If we give the immigrants a favorable milieu, if we tolerate their strangeness during their period of adjustment, if we give them freedom to make their own connections between old and new experiences, if we help them to find points of contact, then we hasten their assimilation" (p. 308).

Five decades after these enlightening conclusions were presented they still are unheeded by millions of American citizens in their individual behavior and in the exercise of public obligations. They are purposely rejected by some and simply unheard of by others. One may perhaps be heartened by the much wider acceptance of the book's message now than at the time of World War I, as evidenced by more recent immigrant and civil rights legislation, judicial decisions, and government civil rights programs. Such changes in government only could have come about in consonance with parallel changes in public opinion. Still, however great the increase in agreement with the conclusions of Thomas, Park and Miller, they are

INTRODUCTION TO THE REPUBLISHED EDITION

not yet widely enough accepted and practiced to justify complacence. Immigrants with divergent heritages still are arriving and adding to the millions already settled here. They still face the same obstacles to full participation in American life. The difficulties of Negro-white relations now overshadow those of immigrant–old-American relations and make them seem trivial by comparison, which they are not either from the immigrant's or the nation's point of view. Nor should it be overlooked that the word "Negro" can be substituted for "immigrant" throughout the book without a need for changing anything but the illustrations.

NOTE ON THE CONTRIBUTOR

Dr. Donald R. Young, now retired, most recently served as visiting professor at Rockefeller University. Earlier positions included the presidency of Russell Sage Foundation, the presidency of the Social Science Research Council, and a professorship in sociology at the University of Pennsylvania. He has also served as President of the National Council on Naturalization and Citizenship and of the International Social Science Council. He is the author of *American Minority Peoples* and other analyses of ethnic questions.

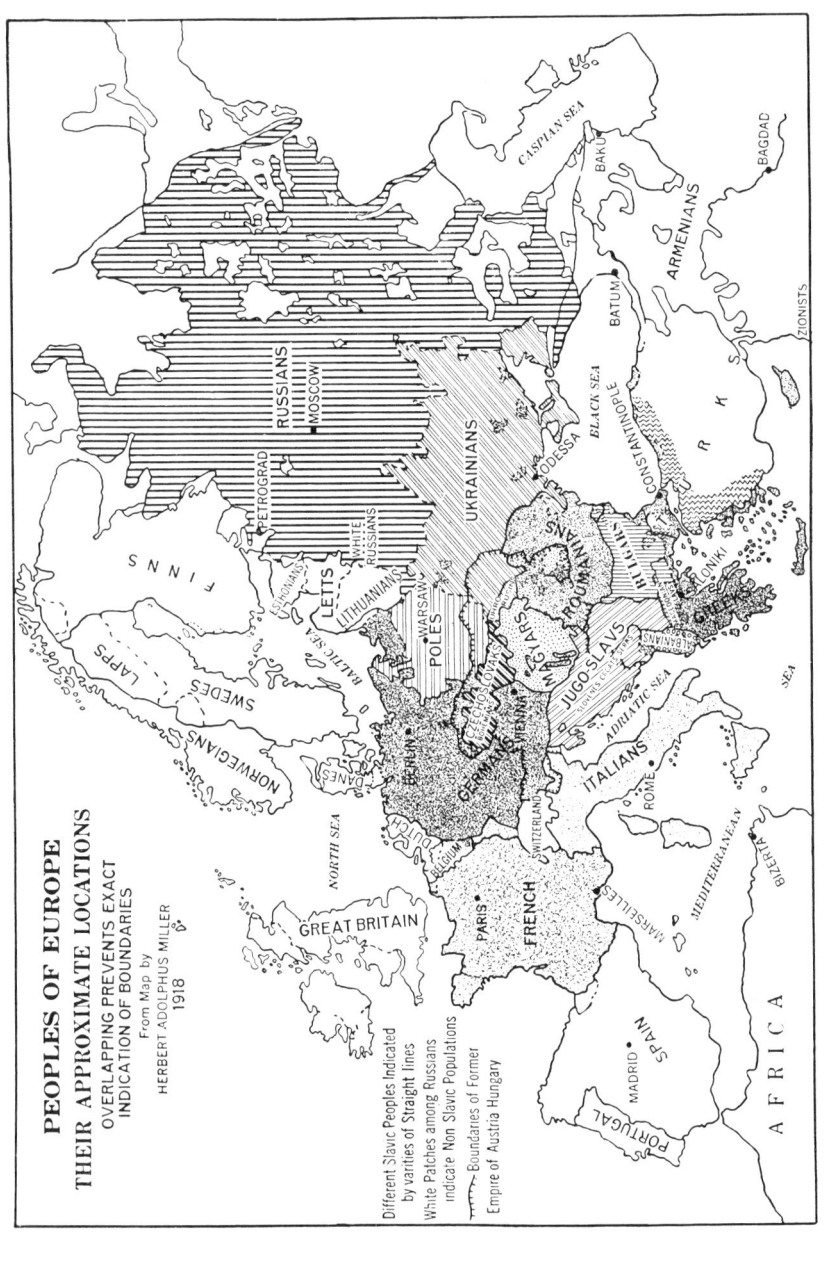

PUBLISHER'S NOTE
TO THE ORIGINAL EDITION

The material in this volume was gathered by the Division of Treatment of Immigrant Heritages of Studies in Methods of Americanization. Americanization in these studies has been considered as the union of native and foreign born in all the most fundamental relationships and activities of our national life. For Americanization is the uniting of new with native-born Americans in fuller common understanding and appreciation to secure by means of individual and collective self-direction the highest welfare of all. Such Americanization should perpetuate no unchangeable political, domestic, and economic régime delivered once for all to the fathers, but a growing and broadening national life, inclusive of the best wherever found. With all our rich heritages, Americanism will develop best through a mutual giving and taking of contributions from both newer and older Americans in the interest of the commonweal. These studies have followed such an understanding of Americanization.

FOREWORD TO THE ORIGINAL EDITION

THIS volume is the result of studies in methods of Americanization prepared through funds furnished by the Carnegie Corporation of New York. It arose out of the fact that constant applications were being made to the Corporation for contributions to the work of numerous agencies engaged in various forms of social activity intended to extend among the people of the United States the knowledge of their government and their obligations to it. The trustees felt that a study which should set forth, not theories of social betterment, but a description of the methods of the various agencies engaged in such work, would be of distinct value to the cause itself and to the public.

The outcome of the study is contained in eleven volumes on the following subjects: Schooling of the Immigrant; The Press; Adjustment of Homes and Family Life; Legal Protection and Correction; Health Standards and Care; Naturalization and Political Life; Industrial and Economic Amalgamation; Treatment of Immigrant Heritages; Neighborhood Agencies and Organization; Rural Developments; and Summary. The entire study has been carried out under the general direction of Mr. Allen T. Burns. Each

FOREWORD

volume appears in the name of the author who had immediate charge of the particular field it is intended to cover.

Upon the invitation of the Carnegie Corporation a committee consisting of the late Theodore Roosevelt, Prof. John Graham Brooks, Dr. John M. Glenn, and Mr. John A. Voll has acted in an advisory capacity to the director. An editorial committee consisting of Dr. Talcott Williams, Dr. Raymond B. Fosdick, and Dr. Edwin F. Gay has read and criticized the manuscripts. To both of these committees the trustees of the Carnegie Corporation are much indebted.

The purpose of the report is to give as clear a notion as possible of the methods of the agencies actually at work in this field and not to propose theories for dealing with the complicated questions involved.

TABLE OF CONTENTS

Introduction to the Republished Edition	vii
Publisher's Note to the Original Edition	xvii
Foreword to the Original Edition	xix
List of Maps	xxiii
Diagram	xxiv

CHAPTER
I.	IMMIGRANT HERITAGES	1
	Heritages Defined	2
	Illustrative Documents	4
	Resulting Antagonisms	16
II.	HERITAGES AND HUMAN WISHES	25
	Four Fundamental Wishes	27
	Primitive Regulation of Wishes	29
	Adjustment to Individualistic Society	40
III.	IMMIGRANT EXPERIENCES	43
	Change in Attitudes	43
	Loss of Status	47
IV.	IMMIGRANT DEMORALIZATION	60
	Early Stages	62
	Extreme Cases	66
V.	IMMIGRANT TYPES	81
	The Settler	83
	The Colonist	92
	The Political Idealist	96
	The Allrightnick	101
	The Caffone	103
	The Intellectual	104

CONTENTS

CHAPTER		PAGE
VI.	IMMIGRANT INSTITUTIONS	119
	First-Aid Institutions	121
	Mutual Aid and Benefit Societies	124
	Nationalistic Organizations	132
	Cultural Institutions	144
VII.	THE IMMIGRANT COMMUNITY	145
	The Italians	146
	The Chinese	159
	The Japanese	167
	The Mexicans	180
	The Jews	195
	The Poles	211
	The Bohemians	219
	The Scandinavians	221
VIII.	TYPES OF COMMUNITY INFLUENCE	225
	The Polish Community	225
	The Jewish Community	234
	The Italian Community	238
IX.	RECONCILIATION OF THE HERITAGES	259
	Required in a Democracy	260
	Similarity of Heritages	265
	Psychology of Assimilation	270
	Tolerance *versus* Suppression	280
	Immigrant Organization Valuable	287
	Perpetuation of Groups Impossible	296
	INDEX	309

LIST OF MAPS

MAP		PAGE
	The Peace Treaty is an attempt to make racial and political boundaries more nearly coincide	*Frontispiece*
1.	The Polish National Alliance has 1,658 branches distributed in 33 states	134
2.	French-Canadian parishes of New England and New York	141
3.	Bowery colony of Italians showing settlements according to native provinces and towns *Facing*	146
4.	California branches of the Japanese Association	168
5.	Location of Japanese business in San Francisco	172
6.	Organizations in the Japanese community in San Francisco	174
7.	Birthplace of the founders of the Jewish synagogues in a congested New York district	201
8.	Density of Jewish population in the neighborhoods of certain Kehillah districts of Manhattan	208
9.	Norwegian Lutheran churches in Minnesota	223
10.	Location of Italian colonists in New York City with sources of emigration in Italy	242

DIAGRAM

DIAGRAM	PAGE
1. Comparison of the Jewish population of New York City with that of other countries	196

OLD WORLD TRAITS TRANSPLANTED

I

IMMIGRANT HERITAGES

DURING the past seventy years the various tribes, races, and nationalities of mankind have been examined in detail by the students of ethnology, and a comparison of the results shows that the fundamental patterns of life and behavior are everywhere the same, whether among the ancient Greeks, the modern Italians, the Asiatic Mongols, the Australian blacks, or the African Hottentots. All have a form of family life, moral and legal regulations, a religious system, a form of government, artistic practices, and so forth. An examination of the moral code of any given group, say the African Kaffirs, will disclose many identities with that of any other given group, say the Hebrews. All groups have such "commandments" as

OLD WORLD TRAITS TRANSPLANTED

"Honor thy father and mother," "Thou shalt not kill," "Thou shalt not steal." Formerly it was assumed that this similarity was the result of borrowing between groups. When Bastian recorded a Hawaiian myth resembling the one of Orpheus and Eurydice, there was speculation as to how this story had been carried so far from Greece. But it is now recognized that similarities of culture are due, in the main, not to imitation, but to parallel development. The nature of man is everywhere essentially the same and tends to express itself everywhere in similar sentiments and institutions.

HERITAGES DEFINED

On the other hand, the different races and nationalities differ widely in the details of their conception and practice of life, and even their behavior in connection with general ideals which they hold in common is often curiously and startlingly different. Thus, "Honor thy father and mother" implies among certain African tribes that children shall kill their parents when the latter reach a certain age. Among these people life after death is conceived as a continuation of this life, under somewhat improved conditions, and the parents wish

IMMIGRANT HERITAGES

to reach the next world while still young enough to enjoy it. Similarly, among many peoples "faithful unto death" does not exhaust the possibilities of marital fidelity; the widow is expected to follow the husband to the next world. When, in 1836, the English governor of India forbade the *suttee* (the practice of burning widows) a petition was presented, signed by 18,000 persons, many of them representing the best families of Calcutta, requesting the revocation of the edict.

These examples illustrate the well-known fact that different races and nationalities attach values to different things, and different values to the same thing. This is the chief factor in the problem of "Americanization," of harmonizing the life of the immigrants with our own. Every human group has developed in the course of its experience a certain fund of *values* particular to itself and a set of *attitudes* toward these values. Thus, a poem, a folk dance, a church, a school, a coin, is a value, and the appreciation of any one of these objects is an attitude. The object, the practice, the institution, is the value; the feeling toward it is the attitude. For the purpose of the present study we call the fund of attitudes and values which an immigrant group brings

OLD WORLD TRAITS TRANSPLANTED

to America—the totality of its sentiments and practices—its "heritage."

ILLUSTRATIVE DOCUMENTS

We add below some documents illustrating further the variety of attitudes and values which exist in the world and which may be brought to America as immigrant heritages. These are used at this point simply as a concrete means of defining heritages. They are not an attempt to characterize the groups in question, though they necessarily do this to some extent. It would be possible to cite in connection with each group examples of both good and bad heritages, as we have done in the case of the Chinese.

1. When I was five years old I began to go to *cheder* [school] . . . Such was my diligence that I went through the *sidur* [prayer book] and the Pentateuch in one winter, and I also began to study "Gemorah." At six and a half, my father brought me into the famous *yeshiba* of Vilna. . . .

The sole source of maintenance for almost all the *yeshiba-bahurim* [pupils] was the system of "day eating," at the homes of some well-to-do or poorer members of the community—at a different home each day. As a rule, the *bahurim* are not residents of the city where the *yeshiba* is situated. To maintain them, each is assigned to eat one day in the

IMMIGRANT HERITAGES

week in certain houses; he thus rotates through seven houses a week. . . .

Reb Simon "Long Robe" was the most remarkable man among the Jews of Vilna. He dedicated his life work to providing the poor *bahurim* who were left without day board with food and other necessities. From early dawn to almost midnight he would stand in the "Jewish street" with a big collection box in his hand, and collect donations for "his children," as he called the *yeshiba-bahurim*. He drew his living from working during the night hours as a grinder of snuff tobacco for a tobacco dealer of Vilna. None knew his birthplace, nor whence he came. . . . He spoke to no one, and to all inquiries made no answer. Even the Christians regarded him with the deepest respect, and deemed him a holy man. . . . So well was Reb Simon known in Vilna that each household that found aught left of the best dinner courses had these remains carried off at once to the synagogue courtyard—to Reb Simon Kaftan, who immediately distributed them among the hungry *yeshiba* youths.[1]

2. When I was seven years of age my father moved his family to Bielostok. At that time I left school and engaged in the reading of Russian novels, books of travel, and of adventure. I remember to have been literally swallowing these books, reading them late into nights and mornings. . . . The gospel of the class struggle, of the wronged proletariat of the world, of the poverty-stricken peasants of Russia, had already at the age of thirteen absorbed my attention. The members of the secret Central Committee of the Bielostok branch of the *Bund* at this time began to use me as a means of carrying on their

---

[1] Eliakum Zunser, *A Jewish Bard*, p. 11 (an autobiography).

OLD WORLD TRAITS TRANSPLANTED

propaganda. One of the members of the Committee arranged with me to have his secret organization code mail sent to my address. I used to pay the letter carrier twenty-five kopecks a month to hand all my mail to me personally, not to leave it with the folks at home. . . .

[At about fourteen] I was introduced to many of the workers in the revolutionary movement, and began to take an active part in it. I attended illegal revolutionary meetings and later assisted in organizing them. I was reading and distributing illegal literature. I soon became a leader among the workers. My activities consisted in talking before circles of workers on the significance of the class struggle and the necessity of overthrowing the then Russian government. I remember distinctly having given a number of talks on the inefficacy of the "terror" as advocated by the social revolutionists. As a member of the *Bund* I did not approve of the terroristic tactics of the social revolutionists.[1]

3. I am a widow. My husband died three years ago. Since then I am struggling to make a living for my family, which consists of five children, the oldest son being fifteen years old, and the baby three and a half.

I have a store and barely get along, for the expenses are great. As I am unable to manage the house and store alone, I am obliged to employ a salesman, who receives as much salary as is necessary for our own livelihood.

If I were to withdraw my son from high school I could dispense with the salesman, but my motherly love and the duty toward the child do not permit me to take that step, for he is a very good scholar.

[1] Louis Bloch, *Autobiography* (manuscript).

IMMIGRANT HERITAGES

So, what shall I do when the struggle for existence is so acute? I must have his assistance in order to keep my business going and take care of the other children; but at the same time I cannot definitely decide to take him out of school, for I know that I would make him unhappy, for he has inclinations to study and goes to school dancing. I lay great hopes on my child.[1]

4. ... I am a son of a [Polish] peasant farmer. Until ten years of age I did not know the alphabet, or, exactly speaking, I knew only the letter B. Father did not send me to school. He was always repeating: "We have grown old, and we can't read nor write, and we live; so you, my children, will also live without knowledge." ... Once my mother took me to church. I looked to the right, a boy, smaller than myself, was praying from a book; I looked to the left, another one held a book just like the first. And I stood between them like a ninny. I went home and said to my father that I wanted to learn from a book. And father scolded me, "And who will peel potatoes in the winter, and pasture the geese in summer?" Here I cried. ... Once, while peeling potatoes, I escaped from my father and went to an old man who knew not only how to read, but how to write well. I asked him to show me [letters] in the primer, and he did not refuse. I went home and thought: "It is bad! Father will probably give me a licking." And so it was. Father showered a few strokes on me and said: "Snotty fellow! Don't you know that, as old people say, he who knows written stuff casts himself into hell?" But I used to steal out to learn more and more frequently. ...

[1] *Forward* (New York Yiddish newspaper), May 6, 1906.

OLD WORLD TRAITS TRANSPLANTED

Once I found on the road an old almanac. I looked at it, and I read on the last page that there was in Warsaw a *Gazeta Swiąteczna* which people order and receive it by mail every Sunday. After that I said to one of the neighbors, not a young man, "Do you know, in Warsaw there is a *Gazeta* which every one, even if not educated, can read?" And that man said to me: "Look at him, at the snotty fellow! He wants a newspaper!" "Do you know, *Kum*," said he to my father, "your son will become a real lord, for he says that he will order a newspaper." "Ho, ho!" said father, "but where will he get the money?" . . .

5. MY ILLUSTRIOUS FRIEND AND JOY OF MY LIVER: The thing which you ask of me is both difficult and useless. Although I have passed all my days in this place, I have neither counted the houses nor inquired into the number of the inhabitants; and as to what one person loads on his mules and the other stows away in the bottom of his ship, that is no business of mine. But above all, as to the previous history of this city, God only knows the amount of dirt and confusion that the infidels may have eaten before the coming of the sword of Islam. It were unprofitable for us to inquire into it. . . . Listen, O my son! There is no wisdom equal to the belief in God! He created the world, and shall we liken ourselves unto him in seeking to penetrate into the mysteries of his creation? Shall we say, Behold this star spinneth around that star, and this other star with a tail goeth and cometh in so many years? Let it go. He from whose hand it came will guide and direct it. . . . Thou art learned in the things I care not for, and as for that which thou hast seen, I spit

---
¹ *Gazeta Swiąteczna* (Warsaw newspaper), vol. 18, no. 31.

upon it. Will much knowledge create thee a double belly, or wilt thou seek paradise with thine eyes? The meek in spirit,

IMAUM ALI ZADI.[1]

6. ... Arson is for the peasant something quite natural, is a *self-redress*, and does not even bring him dishonor in the eyes of his peasant neighbors. Reciprocal incendiarism is such a frequent manifestation of self-redress that it merits particular studies. ... It is civil war. The peasant considers breaking Lent a greater sin. To stop or at least to diminish the number of arsons the bishops in Poland have reserved the sin of putting fire to houses, barns, and stables for themselves—that is, an ordinary priest cannot remit the sin of the incendiary, but must appeal to the bishop or send the man to the bishop to confession, in the same way as with murder. But this does not help much. I would define it as a *feud*, a way of leading civil war. A peasant whom my father reproached for having set fire to his neighbor's buildings said, "I have set fire to his barn, but he could have and still can set fire to mine." ... I have listened to the confession of many even respectable farmers who tried to set fire to their enemies' farm buildings, only they did not always succeed. The variety of the technique of arson is itself worth studying. The motive is frequently the loss of a lawsuit, the seduction of a woman, etc.[2]

7. OUR RESPECTED CATHOLICS AND ASSISTANTS TO THE EMIGRANTS: I beg you kindly to advise me

---

[1] Letter from a Mohammedan official to an Englishman. Sir Austen Henry Layard, *Fresh Discoveries of Nineveh and Researches at Babylon: Supplement.*

[2] Report of a Polish priest. Thomas and Znaniecki, *The Polish Peasant in Europe and America,* vol. iv, p. 119.

in what way I could emigrate to America with my family, for instance, with my wife and four boys from two to fourteen years. One boy, sixteen years old, went to Argentine on May 14th. I intend also to go and to buy land there, because here in Wolyn it is very dear; a *desiatina* [two acres] reaches 500 rubles. What can I buy if I have five boys and only two thousand of money? I could buy perhaps in Russia, but what is the use of it since there are no [Catholic] churches, so my faith will get lost. I have heard meanwhile that in America there are churches enough and our faith will not get lost.[1]

8. One of the [Sicilian] characteristics is the recognition of the principle of *omertà*. What do we understand by *omertà*? *Omertà* is a moral code which has never been written, but which is more or less instinctively present in all Sicilians, in the peasant as well as in the highly cultivated city dweller. Indeed it is more emphasized in the former. . . . The moral code of *omertà* demands firmness, energy, and seriousness, a self-reliant and self-conscious mind whose activities are as far as possible independent of the civil authorities. It seeks help through oneself and not through the courts or police. It has that quality of knightliness which characterizes duelists, who settle their differences between themselves, far from the police courts. Revenge is accomplished quietly, unaided, or with the help of trusted friends.[2]

9. Every year, for the last twelve years, there have been from twelve to twenty murders committed

---

[1] Letter of a Polish peasant to the Emigrants' Protective Association of Warsaw. Thomas and Znaniecki, *The Polish Peasant in Europe and America*, vol. v (in press).

[2] G. Wermert, *Sicilien*, p. 436.

IMMIGRANT HERITAGES

in the square half mile of the North Side Sicilian Settlement of Chicago.[1]

The circumstances are nearly always the same. The victim is shot from ambush, his body riddled with slugs and nails from a sawed-off shotgun or with the entire charge from a revolver; the weapon is found near the body; there are no witnesses and the murderer is never found. A squad of police are sent into the district, premises in the vicinity are searched, the wife or relatives of the murdered man are taken to the station and sweated, an occasional arrest is made, but not more than three or four persons have ever been convicted and sentenced for these crimes. Sometimes the victim is murdered in his own home and not infrequently two and even three men are killed at the same time.[2]

10. In Italy I live in small town—six, seven thousand. It take not much money to live. We pay the rent once a year, only little money. We have fine garden, we live healthy, happy. I obey my mother's word, which is like the God. The people in my town they are serious, human, good heart. We give everything to the poor. When stranger comes to us, he got always the first chair, we make all we could for him. We love the foreigner, especially from North America. The people used to go to him and give him the welcome. We say, "Oh he is Americano, he is from the land of Columbus." The stranger can stay a year, he don't need no money to pay for anything, wherever he go he got everything for nothing.

---

[1] The Chicago *Tribune*, March 17, 1911, enumerates, with some details, thirty-four murders of Italians in Chicago in a period of fourteen months (January 6, 1910, to March 14, 1911), all of them "unsolved."

[2] Marie Leavitt, *Report on the Sicilian Colony in Chicago* (manuscript).

OLD WORLD TRAITS TRANSPLANTED

We work little bit, then we take the leisure. We love very much the music, art, poetry. We love the poetical life—poetry to-day, and to-morrow we take what's coming with the good patience. The way I mean is not only to read the books of the great poets, of Dante that we love more than a father, or Petrarca, Ariosoto, Tasso, Alfieri, and so many others down to Manzoni, Carducci, Giusti, D'Annunzio, but the poetry of the beautiful scenery in the country, the poetry of the music, the poetry of the friendship. Even in the small town we have band and philharmonica. Not to know the musical works of Rossini, like "Barbiere di Seviglia" and "Guglielmo Tell," is not to know anything. We like the music of the great Donizetti and Bellini because they are *dramatici, emotionanti*. We are crazy for "Norma," for "Lucia di Lammermoor." They have red blood, what the Italian like, for the Italian warm heart. We like Puccini, Mascagni. Verdi, we adore him. He was welcome all over for his wonderful heart. He speak the voice of the people, in the big romantic utterance, he speak fearless like a man, he express our own emotions by the great genius. . . .[1]

11. Lindsborg is the center of a Swedish colony of about forty square miles in extent. Its only boast above the neighboring towns is the presence of Bethany College and the annual musical event at Easter time.

Each Easter week its people perform Handel's "Messiah" with a chorus of five hundred voices and an orchestra of forty pieces. With the exception of the soloists, who now are stars of the first magnitude

---

[1] Life history of Alessandro Daluca, a tailor on the East Side of New York. Emily F. Robbins, "If One Speak Bad of Your Mother, How You Feel?" in the *Red Cross Magazine*, September, 1919.

on the artistic firmament, it is entirely a home affair. The membership of the organization is made up of the merchants, artisans, farmers, and housewives of the town and surrounding countryside, together with the students of the college. The chorus is more than thirty years old and has given Handel's "Messiah" eighty-seven times.

Among its members there are those who participated in the first performance, and it is no uncommon thing for three generations of the same family to be represented. From the bass section more than one grandfather hears the voices of his daughter and granddaughter singing among the sopranos and altos. One of the unique features is a children's chorus of three hundred, and the exercises of the Messiah Week, as the festival is popularly called, would be quite incomplete without the concert by this organization. Membership in it is a distinction to which every boy and girl in the community aspires, and it is a red-letter day in the life of the youthful musician when for the first time he is permitted to appear as a member of the orchestra in a public performance of the oratorio.[1]

12. The Finns have much faith in co-operative establishments for the conduct of their affairs, as is evidenced by the numerous co-operative creameries, co-operative general merchandise and grocery stores, co-operative savings banks, and other co-operative institutions. In 1913 there were 2,167 co-operative societies in Finland, with a total membership of 196,000. Into northeastern Minnesota co-operative institutions are rapidly finding their way. While all varieties are not yet represented there, they may

[1] E. F. Philblad, "A Swedish Bayreuth in Kansas," in *American-Scandinavian Review*, May, 1913.

be found in the Lake Superior region as a whole. In addition, the co-operative hotel has grown to be a significant institution.[1]

13. I, Ah Kam, being poor and not having any one on whom to depend, make this agreement, by which to obtain $460 with my person. The middle party in this transaction, Loui Fung, having introduced me to Lang Kai, and having the promise of the latter to pay this debt for me, besides passage money and other expenses, we three are agreed, and to-day the transaction has taken place. Not a cent now is owing to Loui Fung, the money having actually changed hands, first into the hands of myself, Ah Kam; and I am this day handed over to Lang Kai, to be taken to California for immoral purposes. The time of service is agreed to be four and one half years, with no pay for the service on the one hand and no interest for the money on the other. Fourteen days of sickness will not be taken notice of, but fifteen days of sickness will have to be made up by serving another month. In case of pregnancy an additional year has to be served. As to any expected calamities happening that may happen to anyone, that will be left to the decree of heaven. Should I upon arrival at California attempt to escape, or refuse to be a prostitute, I agree irrevocably that Lang Kai should sell me to another at pleasure.

Lest word of mouth should not be proof, this instrument is drawn up to be such.

AH KAM (her mark).

October 1, 1899.[2]

---

[1] Eugene van Cleef, "The Finn in America," in *Geographical Review*, vol. vi, p. 199.

[2] Translation of a bill of sale of a Chinese girl, drawn up in the form of a promissory note. *Report of the U. S. Industrial Commission* (1901), vol. xv, p. 771.

IMMIGRANT HERITAGES

14. [Sister] died last Thursday morning at eight. We did not expect it nor in the least could have dreamed it. About three weeks ago she took a bad cold when she went to Fresno. . . . [Description of sickness]. She was conscious to the end and very cheerful, as she always was. I won't try to tell you how we miss her or how we have lived since. You and she never got on together, but you must have known that she was better in every way than us girls [herself and her sister]. Her music teacher said she had the finger relaxation which the greatest artists succeed in teaching only after years of work. She was the only Chinese girl who could sing well. She had mamma's entertaining ways and she would have become a beauty. She was so popular because of her wit, and then she had to die. I must not let any complaining note come into me, because she would not have liked it. We try to think how beautifully she died and how troublesome a world she escaped. It should comfort us, but it doesn't. We buried her beside my older brother on Friday. The flowers were far more beautiful than anyone had ever seen. It was all as beautiful as such things are possible. The whole thing is almost breaking mamma's and papa's heart. She was their baby. My head is topsy-turvy so I can't remember what I have said and what I have not. Will you give the details to those [her cousins] in China? We can't.[1]

15. Osman Assen . . . said to the judge who questioned him: "Recently I was at the border buying giraffe skins to make shields. About a month ago I returned and my wife informed me that our daughter Fatma, still a young girl, was pregnant. I

---

[1] Letter from a Chinese girl, partly Americanized. Written in English (manuscript).

was greatly displeased and had no peace during a whole night and a whole day. In the evening I told my daughter to come and help me fetch some fodder and wood, and had her mount upon the ass. . . . [In a retired spot] I made her dismount from the ass. I threw her on the ground first and tried to strangle her, then seeing that this did not succeed, with a quick pressure against her head I broke her neck. Before throwing her on the ground I said: 'Think on what you have done. I have brought you here to kill you.' She answered: 'I know I have done wrong. I am in your hands and God's.'

"After I had killed my daughter I set about digging the grave, and two of my cousins joined me, whom I had asked to follow and assist with the burial. . . . Before killing her I asked my daughter who had seduced her, but she would not say. When I returned I informed my wife that I had done what I had said I would do, and what is prescribed in our customs to do. Now I am sorry for what I did."

[Questioned, the mother said:] "My daughter was killed by my husband because, marriageable, she became pregnant. When my husband returned I informed him of what had happened. He assured himself of the girl's condition and then decided to kill her according to our custom."[1]

RESULTING ANTAGONISMS

Some of the attitudes represented by the above examples of immigrant heritages are those which we ourselves have cr under-

---

[1] "Documenti criminalogici," *Archivio di antropologia criminale psichiatria e medicina legale*, vol. xxxvii, p. 71.

IMMIGRANT HERITAGES

stand. The Jewish devotion to learning (document 1) is among these. At the same time this case may be used to illustrate a general principle. The role which a given attitude is able to play in an immigrant group in America is never the same as the one it played at home. Jewish learning as it was pursued in Russia—that is, as a distinction, an artistic, religious occupation—may lead to maladjustment in America. On the contrary, the same attitude applied to a different kind of learning may lead to a superior intellectual status for the whole group in America; or, the attitude may continue to be an organizing force, but in a different field of application. The three documents following illustrate this point.

16. I am forty-five years old, born in a little town in Russia, where my parents brought me up in a respectable way. I studied the Talmud and the Jewish laws until I was thirteen years old, and, being industrious, I drew the attention of a wealthy man who had only one daughter and I became a bridegroom ... and a "board-child" in my father-in-law's home, where I continued to study the Talmud for my mother-in-law's sake and general science for my own sake, to be prepared for the examinations.

[Became a merchant. The pogroms followed. Came to America. Began teaching in a Hebrew Free School.] But my teaching is very tiresome because the children do not want to know the things they are taught in the Hebrew school, which is a hovel —broken benches and cobwebs on the ceiling—and they have no respect for the school when they come from the beautiful, modern public school, and they also do not respect the Jewish teachings, that are really not for them—like the fine books of Moses and translations from the prayers. . . .

So, again I thought: "What can I do to give up my position as Hebrew teacher?" I took a course on how to make eyeglasses and secured a diploma from a college as Doctor of Optics. Unfortunately it is a business that requires peddling with eyeglasses from house to house, and I cannot do that under any circumstances. So a druggist advised me to go to work in a drug store, where after two years I can get an assistant's license and earn fifteen dollars a week, and remain in the drug store for three more years and become a registered druggist and open a store for myself. I went to work in a drug store and then the orthodox officials found it out and I was discharged from my position in the Hebrew Free School.[1]

17. It has been ascertained that the Russian Jews, in spite of their comparative poverty, send more of their children to the high schools of this city, and permit them to stay there longer, than any other ethnic group. It is common knowledge that more than three-fourths of the pupils in the College of the City of New York are children of eastern European Jews.[2]

18. In many cases the rise [of the Jew] to social position through wealth is merely a recuperation of

---

[1] *Forward*, March 26, 1915.
[2] Alexander M. Dushkin, *Jewish Education in New York City*, p. 37.

IMMIGRANT HERITAGES

status previously enjoyed [in Europe] by dint of reputation for learning.[1]

But many of the cases just cited impress us as strange and disturbing, as having no place at all in our scheme of life. We must remember, however, that strangeness itself may be a source of displeasure and prejudice. The un-American shoes and un-American beard of the immigrant arouse these emotions in us. (See documents 35, p. 48, and 38, p. 49.) In general, any practice which is not customary, which is not in our code, is shocking. Thus we customarily carry food to the mouth with the fork and the use of the knife for this purpose affects us unpleasantly, although the fork seems to have no natural superiority for this purpose. Smacking with the lips when eating produces disgust in us, but the Indian, logically enough, smacks as a compliment to his host.

In addition to strangeness, the shock of these examples is often due to the fact that they excite our moral disapproval. But even so, the worst of these practices are not entirely foreign to our experience. A "code of honor," which had the same spirit as the Italian vendetta (documents 8, p. 10, and 9, p. 10), was some generations ago held in

---

[1] I. B. Berkson, *Assimilation: A Critical Study, with Particular Reference to the Jewish Group* (in press).

the greatest esteem by all "gentlemen" of the Western World and did not become entirely strange to us until the past century:

> In the eight years between 1601 and 1609 two thousand men of noble birth fell in duels in France; and, according to Lord Herbert of Cherbury, who was ambassador at this court of Louis XIII, there was scarce a Frenchman worth looking on who had not killed his man in a duel.[1]

The cases of Hamilton and Burr, Jackson and Dickinson, represent this spirit in American history.

Document 13 illustrates the Oriental form of "white slavery." The situation is thus not entirely unfamiliar to us, but it is peculiarly shocking because the naïve and explicit procedure creates the impression that the girl is from the beginning a voluntary participant, and that the practice is normal for this group. It is, in fact, normal in China, under certain conditions and in a certain class. It may even be regarded as meritorious, if undertaken by the girl for the benefit of her family. Our moral superiority in this case lies in the fact that we expect and usually find in the white slave a consciousness of guilt which is here lacking.

---

[1] E. Westermarck, *Origin and Development of the Moral Ideas*, vol. i, p. 508.

IMMIGRANT HERITAGES

(Society wishes to forgive and restore an erring member, but it is not able to do this in the absence of that shame which leads to repentance.)

Document 15 shows another Oriental (Mohammedan) attitude, one which we have had and have, but never so completely. It is only a thoroughgoing repudiation of the girl who goes wrong.

On the other hand, the immigrant finds here strange, unexpected, and inconsistent situations. We are usually not well acquainted with our slums—housing conditions, where three, five, seven, nine families share the same toilet room,[1] the sweatshop, and the general industrial system—or we do not think of them often, but they are totally different from the rural life of Europe, and impress the immigrant in cities painfully. Some of the foreign-language newspapers in America, especially the Italian (as a retort to our condemnation of the Black Hand), constantly seek to find in America phases of life as bad as any we can attribute to the immigrant groups they represent:

19. Now and then the Black Hand of the Americans appears. . . . The payments of tribute to the

---
[1] *Reports of the U. S. Immigration Commission*, vol. xxvi, p. 466.

police . . . the protection by the police of individuals in the *mala vita* [criminals and prostitutes], . . . the sale of liquor and cocaine clandestinely and known to the police—all this graft stinks of the *Camorra*, the *Mafia*—i.e., the Black Hand. . . . The American Black Hand is as well organized as the Italian.[1]

Frequently the displeasure excited by American conditions (often not really American conditions, but immigrant conditions in America) is very violent:

20. . . . In their feelings toward the Americans the Russians, judging by the collected data, may be divided into three groups—those who have learned to love and esteem the Americans; those who are indifferent toward them; and the incensed haters of Americans.

Those who esteem the Americans all write that at first they "did not like them." A visiting teacher opened one's eyes to "the real meaning of Yankee"; another learned to love Americans for their great will power, "the thing that we Slavs lack so much"; the third one became attached to the Americans for their great tolerance and respect toward an opponent in politics and religion, etc.

Those who are "indifferent," write that the Americans simply do not interest them. The Americans whom they meet are a harsh and not always a just people. They are like machine men and "do not appreciate" good craftsmen. Sometimes it is a factory foreman, sometimes it is a house owner, who does not mind molesting his tenants, and, "when

---
[1] *Bollettino della Sera* (New York), December 31, 1910.

IMMIGRANT HERITAGES

the Russian soul goes a-merry," it is a policeman with a none too soft club, and then the judge, who, "expressionless," pronounces between his teeth, "Three, five, ten dollars fine."

The "haters" of Americans are incensed by their compulsory loneliness; they are men whose souls are hidden from Americans, as the Americans' souls are unknown to them. They are the great numbers of immigrants who live in America their old Russian life, only without the soothing effect of the Russian rivers, steppes, and the great Russian forests. It is a soulless, a stifling "American Russia," and they soon feel themselves in a new "prison." They work in shops that belong to foreigners like themselves, reside in immigrant neighborhoods, and are separated as if by a mountain from American thought, American social life, and American struggles. The "America" they live in is suppressing their spirits, and they cannot see behind the walls of their free prison the genuine America.

And sometimes tragical, sometimes comical are their complaints: "America is the most mean and vile country," writes a laborer by the name of Terenty, "and I will try to light the fire of hate toward Americans in every corner of Russia." He lived in America for six years, but during that time the "Americans" he came in contact with were immigrants like himself, who sometimes exploited and mistreated him. A laborer from Ohio, without any evident attempt to be gay, writes: "We have here too many Americans. I worked in other places, and have seen only a few of them. But here wherever you go you see Americans, and they look upon you as if you were a low thing and they were great men. I hate them!"

OLD WORLD TRAITS TRANSPLANTED

Only one of those "haters" displayed some humor, saying: "The Americans are a bad people. You speak to them the plainest Russian language, and you even add a word or two of English for their benefit, and still they do not understand a thing!"

The main difficulty in the relations between Russian immigrants and Americans is that there are almost no such relations. . . .[1]

The first contacts between Americans and immigrants produce, therefore, a degree of antagonism, owing to the element of strangeness and to the different degree of moral worth attached to given values, as viewed by Americans, on the one hand, and by immigrants, on the other. The antagonism produced by mere strangeness is of course in the region of pure prejudice, and has no more moral significance than the displeasure produced by a fashion of dress or a code of etiquette differing from the one to which we are habituated, but this mutual prejudice is, nevertheless, as we shall see, one of the most serious hindrances to the assimilation of the immigrant.

---

[1] Mark Villchur, "The Russian Immigrants and the Americans" *Russkoye Slovo* (New York newspaper), June 10, 1919. The article was based on replies received to a questionnaire printed in this paper at our request.

II

HERITAGES AND HUMAN WISHES

THE attitudes examined in the last chapter were typical for the given groups—that is, they were found to be prevalent in a large number of cases. About 5,000 documents were examined for the Jewish group, about 15,000 for the Polish, and fewer for the other groups. But while they were useful as a means of defining heritages and the problem of assimilation, neither an individual nor a group can be characterized by an enumeration of attitudes taken at random. What distinguishes societies and individuals is the predominance of certain attitudes over others, and this predominance depends, as we shall see below, on the type of organization which the group has developed to regulate the expression of the wishes of its members.

The individual has wishes which can be realized only in association with other human beings, but when human beings come together there is a conflict of wishes. Consequently every man cannot have absolutely what he wants, but must modify, qualify, and regulate the expression of his wishes. The organization of society has always a double character: it makes possible the gratification of the individual's wishes, and even the multiplication of them, but at the same time it requires that his wishes shall be gratified only in *usual* ways, that their expression shall be so regulated as not to interfere unfairly with the expression of the wishes of others. All standards of behavior, all moral and legal codes, all penalties for disorder and crime, all appreciations and rewards which a society bestows on a deserving member, are expressions of this effort to live together.

The factor of individual temperament prevents men from behaving identically—certain wishes predominate in given individuals—but it is the social organization under which men live that mainly determines the behavior inspired in them by their wishes. We can, therefore, gain a better understanding of the heritages of the immigrant groups—why they behave in given ways, why they bring the heritages which they do bring—by examining briefly the nature of the human wishes and the form of social organization which controls the wishes of our immigrants at home.

HERITAGES AND HUMAN WISHES

While the concrete wishes are very numerous, they all fall under one or more of four types or patterns: (1) the desire for new experience; (2) the desire for security; (3) the desire for response; and (4) the desire for recognition.[1]

FOUR FUNDAMENTAL WISHES

Under the desire for new experience we class the tendency to gratify the physical appetites, to secure stimulations and sensations, and to seek their repetition. In its pure form the desire for new experience results in motion, change, danger, instability, social irresponsibility. It is seen in simple forms in the prowling and meddling activities of the child, and the love of adventure and travel in the boy and man. It ranges in moral quality from the pursuit of game and the pursuit of pleasure to the pursuit of knowledge and the pursuit of ideals. It is found equally in the vagabond and the scientific explorer. Gambling is a form of it, and it enters into business enterprise. Novels, theaters, motion pictures, etc., are means of satisfying this desire vicariously, and their popularity is a sign of its elemental

---
[1] See Thomas and Znaniecki, *The Polish Peasant*, methodological note to vol. i and introduction to vol. iii.

force. The individual who is dominated by this desire shows a tendency to disregard prevailing standards and group interests. He may be a complete failure, on account of his instability; or he may be a conspicuous success, if he converts his experiences into social values, puts them, for instance, in the form of a poem, makes from them a contribution to science.

The desire for security is opposed to the desire for new experience. It implies avoidance of danger and death—caution, conservatism. Incorporation in an organization (family, community, state) provides the greatest security. We shall notice later that this desire shapes the organization of the peasants of Europe, which our immigrant groups represent. In the peasant group behavior is predetermined for the individual by tradition. He is secure as long as the group organization is secure, without the exercise of personal originality or creativeness; and security means not only physical security, but a secure economic and social position, without apprehension of disturbing change.

The desire for response is a craving for the more intimate and preferential appreciation of others. It is exemplified in mother love, romantic love, family affection, and

HERITAGES AND HUMAN WISHES

other personal attachments. Homesickness and loneliness are expressions of it.

The desire for recognition expresses itself in devices for securing distinction in the eyes of the public. A list of these devices would be very long. It would include courageous behavior, ostentatious ornament and dress, displays of opinions and knowledge, the cultivation of special attainments, in the arts, for example. This wish is expressed alike in arrogance and in humility, even in martyrdom. The "will to power" is one phase of it. Certain modes of seeking recognition we define as "vanity," others as "ambition." Many of the devices used for securing recognition are also used for securing response.

There is, of course, a kaleidoscopic mingling of wishes throughout life, and a single given act may contain several of them. Thus, when a peasant emigrates to America he may expect to have a good time and learn many things (new experience), to make a fortune (greater security), to have a higher social standing on his return (recognition), and to induce a certain person to marry him (response).

PRIMITIVE REGULATION OF WISHES

Now the simplest attempts to regulate the wishes have always and everywhere—in

OLD WORLD TRAITS TRANSPLANTED

savage as well as civilized societies—taken the form of what is called a "primary-group" organization, and our immigrants, except for the few professionals and intellectuals among them, lived at home under this general system.[1]

"By primary groups I mean those characterized by intimate face-to-face association and co-operation. They are primary in several senses, but chiefly in that they are fundamental in forming the social nature and ideals of the individual. The result of intimate association, psychologically, is a certain fusion of individualities in a common whole, so that one's very self, for many purposes at least, is the common life and purpose of the group. Perhaps the simplest way of describing this wholeness is by saying that it is a 'we'; it involves the sort of sympathy and mutual identification for which 'we' is the natural expression. One lives in the feeling of the whole and finds the chief aims of his will in that feeling." [2]

The obvious value of this type of organization is that it gives solidarity and security to the group; that through group-wise action the interests of all are best secured in the struggle against hunger, cold, enemies, pestilence, and death. It is not a rational

---
[1] The Jew differs indeed from the members of the agricultural communities which furnish the bulk of the remaining immigration, but the Jew lives in fact under a double system. He has a primary group organization connected with his family and the synagogue and at the same time maintains individualized trade relations.
[2] C. H. Cooley, *Social Organization*, p. 23.

form of association; it is customary, and it is capable of assuming the fixity of animal behavior represented in the herd. Every value, every standard of behavior that is fixed by tradition, becomes absolute and assumes a sacred character. Every member is expected to conform and failure to conform produces violent emotions in both the group and the stubborn member. In his volume on the South Slavs, Krauss has given some striking examples of the struggles of the group with the nonconformist.

21. ... Unanimity prevails as a rule, but it also happens that when the question is put by the *domaćin*, all except one may agree to a motion, but the motion is never carried if that one refuses to agree to it. In such cases all endeavor to talk over and persuade the stiff-necked one. Often they even call to their aid his wife, his children, his relatives, his father-in-law, and his mother, that they may prevail upon him to say "yes." Then all assail him, and say to him from time to time, "Come now, God help you, agree with us too, that this may take place as we wish it, that the house may not be cast into disorder, that we may not be talked about by the people, that the neighbors may not hear of it, that the world may not make sport of us!" It seldom occurs in such cases that unanimity is not attained![1]

In another case a member who has been for a time away from the commune and

---
[1] Friedrich S. Krauss, *Sitte und Brauch der Südslaven*, p. 103.

wishes to take advantage of the state law regarding inheritance of property, which differs from the communal practice, is withered by the indignation of the villagers. They tell him he has lost his reason, and eventually he claims this also and asks forgiveness:

22. [The village.] Some strange sin is leading you into an abyss, and has brought you into conflict with the villagers, your brothers. . . . Woe to the brother without a brother! . . . The village is always stronger than the bear. . . . Shake off those strange thoughts and strange clothes.

[Nikola:] Truly, brothers, how shall I answer you? I see myself that I have lost my reason and have sinned against God and against you. And I have mainly injured myself by my wanderings about the world.[1]

23. In the discussion of some question by the *mir* [organization of neighbors] there are no speeches, no debates, no votes. They shout, they abuse one another—they seem on the point of coming to blows; apparently they riot in the most senseless manner. Some one preserves silence, and then suddenly puts in a word, one word, or an ejaculation, and by this word, this ejaculation, he turns the whole thing upside down. In the end, you look into it and find that an admirable decision has been formed and, what is most important, a unanimous decision. . . . [In the division of land] the cries, the noise the

---

[1] Friedrich S. Krauss, *Sitte und Brauch der Südslaven*, pp. 287-291, *passim*.

HERITAGES AND HUMAN WISHES

hubbub do not subside until everyone is satisfied and no doubter is left.[1]

The example cited above from a Mohammedan family in North Africa (document 15), where a father kills his daughter as a matter of course, and the mother and relatives participate as a matter of course, and the girl acquiesces as a matter of course, represents the primary group when the organization is working smoothly.[2] The following documents describe various "primary organizations."

24. The Polish peasant family, in the primary and larger sense of the word, is a social group including all the blood—and law—relatives up to a certain variable limit—usually the fourth degree. The family in the narrower sense, including only the married pair with their children, may be termed the

[1] A. N. Engelgardt, *Iz Derevni: 12 Pisem* (From the Country: 12 letters), p. 315.

[2] We must mention, however, that the community does not determine the character of its members as completely as these instances would indicate. It gives the member those attitudes which are necessary to the common life, but outside of these he may be individualistic, even obstinate and incalculable:

"I have many times pointed to the strong development of individualism in the peasants, to their separateness in action, their inability, or rather, their unwillingness to combine economically for a common cause. . . . Some investigators even suppose that it is contrary to the spirit of the peasantry to act together in any matter. . . . Indeed, to do a thing together, in a lump, as the peasants say, to do it so that each part cannot be reckoned up, is repugnant to the peasants."[3]

[3] Engelgardt, *ibid.*, p. 374.

"marriage-group." . . . The fundamental . . . connection . . . may be termed "familial solidarity," and manifests itself both in assistance rendered to, and in control exerted over, any members of the group by any other member representing the group as a whole. . . . The familial relation between two members admits no gradation, as does love or friendship. . . . Husband and wife are not individuals more or less closely connected according to their personal sentiments, but group members . . . controlled by both the united families. Therefore the marriage norm is not love, but "respect," as the relation which can be controlled and reinforced by the family, and which corresponds also exactly to the situation of the other party as member of a group and representing the dignity of that group. . . .

In all the relations between parents and children the familial organization leaves no place for merely personal affection. Certainly this affection exists, but it cannot express itself in socially sanctioned acts. . . . The behavior of the parents toward the children . . . must be determined exclusively by their situations as family members, not by individual merits or preference. . . . Thus, the parents, usually prefer one child to the others, but this preference should be based upon a familial superiority. The preferred child is usually the one who for some reason is to take the parental farm (the oldest son in central Poland; the youngest son in the mountainous districts of the south; any son who stays at home while others emigrate), or it is the child who is most likely to raise by his personal qualities the social standing of the family. . . .

The reality of the familial ties once admitted, every member of the family evidently feels responsible for,

HERITAGES AND HUMAN WISHES

and is held responsible for, the behavior and welfare of every other member, because, in peasant thinking, judgments upon the group as a whole are constantly made on the basis of the behavior of members of the family, and vice versa. On this account also between any two relatives, wherever found, an immediate nearness is assumed which normally leads to friendship. In this connection it is noticeable that in primitive peasant life all the attitudes of social pride are primarily familial and only secondarily individual. When a family has lived from time immemorial in the same locality, when all its members for three generations are known or remembered, every individual is classified first of all as belonging to the family, and appreciated according to the appreciation which the family enjoys, while, on the other hand, the social standing of the family is influenced by the social standing of its members, and no individual can rise or fall without drawing to some extent the group with him. At the same time no individual can so rise or fall as to remove himself from the familial background upon which social opinion always puts him.[1]

25. When I first came into this world the Rihbany clan experienced the usual rejoicing which comes to a Syrian clan when a man child is born to one of its families. My kindred rejoiced at my advent, not merely because I was a son instead of a daughter, important as that was, but because I was an asset of the clan, a possible reinforcement to their fighting

---

[1] Thomas and Znaniecki, *The Polish Peasant*, vol. i, pp. 87-97, *passim*. The peasant is everywhere changing rapidly in Europe so that the organization here sketched is hardly anywhere found in its pure form. It is, nevertheless, still the dominant fact in peasant life.

strength, which they had to use often against another powerful clan in the town, called Jirdak. In the Jirdak camp, however, a correspondingly great sorrow was felt. On the same night on which I was born they lost by death one of their most valiant fighters. . . . As clans, we lived in accordance with the precept, "Eye for eye, tooth for tooth, burning for burning, wound for wound," and no favor. . . .

Clannish life has its decidedly romantic side. Provided one is able and willing to forget the larger interests of civilization and the nobler visions of nationalism and human brotherhood, and make the rule of his social life the faulty maxim, "My clan, right or wrong," I know of no more delightful social state than that which clannish life affords. As I write, the past rises before me like a bewitching dream. I am carried back to the time when the hearts of all my kinsmen throbbed, beat for beat, with my heart; when everyone of their homes was as much mine as my own fireside, when we lived in life's shifting lights and shadows, "all for each and each for all." The fact that we dwelt among antagonistic clans served only to heighten our heroism, strengthen our clannish cohesion, and intensify the delightfulness of our kinship.[1]

26. There are about four hundred and fifty clans in the [Chinese] Empire. Branches of the most important of them are found in nearly every province. A town, however, never consists of people of one clan alone, as a man is not allowed to marry a woman of the same name. The organization of them is so complete that, while it sometimes secures justice to the innocent, it may besides thwart the designs of

[1] A. M. Rihbany, *A Far Journey* (autobiography of a Syrian immigrant, now a Unitarian minister in Boston), p. 3.

the government, and even of justice. In some parts of the country they keep up bitter and even bloody quarrels from generation to generation; and the chiefs of the clan at Peking are able to prevent the punishment of murder and violence committed by members of it elsewhere. . . . I know of none in California.

The second class of powerful organizations in China is the trade associations, or guilds. These resemble those for similar objects in Europe and America, and therefore need no special description here. They are there, as here, often beneficent in their operations, and yet often oppressive. In a monarchical or despotic government they are useful as a check against its tyranny; but it is still doubtful whether they are not more of an injury than a benefit, since they interfere with healthful competition, remove incitements to industry, and provide opportunities for the arts of intriguing and worthless men, or resorts for the depraved. It is stated that there are a hundred and fifty of their halls in Canton. . . .

The third class is that of town and district councils. This forms the highest advance toward a regular representative government. They exercise the local powers of government to such an extent that the imperial officers rarely dare to rouse them to general resistance. The local administration of justice is left almost wholly in their hands. Police arrangements, and taxation for local purposes, are within their jurisdiction. The elders elected generally are continued as long as they perform their duties with satisfaction to the people. They are allowed a salary of from two to four hundred dollars a year. The elders of a district, which may embrace fifty to a hundred towns and villages, meet in a district council, which has its central hall, and a president and other necessary officers, who receive sufficient salaries. . . .

During the stormy times succeeding the Opium War, foreigners seeking to enlarge their former restrictions often came into conflict with these councils, and proved the extent of the popular power. We were effectually prevented from renting houses, after agreeing to pay the most outrageous, exorbitant rents, by a simple notification from the council of the ward of the city in which they were situated, that if the owner admitted us to the building it would be destroyed, and himself put to death. Nor was the governor-general, with the power of the Emperor to back him, able to sustain us against such a decree.[1]

In America we think of the "feeling of personality" as associated with individually determined acts and policies. The individual acts "on his own," takes great risks, and takes the consequences. But in the case of our immigrants the whole struggle for self-expression has been made as a member of an organization, and the individual has felt himself a person to the degree that he was incorporated in an organization. The primary group maintains the security of the whole community at the sacrifice of the wishes of its individual members. There is little place for new experience, individual recognition, and individual response, because there is little place for individual initiative

---

[1] R. E. Speer, "The Democracy of the Chinese," in *Harper's Magazine*, vol. xxxvii, p. 843.

and responsibility. But the group, as a whole, has an astonishing interest in its own status among the surrounding groups, that it shall be respected and shall prosper and advance, for status means a general, public, and permanent recognition and gives a sense of permanent security. The individual also seeks status, but he must get this as the member of a group. Even the response he seeks in marriage is the response appropriate to him as member of a group. It is on this basis that we can understand completely the letters written by immigrant boys to their parents asking them to send them wives. The parents can be trusted to select girls whose status will not lower the status of the family. This is what the parents mean when they write that they will send a "suitable" wife. They may name the family of the girl, but not state which daughter is to be sent, and the boy may or may not inquire whether they are sending this or that girl:

27. [November 11, 1902.] DEAREST PARENTS: Please do not be angry with me for what I shall write. I write you that it is hard to live alone, so please find some girl for me, but an orderly [honest] one, for in America there is not even one single orderly [Polish] girl. . . . [December 21, 1902.] I thank you kindly for your letter, for it was happy. As to the girl,

although I don't know her, my companion, who knows her, says that she is stately and pretty, and I believe him, as wel˙ as you, my parents. . . . Please inform me which one [of the sisters] is to come, the older or the younger one, whether Aleksandra or Stanislawa.[1]

ADJUSTMENT TO INDIVIDUALISTIC SOCIETY

The form of organization which we have here sketched is common to all the elementary stages of society. In the formation of the state the sentiment for the community was partly converted into allegiance to an individual and through him to the whole territorial group, the state. Russia, before 1918, was in the stage where subordination to the will of the sovereign was as absolute as subordination to the will of the commune, and Japan still represents this stage, formally if not actually:

28. The people believe that it is the Tsar's business to govern them and that for this the Tsar has no need of the people. The Tsar thinks about them, either with his advisers or alone, not sleeping at night for the welfare of the people, but . . . in the understanding of the people the Tsar should govern alone. That is not his right, but his heavy burden. That is how the people look on it. In the history of Russia the Tsar has frequently taken counsel with the people, but there is only that historical form, understood by the people and near it—a *zemsky sobor*. These

[1] Thomas and Znaniecki, *The Polish Peasant*, vol. ii, p. 259.

assemblies said, "This is what we think, but it is your will."¹

29. Mr. H. Kato, ex-president of the Imperial University, in a recent work entitled *The Evolution of Morality and Law*, says . . . in so many words: "Patriotism in this country means loyalty to the throne. To the Japanese the Emperor and the country are the same. The Emperor of Japan, without the slightest exaggeration, can say, '*L'état, c'est moi.*' The Japanese believe that all their happiness is bound up with the Imperial line and have no respect for any system of morality or law that fails to take cognizance of this fact."²

On the contrary, the individualism which is characteristic of Western cultural societies, and which is largely the result of increased communication, means the tendency to construct a scheme of life and relationships based on the intelligent use of all values that can be found anywhere in the world, disregarding to some extent allegiance to persons and localities.

Nevertheless, the primary-group organization persists as an element in all present societies. It is not, as is usually assumed, a survival of the past, but a spontaneous expression arising in all societies, in all classes, never absorbing completely the interests of its members, but still constituting

---
¹ N. M. Pavlov, *Stenographic Report of the Peterhof Conference* (1905), held under the chairmanship of the Tsar, to determine the form of the Duma, p. 127.
² S. L. Gulick, *Evolution of the Japanese*, p. 373.

the most important form of social life for the immense majority of mankind. It is only in a few large cities that the primary group has lost its importance, and even there its loss begins to be felt as a dangerous trend of social evolution, as is shown by the recent attempts to reconstruct the community in American cities.

The need of intimate, face-to-face relations, the desire to be a member of society, is very powerful. Its strength appears in the mental distress of those in solitary confinement and in the tendency to insanity among those completely isolated—the sheepherders of New Mexico, for example. It is seen, stripped of all inhibitions, naked and mandatory, in cases of mental disorder, which sometimes give the opportunity for deeper insight into the nervous system than is possible in normal life:

> I must join some organization as soon as possible, for I cannot fight all hell by myself indefinitely.[1]

Working upon this need, society at home controlled the behavior of the immigrant completely, or attempted to do so, and gave him a complete and rigid scheme of life. We shall next examine the effect of the great American society on this scheme.

---
[1] Letter from a subject of the delusion of persecution. Haines, *Journal of Abnormal Psychology*, vol. ii, p. 379.

III

IMMIGRANT EXPERIENCES

FROM his peasant community, a primary organization such as we have just described, the immigrant comes to a society in a secondary stage of organization in America, based on business enterprise and represented by the state. Actually, the individual, or the family, almost invariably comes to friends and finds some sort of primary group awaiting him here. If he is a Pole, he settles among Poles, and so with the other races. But this new community is only a loose aggregation of acquaintances, not a complete organization, and, moreover, its members have themselves changed in America. They usually take charge of the newcomer, perhaps board him, and instruct him in American customs until "the green has worn off"—"*ausgegrünt*," as the Jews express it.

CHANGE IN ATTITUDES

The first changes in the immigrant are more or less superficial, relating to dress, manners, and the other signs which will betray him as a "greenhorn." But deeper changes come rapidly, more rapidly than we appreciate. Document 30 shows their nature. Usually parents complain of the rapid changes in children, but in this case it is the reverse:

30. I have just taken my wife and child off Ellis Island. The child is five years old. Three years ago I left him at home, where he was reared by my wife's pious parents. Now the little fellow is the defender of God and rebukes me.

He continually questions his mother as to why I eat uncovered, why I do not wash before eating, why I do not make a *brochoh* [short prayer]. He says to her, "Father is a Gentile."

Upon my question as to why it is prohibited to do the above things he replies that God will punish. He will make me ill and I will be tortured in hell. Grandfather, he says, told him so. I attempted to convince him that his grandfather was joking, but he refuses to believe it. He says that God is listening to our conversation through an angel. Once I asked him to remove his cap, but he only did it because he feared me, and began to cry bitterly and became agitated. In short, he is very far from me. He is afraid of me. He cries and tells his mother that father is a Gentile. He wants no Gentile for a father! . . .

How may the poisoned root of fanaticism be torn out of the child's heart.[1]

---

[1] *Forward* (New York Yiddish newspaper), April 21, 1906.

IMMIGRANT EXPERIENCES

On the other hand, these changes may be very limited and slow, owing to the fact that the immigrant continues to live among his own people and has very few contacts with Americans.

31. Although almost five years have passed since I started for America, it was only now that I caught a glimpse of it. For though I was in America I had lived in practically the same environment which we brought from home. Of course, there was a difference in our joys, in our sorrows, in our hardships, for after all this was a different country; but on the whole we were still in our village in Russia. A child that came to this country and began to go to school had taken the first step into the New World. But the child that was put into the shop remained in the old environment with the old people, held back by the old traditions, held back by illiteracy. Often it was years before he could stir away from it; sometimes it would take a lifetime. Sometimes, too, it happened as in fairy tales, that a hand was held out to you and you were helped out. In my own case it was through the illness which had seemed such a misfortune that I had stirred out of Cherry Street.[1]

32. To the small minority of eager, aggressive idealists, whose restless spirits soon break through the barriers of inherited customs and respond with avidity to the challenges of a higher civilization . . . the word "America" soon takes the form of "opportunity," and is understood in terms of incentive and room for soul expansion. The loose composition of a population of many and mutually exclusive nation-

---

[1] Rose Cohen, *Out of the Shadow*, p. 246.

alities, the grotesque manners, and the multitude of saloons and other haunts of vice and crime in the "lower regions" of American cities, where the foreign colonies are generally located, soon tend to awaken in the mind of that foreigner who finds himself yearning for a better order of things, the significant question, "Where is America?"[1]

33. Finally father, choosing his words carefully with difficulty, said to Doctor McFarland: "Sir, do you know you are the first American gentlemen who has spoken to me in America?" It was true. In all the years of his life in America, father, the scholar, the dreamer, had never really met a real American. He had met people who spoke English, the language of America. They were the bums in our narrow streets, the crooked politicians in our ward. There was not one man whom father knew as an American who was a gentleman.[2]

Nearly all immigrants have idealized America. They have usually had glowing pictures of it, and are disillusioned by the conditions they find here.

34. All the time I hear about the grand city of New York. They say it is something to surprise everyone. I learn New York is twice, three, four, ten times bigger than Italian city. Maybe it is better than Milano. Maybe it is better than Naples. "The land of the free and the home of the brave" —I am young and I think that is beautiful land. I hear such fine words like "liberty," "democracy," "equality," "fraternity," and I like this high prin-

---
[1] A. M. Rihbany, *A Far Journey*, p. 46.
[2] E. C. Stern, *Mother and I*, p. 113.

IMMIGRANT EXPERIENCES

ciples. The people say it is the country where you are your own boss, where you may receive money on your word, where there is trust and confidence, so that America look like a blessed country, and I think I am going to great city, to grand country, to better world, and my heart develop big admiration and a great, noble sentiment for America and the Americano.

I arrive in New York. You think I find here my idea? . . .[1]

LOSS OF STATUS

But the most serious condition results from the loss of status and the consequent diminished sense of personality when the immigrant encounters American conditions. He brings with him certain habits, customs, and traditions, including language, dress, social ritual, sentimental ideals and interests, and a sense of moral worth, and it was in connection with these that he had status at home (the recognition of his group) and a sense of personality (recognition of his role in the group). He brings with him, in fact, (1) a self-consciousness, which is consciousness of his status in his group; (2) a group consciousness, which is consciousness of the status of his group among other groups; and (3) a national consciousness which is

---

[1] Alessandro Daluca, *Life History*. See document 10 and note, p. 11.

consciousness of the status of his national group among other nations. His feeling of personality is dependent on this whole complex of ideas.

When the immigrant comes to America, not only must he leave behind the community which was the basis of his personality and self-respect, but here the very signs of his personality (dress, language, and so forth), which in his own country were the signs of his self-respect, are regarded with contempt and made the occasions of his humiliation. In Europe, the question of personality was not the subject of much reflection, because everything was habitual, but here the realization of incongruities between himself and American life makes the question of personality acute:

35. [He had long wondered why he was always refused work.]—At last a butcher in the upper eighties gave me the answer with pungent frankness. . . . He looked me over from head to foot, and then, with a contemptuous glance at my shabby foreign shoes (the alien's shoes are his Judas), he asked me whether I supposed he wanted a greenhorn in his store. I pondered that query for a long time.[1]

36. [At the University of Missouri] In the first two months I had and lost a half-dozen roommates. Do what I might, I could not make them stay with me. There were never any hard words; we always parted

---
[1] M. E. Ravage, *An American in the Making*, p. 93.

IMMIGRANT EXPERIENCES

as "good friends." But almost from the first day they would hardly talk to me, and before the week was out they would find some excuse for moving or asking me to move. I spent many sleepless nights in trying to figure out the thing. [At this time no one knew that he was a Jew.] [1]

37. When I was twenty-five years old I sailed [from Austrian Poland] for America, with nine suits of clothes and about $200. My first job in this country was in a factory where they painted ribbons for typewriters. The factory was not far from the South Station in Boston. I worked ten hours a day for $4 a week. My ten suits were soon spoiled, for I was ashamed to wear overalls, and one after another my suits were ruined at work. Finally the only suit I had left was a Prince Albert affair. I went to work in that. I remember passing a line of fellow workers leaning against the building, smoking their pipes. When they saw me coming in my Prince Albert, they took their pipes out of their mouths and bowed low to me, saying, "Me lord," as I passed. [2]

38. I found that father was already at home. As I came into the room I saw him resting against the wall, clipping his beard. I was so surprised and shocked to see him actually do this thing that I could neither speak nor move for some minutes. And I knew that he, too, felt embarrassed. After the first glance I kept my eyes steadily on the floor in front of me, and began to talk to him quietly, but with great earnestness: "You had been so pious at home, father," I said, "more pious than anyone else in our whole neighborhood. And now you are cutting your beard. Grandmother would never have believed

---
[1] M. E. Ravage, *An American in the Making*, p. 207.
[2] Frank Wiech, *Lawrence American*, June 4, 1919.

it. How she would weep!" The snipping of the scissors still went on. But I knew by the sound that now he was only making a pretense at cutting. At last he laid it down and said in a tone that was bitter yet quiet: "They do not like Jews on Cherry Street. And one with a long beard has to take his life into his own hands."[1]

39. In the shop . . . the only inequality I had ever felt was that of age . . . while as a servant my home was a few hard chairs and two soiled quilts. My every hour was sold day and night. I had to be constantly in the presence of people who looked down upon me as an inferior. I felt, though in a child's way, that being constantly with people who looked upon me as inferior, I was, or soon would be an inferior.[2]

40. One day a well-dressed strange young man came in. He made sure of our name at the door and then came and sat down at the window, opened a little book and began to question me about my family, my father's name, his trade, how long he had been out of work, how much he had earned, how long mother had been ill, and so on. . . . "Do you need anything?" he asked. . . . "Do we need anything?" It seemed such a strange question and I did not answer, and he repeated the question in Yiddish. I finally did understand and I heard myself say, "No." Still thinking that I did not understand, he asked: "Do you need any clothes?" I shook my head. "Do you need any shoes?" He looked at mine. "No." "Have you everything?" "Everything," I repeated, but I could not look at him. . . . In the evening when father was home our neighbor

---
[1] Rose Cohen, *Out of the Shadow*, p. 106.
[2] *Ibid.*, p. 180.

IMMIGRANT EXPERIENCES

brought in four dollars. "A strange young man left it," she said, and the next day there was a half ton of coal.[1]

41. The first family where I worked knew perfectly well that I spoke French and German. I heard them mention the fact to a guest at the table—but to them I was not any more interesting an object than any peasant girl who could neither read nor write. They might have known that I must have had some sort of education, for the average immigrant girl does not speak many languages. Our relations were entirely impersonal. I found out how foreigners are regarded by the old-line Americans, and I cannot say that it made me feel any more friendly toward America. I was still of the Old World, and who can blame me?[2]

42. There is much Italian talent which Americans do not recognize as yet. The best workers at Tiffany's are Italians. The best designers among garment workers are Italians. I do not understand why Italians have been treated in this country as they have been. I go to a store, and they say to me, "Are you French?" I say, "No." They say, "Spanish?" "No, I am Italian." And then there is immediate coldness and contempt.[3]

43. More than to any other of their heritages, the Italian immigrants hold to their music. When they are in their homes or the homes of their friends they sing their folk songs, but they are ashamed to sing this music when they are in gatherings of Americans. . . . The reason the young people buy ragtime

---

[1] Rose Cohen, *Out of the Shadow*, p. 166.

[2] *Autobiography* of a Finnish girl of Swedish descent (manuscript).

[3] Signora de Blasio, Italian Industrial School, New York (interview).

music is that they do not want to be different from their American friends. When they visit their friends in American homes they find that ragtime music is the music that is played, and they don't want to be humiliated by being different from their American friends. Therefore they buy the same records that their class of Americans do.[1]

In document 44, below, we have a different case of anxiety about status. The family belongs to the type called by the Jews "*allrightnick*" (mentioned in Chapter V); it has penetrated the American environment probably as far as the Bronx, and the writer's anxiety concerns her status in the new situation:

44. I have a nice home, fine clothes, a good husband, and yet all this cannot satisfy me. The reason is that I am uneducated; also my husband, who is even more ignorant than myself. He cannot even write Jewish nor speak properly to anybody. You may, then, picture my anguish!

We live in a very rich neighborhood, among wealthy, intelligent people. I can keep up with their styles, clothes, and furniture, but not with the English language. My misfortune is still greater because I am a good judge of myself. When my husband or I say something that is not expressed properly, I immediately recognize the error and I imagine everybody smiling. And my pain is still more acute over the fact that we came here as children. My husband was nine years old and I eleven. But very unfortu-

---
[1] R. N. O'Neil, *Report on Syracuse, New York* (manuscript).

nately there was no law against child labor at that time. Just imagine a nine or eleven year old child working to-day!

I received a little education in Europe up to my tenth year. I know a little of German, Polish, Russian, and—as you see—Jewish. I can also read an English book and write also—though I am spelling defectively. But what troubles me most is speaking. Am somewhat familiar with the street English, but unable to converse with an intelligent person. My husband does not even know that much. He is a very able business man and no more. Owing to his ignorance I have neglected what I did know, for I did not wish to be superior to him. My desire had always been to marry an educated man and learn from him.

Perhaps you can show us a way to educate ourselves. Some may regard this as folly and remark that I am too comfortable and do not know what I want. My husband is unconcerned, but I am dejected and feel inferior even to the one I am superior to. I must add that we have been married twelve years, have three children. But I am so young— only twenty-nine![1]

The subject of document 45 had a superior standing at home; he was a learned man, and the first experience here is bitter. Obliged to live scantily in New York, he went to a five-cent lodging house kept by one of his countrymen in the Syrian colony. Later, advised by his friends, he takes up peddling.

[1] *Forward*, July 20, 1917.

45. As I lay awake under Moses's roof that night I thought of all the good things I had ever enjoyed in my life, of all the poetry I had learned, of the pride with which my breast had heaved as a "learned man" among my kindred. Now I was in the New World, which did not seem to take immediate notice of my worth, tucked in a dingy corner, nay, crucified between two thieves [fellow lodgers]! . . . Call it pride, vanity, or whatever you please, whenever I thought of peddling "jewelry and notions," death lost its terror for me. The mere sight of those crude, greasy peddlers nauseated me. Come what might, I would not carry the *keshah* [a colloquial Arabic name for the peddler's pack].[1]

Rihbany (document 45) was a man of action and adapted himself rapidly and completely to American conditions. But certainly the most difficult and painful situation is that of the superior person who is inclined by temperament and training to analyze his emotions and rationalize his situation in America. Document 46 indicates the degree of nervous shock possible in such cases:

46. The first period was characterized by a loss in emotional life. There was: (1) a fading of emotional tones [*Gefühlsbetonung*] and a gradual reappearance. I forgot for some years that birds sing, flowers have odor, stars shine. I lost interest in theater, concert, fiction; (2) a replacement of emotional

---

[1] A. M. Rihbany, *A Far Journey*, p. 194.

IMMIGRANT EXPERIENCES

standards by opportunistic notions. I did not think of what I liked or disliked, but of what was advantageous or disadvantageous. There was a decided shifting from emotional to rational motives. I found it very difficult to adopt a new code of conduct because of an entirely foreign emotional basis. . . .

After some years of life in America a reconstruction of my emotional life took place. I was building up another emotional basis. Some of the means to it were: (1) a groping for new interest (literature, bibliography, history, world politics, science); (2) participation in public interests and activities (*Vereinigung alter Deutscher Studenten in Amerika*, Bibliographical Society, Rifle Club, Military Work); (3) new social contacts (clubs, society); (4) my family interests.

The transition period caused by my emigration lasted nearly twenty years and was retarded by the Great War. A return to normal emotional life showed itself by the absence of dreams in which I saw myself back at home again. Such dreams were extremely frequent at first. Now all my plans and hopes centered in America and the desire for a permanent return to Europe ceased. Also the fear of isolation in America ceased and a sentiment of coherence with the new country and identification developed and has probably completely established itself. . . .

A very serious handicap in my new life in America was the loss of confidence in my judgment which the shifting from one emotional standard to another one caused. Whenever we must decide quickly we judge subconsciously. The subconscious life was destroyed and badly disorganized. I never knew if my reactions would be in line with the new code of conduct and had to think and reflect. Whenever I decided on the spur of the moment I found myself out of sympathy with my environment. I did not feel as they felt and therefore I felt wrongly according to their standards. To act instinctively in an American fashion and manner was impossible, and I appeared slow and clumsy. The proverbial slowness of foreigners is largely due to this cause.[1]

Document 47 is typical of the experience of the unsophisticated immigrant who loses in America that security assured to him at home as a member of an organization. Taken in connection with the foregoing experience, it indicates the motive for the spontaneous formation of the immigrant organizations—mutual aid, nationalistic, and so forth—in America, which we shall notice later.

47. I have been five years in America. For four years I lived in Cleveland and now I am in Chicago. When I came to Chicago I did not have anybody. I got off the train, took my wife and three children, and we walked about the city until we came to the Jewish neighborhood. We stopped on a corner and were talking it over. We decided to look for rooms in order to have a home where we could lay our heads down. We found three rooms for $7 a month. Then I left my wife and children in the vacant rooms and I went to buy some furniture, and I was told to go to a certain store. I went in there and I was treated cordially. I told them I want some furniture

---

[1] Autobiography of an Austrian-German university man (manuscript).

IMMIGRANT EXPERIENCES

only of the cheap kind, because I am still green here and they should not overcharge me. So they said: "We have only one price, and cheaper than anywhere." So I believed them and I took, like a poor man, not what was necessary, only what we had to have. The prices they quoted were really not very dear and they told me to come back on Saturday for my bill. In the meantime they took a deposit from me, $50, and I was to pay $2 a week. Then I came home and ate and I went to look for a job and I found one at $9 a week. I was very pleased with Chicago. The next morning I went to work. I had left $4.75.

When I came home after my first day's work I found my home fixed up with the furniture that they had sent up. We had our supper with great happiness. Sabbath (Saturday) came and I went up for my bill and handed them $2, the first payment. They entered it in their books and they gave me a book. When I looked in the book, my eyes became dark! The bill amounted to $235.98! For half an hour I could not speak and when I came to myself and I asked them, "What is that?" they said, "We told you the prices before." The prices were entered correctly but with a "slight" difference. For instance: The bed does cost $15, and they entered $15 but they had added springs, $10, and a mattress, $10. A stove is $28, as in my book, but a mantel for the stove $15 more. And so on for everything. But I saw that it was over and I went home. To my wife I did not disclose the real bill. She would not shout at me, but I did not want her to be vexed over it. I used to pay $2 every week and was considered a fine man in the store. And so I paid a whole year and never missed a week. Fifteen weeks ago I lost my job and I could not get another one so quickly. And I disliked the work, too, so I wanted to learn a good trade, and I saw an advertisement in the newspaper that they are teaching a good trade, and they are furnishing a steady place, and it takes two weeks. I went up there and they told me that they give a place and it takes two weeks, only it costs $50 for the course and the payment is in advance. If I had seen that I was dealing with *Schnorrers* I would have gone away. But here I saw an office with twenty bookkeepers, with a whole business, so I went home and talked it over with my wife and we decided that I should go and learn the trade. But I did not have no $50, so, as we still had some pieces of jewelry that we had brought from Cleveland, we pawned them and gave them $50, and the next day I went to work there.

When I went into the shop everybody began to laugh at me. But I did not pay any attention to them. When I spoke to the foreman, the instructors, I saw that it does not take two weeks, but two years, and that they do not give any place, and that one must know good English. I realized that I fell in with $50! I came home half dead and half alive, and I could not eat any supper that night. The next morning I went up there and I told them that this work is not for me, that I am green yet for this kind of work, and I wanted them to deduct $10 for the day and to refund me $40. So they began to send me from one to the other. The one to whom I gave the money wasn't there any more. In his place there was already another. I stood there, talked and cried it did not help me and I went home.

The next day I went up there again and they told me the same as yesterday. I began to go there every day and I began to shout, so they called a policeman and wanted to arrest me. I went to a lawyer and he wanted $15 beforehand, win or lose. I did not have even fifteen cents. I went to the Jewish Protective Association and told them my story. They told me that they can do nothing for me because I am not entitled to get my money back. So it means that I have lost $50! If I had lost it I would not have been so sorry; maybe another poor man would have found it. But here I see how they are running out in their automobiles, going to the best hotels, to the largest theaters for my hard-earned $50.

But that is not all. Listen further. Now it is already fifteen weeks that I am not working. In our city there is a big crisis. Sometimes I strike a job and I make $4 or $5 a week. From these earnings I cannot take $2 a week to pay for the furniture. So I went to them and I asked them to wait. They promised me. But when I went away to-day to look for a job and when I returned I found something that shocked me so that I nearly lost my mind. The house was vacant; they had taken away everything from my house; my wife was lying on the floor, her hair disheveled; two men were holding her and two men were taking everything out. Now it is winter and we are without a stove and without anything.

Again I went to the Jewish Protective Association and they say that the furniture dealer is lawfully right.

To find work in Chicago now is impossible. I haven't even a penny. Naked and shoeless, of what good is my life in this world? So I decided to end my life, but before I do that I want to avenge myself on the two murderers. But I am asking you, publish this letter, let the people know the life of the poor, what the rich do with their hard-earned money![1]

---

[1] *Forward*, January 26, 1914.

IV

IMMIGRANT DEMORALIZATION

HUMAN nature is such that society has an extremely difficult task to make its individual member "good"—that is, to regulate and organize his wishes and make him efficient. Even when the population is homogeneous, the traditions unbroken, the institutions of family, community, state, church, school, etc., complete, it is a task which society never accomplishes perfectly; we always have some disorder and crime.

"Good" behavior, conformity to accepted standards, is secured in any population by what we may call a *common definition of the situation*. The "shalt nots" of the Ten Commandments are definitions of the situation. The "don'ts" of the mother, the gossip of the community, epithets ("liar," "thief"), shrugs, sneers, and "bawlings out," the press, the pulpit, legal decisions, etc., are common methods of defining the situation.

IMMIGRANT DEMORALIZATION

At home the immigrant was almost completely controlled by the community; in America this lifelong control is relaxed. Here the community of his people is at best far from complete, and, moreover, it is located within the American community, which lives by different and more individualistic standards, and shows, as we have seen, a contempt for all the characteristics of the newcomers. All the old habits of the immigrant consequently tend to break down. The new situation has the nature of a crisis, and in a crisis the individual tends either to reorganize his life positively, adopt new habits and standards to meet the new situation, or to repudiate the old habits and their restraints without reorganizing his life—which is demoralization.

There is, of course, violation of the traditional code, "breaking of the law," in all societies, and there is at present a general problem of demoralization in the regions from which our immigrants come, particularly where the peasant population has come into contact with the industrial centers or practices seasonal emigration (as from Poland to Germany); but the demoralization, maladjustment, pauperization, juvenile delinquency, and crime are incomparably greater among the immigrants in America than in the corresponding European communities.

EARLY STAGES

In document 48 below, the girl is not yet demoralized. Her habits are disorganized and it is a painful situation, but she is evidently trying to make the transition to a new group—to become Americanized. She may marry and become an *allrightnick* (see document 81, p. 102), or she may abandon the family and become wayward. A too rapid Americanization is usually disastrous. Document 49 presents another painful and abnormal situation, as result of the same process of rapid change in children. The humoristic fiction extract (document 50) illustrates the condition of the individual whose life is no longer regulated by the community norms and who is not yet able to stabilize his life on any other basis:

48. [Her husband, a business man in Russia, contracted for standing grain and was ruined. Her sister in America offered to take her daughter until she had "worked herself up" and could send for her parents.]

So we sent our sixteen years old daughter to America and we remained at home. I cannot describe to you the way I felt when my daughter left us. Many nights I did not sleep and shed many tears before I received a letter from her that she had arrived safely.

IMMIGRANT DEMORALIZATION

We thought that we should be able to follow her within a short time, but it was not so. My daughter came to America, but she did not meet with luck and it happened that our condition improved, so we wrote to our child to come home.

This was three years after she left us. We wrote one letter after the other and we begged her to return, but she did not want to. She wrote that she liked America and did not even think of returning home. I am a mother, and a faithful mother at that, and I was longing for her, and when I saw that she did not want to return, I began to persuade my husband to go to America. He did not care to go, but I talked so much and argued and pleaded with him that he consented and we emigrated to America. It was not so soon; a few years had passed, and when we arrived we did not recognize our daughter. She was grown up, tall, pretty—a pleasure to look at her.

My husband began to earn little by little. We fixed up a nice home and I was happy because I could see my daughter. But soon I realized that my big pretty daughter is not the girl I knew; she has changed entirely. During the few years that she was here without us she became a regular Yankee and forgot how to talk Yiddish. I talk to her in Yiddish and she replies in English. With much difficulty I induce her to speak a word in Yiddish and I succeed only when there are no strangers in the house. When strange people come to us, my daughter will not say a single Yiddish word.

So I ask her: "Daughter of mine, talk Yiddish to me and I will understand you." She says that it is not nice to talk Yiddish and that I am a greenhorn. And that is not all. She does worse things. She wants to make a Christian woman out of me. She does not like to have me light the Sabbath candles, to observe the Sabbath. When I light the candles she blows them out. She does all the things that I do not want, that cause me the greatest heartache. And she argues with me. She says that because I and my husband are pious and have a Jewish home, she can never invite a boy acquaintance to her house; she is ashamed. She makes fun of me and her father. She calls us greenhorns and is ashamed of us. Once I saw her standing on the stoop with a boy, so I went up to her and asked her when she would come up and eat something. She did not even reply, and later when she came up she screamed at me because I had called her by her Jewish name. But I cannot call her differently. I cannot call her by her new name.

Dear Editor, it is impossible to describe the troubles that she causes us, and as much as I ask her to be a good daughter, it does not help. Please write a few words for my daughter.[1]

49. I, an old seventy-year old Jew, am asking you for a little space to tell you my troubles. I have hardly begun to write and my tears are coming down already.

Just listen what children are. At home I was a business man. In Russia I have played a big part, employed many people, contributed much to charity, and had a good name. My house was always open for the needy and hungry. The best people of our city came to my house. In short, I had everything that one could wish for. . . .

[Business failed, but saved money and on it his sons and sons-in-law have become prosperous in America.] My daughters go to the country every year. Naturally it costs them a large sum of money.

---
[1] *Forward*, July 9, 1917.

IMMIGRANT DEMORALIZATION

First, they go with their children, my grandchildren; second, they buy extra dresses and they go to a swell place where they pay high prices. And my sons-in-law go to them every Saturday and return Monday morning. Until now I would remain at home with the servant girl. She would wash and cook for me. But this summer they took the girl along with them and on account of her I went too.

Now I am cursing every day my old years. I am worse off than a beggar, because a beggar when he does get a piece of bread he can eat it wherever he wishes, but I cannot. They, my children and my grandchildren, told me that I should not sit and eat with them at the same table because I do not know English and I have a long gray beard, and to sit with such a father or with such a grandfather is a shame. . . . So they told the hotelkeeper to make a separate place for me in a hut not far from the springs. And so I am getting my meals just like a dog. They do not talk to me, they do not take me along whenever they go out for a walk; they do not want to introduce me to anybody and so on. . . .

So I decided to ask my children for a few hundred dollars and I will return to Russia. And there I should close my eyes far, far from my children and die among strange people on a strange bed.[1]

50. Because he was too lazy to go to preparatory school to gather "counts" like his older brother, and his mother made his life miserable, he read Yiddish papers and was an anarchist. And because he was an anarchist he wanted to like music, and he let his hair grow until it was big enough for both an anarchist and a violin virtuoso. Bertha felt he was the right man for her, so she no longer looked with disfavor

---

[1] *Forward*, July 15, 1914.

upon Yiddish papers, ceased buying the *Times* every morning, and donned an anarchist blouse with a black tie. When his mother saw their intimate relations she discharged the girl from the shop. If they had no serious intentions until then, this action served to bring them closer together and they went to live in a free union. . . .[1]

EXTREME CASES

In document 51 we have a definite demoralization, but in its first stages; while in document 52 the demoralization is complete. In this case there had been no organizing influence of family and community, no definition of the situation in social terms, and the boy shows the predatory disposition natural to boys, one which in tribal times, on the frontier, and in war makes the hero:

51. DEAR SISTER: I write as to a sister and I complain as to a sister about my children from the old country—those three boys. I did not have them with me, and I grieved continuously about them; and to-day again, on the other hand, my heart is bleeding. They will not listen to their mother. If they would listen, they would do well with me. But no, they wish only to run everywhere about the world, and I am ashamed before people that they are so bad. They arrived, I sent them to school, because it is obligatory to send them; if you don't

---

[1] F. Stock, *The Day* (New York Yiddish newspaper), January 14, 1917.

IMMIGRANT DEMORALIZATION

do it the teacher comes and takes them by the collar. So they have been going, but the oldest was annoyed with the school. "No, mamma, I will go to work." I say, "Go on to school." But "No!" and "No!" Without certificates from the school they won't let them work. I got certificates for the two oldest ones: "Go, if you wish." They worked for some time, but they got tired of work. One went with a Jew to ramble about corners (trading or amusing himself?), and for some days was not to be seen; I had to go and search for him. The worst one of them is Stach; the two others are a little better. They were good in the beginning, but now they know how to speak English and their goodness is lost. I have no comfort at all. I complain [to you] as to a sister. Perhaps you will relieve me at least with a letter, if you write me some words, dear sister. . . .

Stach has been bad, is bad, and will be bad. So long as he was smaller he remained more at home. I begged him, "Stach, remain at home with your mother." No, he runs away and loafs about. Well, let him run. I had his eyes wiped [had him instructed] as well as I could; he can read, write, and speak English, quite like a gentleman. You say, "Beat." In America you are not allowed to beat; they can put you into a prison. Give them to eat, and don't beat—such is the law in America. Nothing can be done, and you advise to beat! Nothing can be done; if he is not good of himself, he is lost. . . .

I regret that I took the children from our country so soon. In our country perhaps they would have had some misery, and in America they have none, and because of this many become dissolute. In America children have a good life; they don't go to any pastures, but to school, and that is their whole work. . . .[1]

52. When eleven years old [father still living] Walter Dyganski was brought to court in company with three other boys, accused of breaking a padlock on a grocery store and attempting to enter the store at 4 A.M., March, 1909, and also of breaking a padlock on the door of a meat market and stealing thirty-six cents from the cash till. Put on probation.

August 19, 1910.—Brought to court for entering with two other boys a store and stealing a pocketbook containing $3. "He admitted to the officers he and his company were going to pick pockets downtown. He is the leader of the gang." The officer believes he is encouraged in his acts by his mother. . . .

Sent to St. Charles.—Ran away March 17, 1913. By breaking a window got into a drug store with two other boys and stole a quantity of cigars and $1.61. Having taken the money, he gave one boy 10 cents and another 5 cents. He gave away the cigars—eight or nine boxes—to "a lot of men and some boys." Spent the money "on candy and stuff." Committed to John Worthy School. . . .

October 27th.—His conduct has improved greatly; released on probation. Work was slack; boy changed three positions within a month.

December 23, 1913.—Accused of having broken, with an adult boy nineteen, into a clothing store and filled a suit case they found in the store with clothing and jewelry. Caught in shop. The officer said: "He would like to imitate Webb. He would like to kill somebody." According to his own confession: "It

---

[1] Thomas and Znaniecki, *The Polish Peasant in Europe and America*, vol. ii, pp. 219–223.

was six o'clock at night. I was going to confession. I met a boy and he said, 'Come out with me.' About nine o'clock we came to a clothing store, and we walked to the back, and seen a little hole. We pulled a couple of the laths off and as soon as we got in we got caught." But the officer said that previous to this they had burglarized a butcher's store and took from there a butcher's steel, and bored a hole in the wall with it. Committed to John Worthy School. Released June 26, 1914. . . .

July 19th.—Shot in a back alley twice at a little boy and once hit him. Broke with two other boys at night into Salvation Army office, broke everything he could and "used the office as a toilet room." Next day broke into a saloon, broke the piano, took cigars. Before this, July 14th, broke a side window of a saloon, stole $4 and a revolver. At the hearing Walter said about shooting the boy: "That boy was passing and I asked him for a match, and I heard the boy holler. I took a revolver off him [his companion] and fired a shot and hit the boy." His mother testified that he had spent only three nights at home since the time of his release from John Worthy School. He was arrested after the first offense, but escaped from the detention home. Committed to John Worthy School. . . .

[Letter of Mr. Millkan, John Worthy School, January 4, 1915:] ". . . I wish to recommend for release . . . Walter D. He has been at the Worthy School 568 days. . . . I am putting him on the list, not because I feel that he will make good on the outside, but because by keeping him here we are removing all possibility of his making good, and I feel that for his sake he should be given a chance. If he returns to the court he should be sent to Pontiac, where he can be kept from society entirely. He is bright enough, but a sullen, surly character." . . .

Released after March 26th.—Committed a burglary in a grocery store, April 17th. Shot a man with a revolver in the left arm April 4th; held up, with three other boys, a man on April 11th, and robbed him of $12. Caught later, while the other boys caught at once. Held to the Grand Jury, found "not guilty," and released June 16, 1915.[1]

Our documents show that the disorderly behavior of the immigrant is often connected with some misapprehension of what he sees and hears here. In seeking to imitate the new environment he naturally selects the more pleasurable aspects—those giving expression to his suppressed wishes, perhaps gratifying the natural tendency to vagabondage.

53. Mary Ceglarck *vs.* Joseph Ceglarck. Married twelve years. During this period he deserted her more than a dozen times, but always returned after a month or so.[2]

But frequently he really misunderstands our institutions, seeing an identity in situations which have only a superficial or nominal resemblance. So much is heard of divorce in America that the immigrants have developed a tradition that we have no marriage

---

[1] Records of the Juvenile Court of Cook County, Illinois.
[2] Records of the Chicago Legal Aid Society.

IMMIGRANT DEMORALIZATION

—only temporary relations. A boy writes to his parents in Poland:

54. You write me whether I am married. Well, no. America is not the old country where it is necessary to marry for your whole life. Here it is not so.[1]

An analysis of the puzzling cases of immigrant crime shows that the perpetrators often introduce features which they think are a part of the proper procedure in the case, but which show a misapprehension of the motives of the American models which they think they are imitating:

55. On October 20, 1911, Walter Shiblawski, Frank Shiblawski, Philip Suchomski, Thomas Schultz, Philip Sommerling, and Frank Keta (all boys) held up and killed Fred Guelzow, a farmer, who was bringing a load of vegetables to Chicago. They had two revolvers, a bread knife, a pocketknife, and a large club. They had been reading novels and planned a hold-up. When Guelzow was ordered to hold up his hands he promptly did so. They took his silver watch and chain, then killed him, mutilated him horribly with bullets and knives, and cut off a piece of his leg and put it in his mouth.[2]

It appears from the complete record that the boys were not satisfied with the mere

---
[1] Thomas and Znaniecki, *The Polish Peasant*, vol. ii, p. 287.
[2] The details are in the records of the Coroner's office, Chicago.

hold-up. They were nonplused to find that it was all over and there had been no killing. It was not complete and did not correspond to a hold-up as they had come to understand it. So they added the details which were lacking. The immigrant child is more likely than an American child to follow the suggestion gotten from picture shows.

The person who has been completely controlled by a group, whose behavior in a limited number of possible situations has been predetermined by his community, tends to behave in wild and incalculable ways, to act on any vagrant impulse that invades his mind, when withdrawn from the situations he knows and removed from the background of a permanent community. The result is behavior that is incomprehensible because it follows no known pattern:

56. On August 29th at 3 P.M., I was in the house, the following people being present: Joseph Stanczak, his wife, Josephine Okrasina, and myself. We drank some beer and got pretty well intoxicated. I did not drink anything. The two Stanczak brothers were arguing over $100. About nine o'clock I went to bed, but I could not sleep. I stayed in bed until eleven o'clock. I got up, put on my trousers, and sat on the side of the bed until 1 A.M. And Constantine Binkowski came into the house through the kitchen door. I seen him through the bedroom door

which was open. I went into the kitchen and took hold of Feliks Stanczak and put him outside through the kitchen door which I locked about ten minutes later. Joseph Stanczak took a bottle, a pail, and went out. When Joseph Stanczak went out Constantine Binkowski came into the bedroom where I was and told me I had better get out of the house or the two brothers would lick me. So I took my hat and coat and shoes and went out alone leaving Mrs. Stanczak asleep in the kitchen bedroom. Josephine Okrasina was sitting at the kitchen table and Constantine Binkowski was standing in the kitchen. I went over to Peter Altman's house . . . first floor; and old lady Binkowski let me in. There I put my shoes, coat, and hat on, and went back to Stanczak's and entered by the rear door. Finding the two Stanczak brothers, Joe and Feliks, I said: "If you are so strong, why, commence now." Joseph ran toward me, struck me with his fist right by my right ear. I had a file which I carried inside with me, and pulled it out of my pocket and struck Joseph on the head with it. He fell down on his side and then Feliks ran toward me and I struck him twice on the head with the file. And he staggered against the stove and called out, "Women, help." Feliks ran into the bedroom and Joe was about to get up. When I seen him getting up, the file slipped out of my hand and I grabbed the chair and beat him with it on the head. The chair broke in pieces and he fell down again. I don't know how or when the women got out, but they were gone at that time. I went into the front bedroom and got my revolver which I had bought from a pawn man a few months before. . . . I bought it with the intention of killing Joseph Stanczak after a fight I had three months ago.

I then went to Joseph Polowski's. . . . I got there about four o'clock . . . and I slept until about noon. Got up and ate breakfast, and left there and rode to Stephen Malecki's, Twenty-sixth Street. I got there about 2 P.M., I changed into my Sunday clothes and left there about 4 P.M. I went downtown to see a show on State Street. I left the theater at 9 P.M., and then I came home to Peter Altman's . . . and slept in the kitchen until eight o'clock in the morning— August 31st. Then I got my revolver and went to Joseph Stanczak's. I entered by the kitchen door and went into the bedroom where Joseph Stanczak was sleeping and fired three shots at him. He was asleep. There was nobody else in the house at the time and nobody knew my intention that I know of. I then went to (Altman's) house, where I sat on the porch while I emptied and cleaned the revolver and then went to the attic and hid the revolver. . . . After hiding the revolver I went down to Altman's and went in and sat there until 5.30 A.M. Then I went upstairs to Stephen Vickes, where he made up a lunch for me, and I went to work at the car . . . shop. This was September 1st. I worked all day and went home and slept in Altman's house and went away. I ate my supper at Stephen Weybeck's, Twenty-sixth Street. They mentioned that Joseph Stanczak was dead, but I didn't answer when they told me. I went down to Stanczak's place and Josephine Stanczak and Josephine Okrasina and Binkowski was there. And Binkowski told me that Joseph Stanczak was dead, and I answered that his time was come. The women were in bed asleep and I went to bed and slept with little John Stanczak [his victim's son]. And no more said about the death. The morning of September 2d I got up at 9.30 and went

IMMIGRANT DEMORALIZATION

to work. I worked until 1.30 P.M. At the time I was arrested. . . .

Question.—Did the wife of this man ever make you an offer of $25 to kill him?

Answer.—No, she did not.

Question.—Weren't you living with her just the same as if you were married to her?

Answer.—No, never.

Question.—Why did you do this?

Answer.—I done this just because I knew that this man lived long enough. He killed one in the old country. He cut a man out there with a razor.

Question.—Was this man in the old country that was killed by Joseph Stanczak a relative of yours?

Answer.—I don't know this man at all.[1]

We learn from other sources that Opalski was disturbed by the fact that he was not immediately recognized as the murderer, and, so to speak, claimed the crime. We have other documents showing that immigrants have been pronounced insane by our courts, because their behavior showed no sort of consistency, who at home would probably have remained normal, though perhaps difficult, members of their communities.

Another type of demoralization occurs where a socially produced inhibition yields to the prompting of an instinctive appetite:

57. Defendant, Lithuanian, naturalized, fifteen years in America. Testimony of Mrs. White: "I

[1] Confession of Joseph Opalski, records of the Chicago Criminal Court.

live down stairs from where these people lived upstairs. . . . She [defendant's daughter, twelve years old] came on Sunday morning, 28th of February, and looked as though she had been crying. I says: 'Anna, what is the matter?' She says: 'Well, if I would tell you, my papa would be put in jail.' I says: 'What did he do?' 'Oh, he did something bad to me, he did really wrong.' And I questioned her. . . . I said, 'Could that be so?' . . . I thought that was pretty dangerous, and as I have a ten-year old girl myself, I thought it best to go to the station."[1]

Communal habits of life and the disposition to regard any countryman as a friend, make it easy for the immigrants to exploit one another in various ways, and some of them make a business of doing this:

58. Defendant Kasimerz Marzec was engaged to be married to Katie Dupak, who went with him three years. On his promise of marriage he got from her $200 in cash. She bought him a suit of clothes valued at $25; he took her watch, $20; she bought a couple of rings valued $10, which he took along with him. The baby was born and the midwife bill was $10, and the baby died later and she paid $50 for the funeral. Then there was the meats and everything ordered, $77, for the wedding feast. She paid all this for him. They were to be married September 10, 1915. He left on September 8, 1915, for parts unknown. He got back September 18, 1916, and was arrested in Chicago. He said he

[1] Records of the Chicago Criminal Court.

IMMIGRANT DEMORALIZATION

caught her talking to some other fellow. . . . The child was born in December, 1915. . . . [Before leaving he married another girl and went with her to Philadelphia.] [1]

59. I am a married man and live contented with my wife and two children and could be happy for a long time were it not for the trouble that corrupts my life, and that is my conscience, which burns with a hellish fire in my heart, which gives me no minute's rest and which will soon make me give up my happy life.

For the past few years I was in business for myself . . . and always worried about a livelihood until this summer. I am now an agent for lots and sell them to the poor workers of New York. I make a lot of money in my present business. I make more than I ever could make and this is the cause of my trouble; for I do not consider myself as agent, but an accomplice of a band of robbers who are robbing people right and left in the name of business.

The lots that I have sold are very far away, but it is so trickily done that the trip with our victims shall not take over thirty to forty minutes, and when we arrive at the station the victims are packed into autos or large wagons and when they are dragged out of the vehicles—tired and full of illusions about fortunes that they will now secure (we, the agents, are filling their heads with it during the trip), they are relieved of their money so easily that it is really a shame. You can imagine what it means when the chief of the gang himself exclaims—after raking in all the money—in English, and with a villainous smile: "It's really a shame to take the money, by Jesus." They are stripped of all the money they

[1] Records of the Chicago Criminal Court.

possess, from $1 up. Even if the lots were sold by a reliable company they are being charged $200 for every $5 worth.

How, then, can one witness such robberies? And you ought to see the agents! It is a rather mixed gang. Some are apparently born for that; they are stout-faced and of large physical proportions so that one can at once tell that they had never earned an honest cent; and then there are Jews with *peyos* [side locks] and whiskers, dressed in half-silk coats, with pious faces, who always speak with God's help.

I laid my eyes upon an Essex Street Jew and his son. They are quite green in the country, but not in the business. I do not want to bother you or I could fill a volume on this little Jew.

Among the gang there is also a Brooklyn woman who knows how to lure innocent victims and extract the last hard-earned pennies from the poor workers.

Well, I think you know enough to comprehend my situation. I know how dirty is this sort of business. You can imagine how bad I feel that when a friend of mine asks my advice as to purchasing some lots in Brooklyn . . . I asked him to purchase from me.

I have acquired gold out of dirt and dirt out of gold. I am satisfied to give up my dirty fortune if I could only get some good advice as to what to do. . . .[1]

60. I am a girl from Galicia. I am neither old nor young. I am working in a shop like other girls. I have saved up several hundred dollars.

Naturally, a young man began to court me, and it is indeed this that we girls are seeking. I became acquainted with him through a Russian [Jewish] matchmaker who for a short while boarded with a

---
[1] *Forward,* July 25, 1906.

IMMIGRANT DEMORALIZATION

countryman of mine. He is really handsome and, as the girls call it, "appetizing." But he is poor, and this is no disgrace. He became dearer to me every day.

One day he told me he was in want, owing to a strike, so I helped him out. I was never stingy with him, and besides money also bought him a suit of clothes and an overcoat. . . . Who else did I work for if not for him? In short, we became happily engaged. . . .

Some time after, we hired a hall in Clinton Street and we were on our way to the bank to draw some money for the wedding expenses and also to enter the savings in both our names. On the way we passed some of his countrymen who were musicians, and we needed music, so we stopped in. He introduced me as his bride. I offered to have them play at our wedding.

Incidentally, I inquired about my fiancé, and they gave good opinions of him. Only a musician's boy pitifully gazed at me and remarked, when my fiancé was not near us: "Are there not enough people from the old country to ask for their opinion?" I understood the hint and asked him for an address, which he gave me.

Meanwhile, we were late for the bank, and fortunately, too! I could hardly wait for evening when I rushed over to his countryman and inquired about him. They were surprised at my questions and told me he had a wife and three children in —— Street. As I later found out, she was the same woman whom he introduced to me as his boarding mistress. . . .

I cannot describe my feelings at that time. I became a mere toy in the mouths of my countrymen.

But what more could I do than arrest him. But his wife and children came to court and had him released.

I found out of the existence of a gang of wild beasts, robbers, who prey upon our lives and money. I then advertised in a Jewish newspaper, warning my sisters against such a "fortune" as befell me. I was not ashamed and told my misfortune wherever I came and gave warnings. The East Side has become full of such "grooms," "matchmakers," "mistresses," "sisters," and "brothers." Inquire of their countrymen. There are plenty of their kind.

A girl from my country also married one of the band, the one who was my former matchmaker. To the warnings that he had a wife and child in Europe she replied, "Well, if she comes she will be welcome." And good countrymen did indeed send for her and she came with a four-year-old boy. Her predicament is horrible to describe. She is poor and lonely and my countrywoman did not welcome her as she boasted, and her husband said, "Whoever sent for you may support you."

So she was forced to adopt the American method; she had him arrested . . . and he was sentenced to five years in the workhouse, where there are no slack seasons nor strikes. Who is to blame? [1]

[1] *Forward*, June 7, 1906.

V

IMMIGRANT TYPES

EACH immigrant brings to America an individual correlation of the wishes which rule human conduct (see Chapter II). In one the desire for recognition predominates; in another the desire for security; and so on in many variations. This individual organization of wishes is what we call character. Likewise each immigrant group as a whole brings a more or less marked character. And while we do not ignore the fact that character is partly due to temperamental qualities—the characteristics of the Swedes, the Jews, the Italians, may be connected with their original, inborn, temperamental dispositions—it is nevertheless certain that character in both individuals and groups is mainly built up by the process which we have referred to above as "the definition of the situation"—by gossip, conversation, disputes, doctrines, by the whole of the experiences and social influences which modify, qualify, and organize the wishes. Thus, the

Sicilian *omertà*, the Catholic church and confessional, the Lutheran faith, the doctrine of anarchy, the principle of democracy, are more or less dominant in defining the situation in certain groups and tend to characterize partially these groups and their members. We are able, therefore, to distinguish roughly various immigrant types, representing different heritages. It is not true, however, that we can treat any given immigrant group strictly *en bloc* from the standpoint of heritages. We find a great homogeneity in this respect in certain groups (and we are inclined to assume more than exists), but in all groups certain individuals resemble individuals in other groups more than they resemble the average member of their own group. Thus a Jewish intellectual probably has more in common with an intellectual of any other group than with a ritualistic Jew. Certainly the difference between an intellectual Pole and a Polish peasant is as profound as possible. In general, where the process of defining the situation rationally instead of customarily has been introduced, a wide divergence will be found between individual members in a group.

In this study we do not attempt to characterize immigrant groups in their totality. We are able to study only the *types of*

IMMIGRANT TYPES

attitudes brought to America by immigration, and the following indication of types is made from this standpoint, though it will become evident, here and later, that certain attitudes are more or less peculiar to certain groups. The terms used below are more or less arbitrary and the types are usually not pure.

THE SETTLER

All emigration represents some crisis in the life of the emigrants. The decision to leave home is usually precipitated by some incident of immediate significance, probably one destroying the economic basis of life—as where the hereditary land fails to support a growing family, or the property of a Jew is destroyed by a *pogrom*. What the peasant immigrants call "securing an existence" is practically always a motive. And the whole attitude of the immigrant in America is frequently determined by the type of experience at home which has led him to come here. The settler either sets out with a resolve to break with the past permanently, to seek a home in the new country, and transfer his interests to it, or this may become his attitude, perhaps, after a series of hardships here. Extremely and permanently hard economic conditions, such as exist in Sweden and Norway, are favorable to this decision. In general, when the organization of life at home, the traditional attitudes and values resemble our own, the decision to make a home in America is more natural.

61. In Hungary I had a wife, two children, house, six acres of land, two horses, a cow, two pigs, and a few poultry. That was my fortune. This same land that afforded an existence to my father and grandfather could not support us any longer. Taxes and the cost of living in the last few years have advanced so greatly that the expenses cannot be covered from as much as a small farm can yield.

[Things became worse, an early spring storm killed his crop, he had to buy his bread for money.] My horses were killed from disease. I had to sell my cow to buy winter clothes for the family. There was no money to work the land and without horses and work the land will not produce. I had to mortgage my home. . . .

As a farm laborer in Hungary can earn only enough for bread and water, how is he to pay the taxes, living expenses, and clothing? There was but one hope, America, the golden land of liberty, where the rivers and mountains are full of gold. . . .

We will never go back to Hungary. It only deprived us of our home and land, while in America the soil covers our child. We have a home, money, and business, everything acquired in America. We lost everything in Hungary. We love Hungary as our native land, but never wish to live in it again.[1]

62. My first recollection is that we lived in a

[1] Janos Kovacs of New York City (interview).

very small hut in the most abject poverty. When I was about seven years of age I had to go out and look after infants—that was my first occupation—and then I had to tend geese, pigs, and sheep. Then I worked on the estate until I was fourteen years of age, when I was confirmed. I also had a little schooling, nine months altogether, two days in one week and three days in the next. The school children were too many, so the boys and girls had to attend school every other day. After I had been confirmed I hired out to a dependent farmer, who leased a large farm. My wages were fixed at twenty-five *riksdaler* ($7), one pair of boots, two shirts, and one pair of mittens a year.

Then I went to another dependent farmer, where I got herring five times a day, must be at the estate at four o'clock in the morning, and work to half past eight at night, when I had to walk one and a half (English) miles, get a little porridge and milk and four hours' rest.

I left my parents' home the 4th of April, 1871, and landed in New York the 4th of May the same year. Now at last I was in land of promises, without relatives, without friends, and almost without money. I wandered about like a deaf and dumb man. My ticket was to Chicago and I started for that city, but by some mistake by the railroad people I was sent astray. [At last reached Chicago, dug graves in Rosehill Cemetery, contracted malaria there.] Now I was in the worst situation I ever have been in my life—sick, and without money and friends, with a two-hundred-*riksdaler* mortgage on my muscles for my ticket to this country. As in a dream I went up and down the streets in Chicago. Was this the so highly praised America?

At last I left Chicago and went to Pennsylvania,

where I worked on the railroads for about four years. Then I married a girl from my own home country. She had a little money and I had saved some, so we bought a small place of 20 acres, which we started to work up, bought three cows, one horse, and some farm implements. We kept this place for two years, when we sold it and bought another of 120 acres for $1,000. I sold 50 acres of this and that made us free from debt. Now we worked on this farm for a couple of years, when a sawmill in our neighborhood was offered for sale and we bought it for $2,000. Now I sawed timber both for myself and others, so within two years I had paid for the mill, but then it burned down and I had no insurance. I built up the mill immediately and started to saw again. Now I started to buy larger and smaller pieces of woodland and all went well. I sold my old place, bought a bigger and better one, started a country store, bought building lots in the cities, and started to build houses in Youngsville and Jamestown, New York. To-day I have 300 acres of land, a good farm, a good sawmill with planing machinery; two stores, eight city houses, and ten lessees, who pay me $900 a year. In the meantime I have brought up eight children, some of whom are married now. I am taxed about as follows: my farm, $3,000; woodlands, $2,500; sawmill, with accessories, $3,000; horses, other cattle, and farm implements, $1,500; timber on land, $3,000; city property in Youngsville, $10,000; in Jamestown, $2,500. If I had remained in Sweden I should probably be a hired man, or at most a dependent farmer.[1]

---

[1] Communication to the Swedish Emigration Commission, *Statistiska Central Byrån: Emigrationsutredningen (Bref från Svenskas i Amerika)*, part 7, p. 186.

IMMIGRANT TYPES

63. [Born on a small farm in Saxony, worked from fourteen to eighteen hours a day. Had a small inheritance. Started a small business and lost everything.] I longed all the time for my first profession, *farming;* but there was no prospect at all to become independent, because one acre of good land costed from $400 to $500. It happened occasionally at that time I saw some papers and pamphlets, printed in America, the contents of which were quite inviting for emigrants. The prospects were painted in the brightest colors. . . . Finally we decided if three quarters of the reports we read in those papers and pamphlets were exaggerated and only one quarter the truth, still the prospect would be inviting. So we resolved to emigrate. We thought it advisable I should go alone first and look around somewhat. . . . [Bought farm at Eau Claire, Wisconsin, returned to Germany and brought back wife and four children.]

By and by I found out my place was a so-called "run-out farm." The former owner worked in the winter time in the logging camps where he earned cash wages and took to farming only as a side line. On the 120 acres available land, only about 50 were under cultivation. He raised everything, but preferred crops with the least work—wheat, oats, and timothy hay; that meant stuff he could sell any time. The worst of it was he did not care to give the land anything back and so finaly the land refused to give continually good crops. In fact, at the time I started on that farm, some crops did not yield the seed back. My harvests were the poorest among the poor in the whole neighborhood. In those circumstances I got aware not even that quarter of the fine reports I had read in Germany was true.

But what could be done? I was here and could not go back. I was not discouraged, but I had to change the method of farming here to that I had followed in Germany, where I had worked land valued up to $500, paid the interest, and laid something by for "rainy days." Of course it took years before I was acquainted with the different kinds of soils I had on my farm, but finaly I had the best success. After years of intensive farming, no other farmer was able to beat me in the yield of any crop per acre. I tried my best to inform my neighbors how they could improve their crops, but when I found out my advice was not wanted I had to let them alone; but I had the satisfaction, when they could not help to see my success, to see one after the other to accept some of my methods. I got acquaint with smart (!) business men in the cities who told me the same thing as those reports in the papers and pamphlets I mentioned above, that it would be entirely superfluous to bother oneself with the learning of the English language, because I could sell everything I had for sale to them, and also everything I needed to buy, I could have from them. For years I was foolisch enough to believe that, but meanwhile I took the chance to join my children in their studies in their Englisch schoolbooks and from that time I had better success in selling my stuff. I acquired private customers, received cash, and was able to buy only what I needed, and was not compelled to take goods which I did not need, but had to take in order to balance my bill of trade in the store.

By and by I noted the condition of my pocketbook and my bank account constantly improved in spite of the very low prices I received for my goods. For instance, I had to sell for years most of my eggs three

IMMIGRANT TYPES

dozen for a quarter, and a pound of butter from ten to fifteen cents. All other products in same proportion. I got aware there was no chance to getting rich on the farm, but working hard with my good wife and obedient children—was able to meet my obligations and knew I was on the road of progress. Of course our personal living was fine, and when I corresponded with relations and friends in Germany I truthfully stated I live in a country "where milk and honey flows."

Right here I make the statement that I am convinced the main reason for my success consisted in the fact that I kept correct accounts about all my affairs. This enabled me to decide the best crops adapted to my soil, the best for the market, the best live stock, etc. In short, it gave me the most reliable information of everything pertaining to the management of my farm. I have started with those records already in the year 1866 and keep it up until to-day. There is no guesswork in all my affairs. I am able to give the minutely accounts of everything pertaining my farming and also about my household.

After I had been here over five years, one day two of my neighbors came to me (both Frenchmen) and asked if I intended to stay. "Why! sure," I said. "Would it not be foolish otherwise to spend my time and money on this farm?" "Very well, then, it is time to do your duty and make application for citizenship and take part in the public and political life of this country." I was quite perplex, it never occurred to me to have any duties besides to run my farm and pay my taxes. Knowing my neighbors to be very honest and explicit men, I followed them to the clerk of the court where they acted as my spokesmen. I received my first paper and took now active part in the several elections and other kind of public affairs. After a few years more I received my paper as a ful-fledged citizen. In short succession my neighbors elected me as road commissioner, as a member of the school board, and a member of the town board. Finaly they elected me to the office of town clerk. That was now quite hard for me. My English was hardly sufficient to converse with my neighbors about the most common things, much less sufficient to fill that office. As I had no spare time, I had to spend many nights in studying the English language, and I tell you it wes hard work, because I was already an old boy of fifty-five. I was re-elected to that office for five years and mostly unanimously, so I have good reason to believe I did my duty. . . . I am now seventy-one.

It is now thirty-one years I live in this country and have never repented to come here. I correspondet much with parties of Germany, and in my answers I never failed to emphasize the importance for every newcomer to learn the English language as soon as possible. Other correspondents might be correct by saying it is not absolute necessary, but I say it is very beneficial and therefore highly important to understand the official language.

This is a short biography of my existence, and I am astonished to note what a long story it is. I am afraid you will feel very tiresome by reading it, therefore I repeat if it is not what you want, drop it in the waste basket and no harm done. At the other hand if it proves to be what you expect from your correspondence, then I inform you I could be much more in detail if you will have the kindness to name the particulars you want me to answer.

Please excuse my still very faulty English and the

IMMIGRANT TYPES

many errors in the foregoing. It is not long since I learned to use the typewriter in order to avoid the cramps in my hand by the use of the pen.[1]

The settlers described above are of the pioneer type. In addition, the political refugee and the fugitive from justice may have the psychology of the settler, or, as we shall note presently, they may belong to other categories:

64. [Father] had scarcely ever known what it meant to be free from anxiety. First, from early childhood it was the fear of the army where he would be compelled to violate the laws against God, "Thou shalt not kill," and the fear for the blind and helpless mother he would have to leave behind. In this fear he grew up to manhood. And then with blood money, borrowed and saved on bread and his mother's tears, he bought a false name. Then his life was in constant fear of human beings, often in fear of his own shadow. Then being found out, and all seeming lost, his escape to America, then the struggle of a stranger in a strange land, which led to only a hand-to-mouth existence, without any change, without hope of change.[2]

65. I have been already ten years in this blessed country, where there are no passports.

I am doing honest labor as a machinist's assistant. In Russia I was a plain criminal. Yes, a criminal. I am openly saying so, for that was in my far-away past. And it seems to me that I am speaking not of myself, but of another unfortunate man, whom

---
[1] Reinhold Liebau, *Autobiographical Sketch* (manuscript).
[2] Rose Cohen, *Out of the Shadow*, p. 211.

circumstances made a thief and a forger. . . . I knew well what the criminal prison means . . . America accepted me as I was. America gave me a chance to stand on my own feet. I was taken in with my shameful past, as if I were equal to the best. And I have repaid America with respect that only death itself can take away from my heart.

Excuse me for not signing my name. My Russian name I have, indeed, thrown out together with my Russian past, and as to my American name it is a clean one, and is not guilty for the past of the one who carries it. A SON OF THE DON.[1]

THE COLONIST

We may distinguish two general types of success, according to the standard in the mind of the individual. The one is associated with an extraordinary gratification of the wishes, or of some of them—for example, the "will to power"—the other with their limitation. The small shopkeeper may be as successful in his way as a Napoleon, because his wishes are limited. The typical settler has been accustomed to a severe limitation of the wishes in the home country and relative hardship here is considered success. But in the first generation of immigrants this success is never felt as complete. The economic success may be complete, from any standpoint, but there

---

[1] Letter to the newspaper *Russkoye Slovo* (New York).

IMMIGRANT TYPES

are sentimental losses. In the Swedish volume containing document 62 above, there are 128 short life histories of immigrants, and the most general attitude in them is: "I have been successful. I have property. My children have superior advantages. But *I have lost my life.*" This means, of course, not only that the writer has had a hard time here, suffered sentimental losses, but that he has regretful memories of home conditions, of occasional leisure and festivities, of joys and sorrows shared by an intimate group.

We define the colonist as one in whom these memories of home are, from our standpoint, "over determined" (to use the psychoanalytic phrase): one who never forgets nor wishes to forget, whose allegiance is to the home country, whose superior values are the home values. The English are historically great colonizers, and they furnish good representatives of this type in America. The German is also likely to show the colonist's attitude, and the same is true of the French, and of any people who have an eminent position among the nationalities. Their representative feels something akin to the pride in family. These are often very fine types, but the old loyalty yields stubbornly to the new, and the subject is usually careful to let you know that he is

OLD WORLD TRAITS TRANSPLANTED

contributing more to America than America is contributing to him:

66. Major Ian Hay Beith, in his delightful little essay entitled "Getting Together," gives some advice to an Englishman as to what he should remember in conversing with an American, and to an American as to what he must bear in mind in talking with an Englishman. To the Englishman, he says: "Remember you are talking to a man who regards his nation as the greatest nation in the world. He will probably tell you this." To the American, he says: "Remember you are talking to a man who regards his nation as the greatest in the world. He will not tell you this, because he takes it for granted that you know already." . . .

[One contribution which an Englishman is able to make to America] is the historic memory which British birth and education give to a man. He inevitably escapes the shallowness of a retrospect that is bounded by 1776 or 1619, or even by 1492. . . . [Another] contribution which every immigrant can bring to America consists in the positive good which he has derived from the civilization of his native country. It is at this point that one may seem to be setting oneself up, in a ludicrously pharisaic fashion, as an example. I must therefore beg the reader to understand that . . . I am thinking not of what I am, but of what any Englishman ought to be.[1]

67. We did not enter the American nation as a banished or persecuted race, seeking aid and protection, but as part of this nation, with equal rights, and as part of a noble people which for more than two hundred years has found a second home here

---
[1] Horace E. Bridges, *On Becoming an American*, pp. 39 and 43.

IMMIGRANT TYPES

and, in common with the kindred Anglo-Saxon race, had founded and developed this state. . . . We protest most energetically [against the ideal of the "melting-pot"] not only because we regard this uniformity as equivalent to the destruction of all that we regard as the holiest part of our people and its culture, but because the undertaking itself appears to the German spirit as repulsive as a desecration.[1]

68. Emerging from the colony is one pole of the dreams [of the Hungarian-American leaders]. The other is recognition in and by the old country; the desire to attain status, to show that they have made good. In pre-war times this desire, always very vague, crystallized mainly around the hope of a governmental recognition of some sort or other, perhaps a knighthood of the Order of Francis Joseph, or some similar decoration [2]

69. The Sixty-ninth Street group is the central group of the Sicilians who come from the village of Cinisi, and those who remain in this group intend to return to Cinisi; in fact, most of those who are in New York intend to return. Those in the interior cities do not have this intention. My cousin from New Orleans remarked about this fact—namely, that those in New Orleans are settled and never talk of Cinisi, while here he was surprised to hear them constantly talking of the home town.

The reason for this is evident. Here they are nearest to Cinisi. Here they receive letters and talk to the new arrivals. All those who return from Detroit, Chicago, or anywhere else, pass New York and this reminds them.

---

[1] J. Goebel, *Der Kampf um deutsche Kultur in Amerika*, p. 11.

[2] Eugene S. Bagger, *Hungarian Intellectuals and Leaders* (manuscript).

OLD WORLD TRAITS TRANSPLANTED

In this way the town of Cinisi is always in their minds.[1]

70. The intellectual atmosphere prevailing in Polish-American circles is purely and exclusively Polish. In every home the conversation runs on Polish topics, the library is full of Polish books, pictures reproduce Polish paintings, Polish music is played, Polish dishes served. I heard a lady of this circle pride herself on the fact that when a prominent Pole from Cracow, who had just come to this country, visited her (she lived then in California with her husband, in a purely American town), she could talk with him about the latest literary and artistic events in Cracow, and he felt in their home as if he had never left Poland. At this moment, I have not met a single person belonging to this circle who did not talk about returning home in the near future; some have been here for fifteen years. At the same time, every one hastens to prepare some American values which he thinks may be useful in Poland. One studies American economics, another American legislation, a third some special line of industry, a fourth the American newspaper technic. There is one who is organizing an entire factory, on the co-operative basis, and expects to transfer it to Poland—machinery, capital, workmen, and all.[2]

THE POLITICAL IDEALIST

Members of the "oppressed and dependent" nationalities of Europe bring to Amer-

---

[1] Gaspare Cusumano, *Study of the Cinisi Colony in New York*, (manuscript).

[2] Florian Znaniecki, *Study of Polish Organizations in America*, (manuscript).

IMMIGRANT TYPES

ica forms of the Freudian "baffled wish" and of the "inferiority complex." They are obsessed by the idea of the inferior status of their group at home, and wish to be a nationality among other nationalities. Their organizations here seek to make America a recruiting ground for the battle in Europe. Consequently they wish first of all to save their members from Americanization, to send them home with unspoiled loyalty, or to keep them a permanent patriotic asset working here for the cause at home. They regard America as merely the instrument of their nationalistic wishes. Their leaders wish also to get recognition at home for their patriotic activities here, and superior status on their return. They speak of the penetration of America by their own culture. Thus the Poles, the most ambitious of them, call the Polish-American community the "fourth division of Poland," and refer to the whole body of Poles in America as "*Polonia Americana*." At the same time the material position of the leaders of these groups—the editors, bankers, priests—depends on keeping the group un-American. We find that the aims of these nationalists are often more explicitly and naïvely stated in communications sent to Europe than in their American publications.

71. This great current of [Lithuanian] emigration would have been lost for the Lithuanian national cause, would have been submerged in the ocean of a great foreign nationality, if some great patriots had not succeeded in organizing it and rendering it refractory to assimilation by forming it into groups and associations, by teaching it the maternal language, by creating parishes, schools, and Lithuanian newspapers, by the development of pride of race, respect for the traditions and customs of its ancestors, and above all the love of native land.[1]

72. The most powerful bond which unites emigrants of the same nationality in a strange country is constituted by religion and the church. Pious people like the Poles, the Slovaks, the Lithuanians, etc., carry with them their profound religious sentiments. In their churches they feel at home; the church is for them a corner of their distant country. Thus in America religion is the most powerful source of resistance to Americanization, to assimilation.[2]

73. The task of the intellectual Ruthenians will be the easier since many Ruthenians live in America and after having amassed a certain sum return to their country. What is not permitted in the country of the crown of Saint-Etrienne is permitted in the free land of Washington. If the Ruthenian national idea is firmly planted in America it will extend to Hungary.[3]

74. The ultimate meaning of all activities [of the Alliance of Polish Socialists] is connected with the

---

[1] Jean Pelissier, *Renaissance nationale Lituanienne*, p. 107.

[2] A. Kaupas, "L'Eglise et les Lituaniens aux États-Unis," in *Annales des Nationalités*, vol. ii, p. 233. The writer is the editor of two Lithuanian papers in America.

[3] Y. Fedortchouk, "La question des nationalités en Austriche-Hongrie," in *Annales des Nationalités*, vol. iii, p. 56.

IMMIGRANT TYPES

future of Poland, not of America, and the political and social interests of its members are concentrated mostly around the question of returning to Poland and helping to organize Poland. . . . They have resigned all hope of playing a political role in this country, as a party, and consider their organization as a training school and a center of future influence.

. . . Any characterization of Polish life in this country which can be written at this moment is in a large measure "mere history," as a prominent Chicago Pole (Zaleski) expressed it. The war and the consequent liberation of Poland is bound to bring a radical change of the entire direction of evolution of the Polish-American society. The patriotic exaltation produced by Poland's oppression, by all the preparations for national struggle, by the expectation of Poland's freedom, will decrease very soon among those who decide to stay in this country; there will no longer be the feeling of duty to preserve Polish ideals intact, no feeling of guilt will be connected with Americanization.[1]

Another group of political idealists, embittered against the social order represented by the state and by private property, perhaps disgusted with humanity, are the propagandists of some revolutionary scheme—bolshevism, anarchy, communism—for the redistribution of values. They continue in this country a struggle against organized society which they had been carrying on at

---

[1] Florian Znaniecki, *Study of Polish Organizations in America* (manuscript).

home. They bring here and exploit grievances and psychoses acquired under totally different conditions. We are sufficiently familiar with the type:

75. I hated the rich because they are murderers, and the poor because they would become such if they had the opportunity.[1]

76. ... We must mercilessly destroy all the remains of governmental authority and class domination . . . all legal papers pertaining to private ownership of property, all field fences and boundaries, and burn all certificates of indebtedness—in a word, we must take care that everything is wiped from the earth that is a reminder of the right to private ownership of property. . . .[2]

76a. The bourgeois is useless and the government is unnecessary for the development of the commercial and industrial life of the people. . . . It is better to die, and if we are going to die . . . why don't we seek those who are responsible for such disorders and iniquities and execute them?[3]

77. ... We have nothing against the blindness of the bourgeoisie and expect nothing else from them. Because the bourgeoisie, which includes lawyers, priests, physicians, writers, merchants, etc., have the same habit as a prostitute; she sells herself to the one who pays more money. . . .[4]

78. We will strive for a revolution and we will

---

[1] Letter to *Forward*, February 4, 1918.

[2] *Novomirsky: Manifesto of Anarchists—Communists.* Reprinted in the New York *Times*, November 10, 1919.

[3] *Cultura Obrera* (Spanish newspaper, New York), November 17, 1917.

[4] *Robotnik* (Ukrainian newspaper, New York), April 17, 1919.

IMMIGRANT TYPES

carry it through to the end, until every remembrance of you shall be obliterated.[1]

79. ... The real cause [of the war] was the same damned trinity—rights [law], ownership, and state [rule]. ... Down with rights! Down with ownership! Down with the state! Let this be the death of this three-headed monster. Long live anarchism! In anarchy humanity will find happiness and eternal well-being.[2]

80. ... Will you be meek and slavish? Will you wallow under the iron heel of your masters? Or will you tear your way by the revolution to a better and happier life? ...[3]

THE ALLRIGHTNICK

This term is one which the Jews of the New York East Side apply to successful members of their race who have found a comfortable berth outside of the Jewish community and within the cosmopolitan group of the "Americanized" Americans. There are, however, other and deeper implications in the term. Here it is used to characterize an opportunistic type which is not peculiar to the Jewish race—namely, the individual who realizes a very natural ambition to gain access to and some sort of recognition, or

---

[1] *Der Industrialer Arbeiter* (Jewish newspaper, Chicago), March 31, 1919.

[2] *Khlieb i Volya* [Bread and Freedom] (Russian newspaper, New York), April 3, 1919.

[3] *Il Diritto* (Italian newspaper, New York), March 8, 1919.

at least toleration, in the native American community, or what passes for it, but who does so at the sacrifice of the ideals of his own national and family group. In the case of the Jew, the *allrightnick* may simply be a man who has been a socialist, who has gone into business and become a bourgeois. The mental type is a familiar one, found wherever the transition is made from one cultural group to another, as in the case of the missionary convert.

81. . . . The poor Jew whom I now scrutinized more closely wore an old shabby coat, an old cap, his hands were black from dust and cold. And his face—what a face! Pale, bony, wrinkled. In each wrinkle there was compassion. And this Jew who sells cookies on the street has three sons and a daughter—all fairly prosperous!

"How is it possible?" slipped off my tongue.

"You mean, of course, why I am not living with them? . . . I did not want to live with them. You understand, I cannot live among machines. I am a live man and have a soul, despite my age. They are machines. They work all day and come home at night. What do they do? Nothing. Wait for supper. During supper they talk about everything in the world—friends, clothes, money, wages, and all sorts of gossip. After supper they dress up and go out. Where to? Either the theater, banquet, or movie. Or else their friends call and they drink, eat, and play cards; or they start the machine and it, plays and they dance. The next day again to work and so on for the rest of their life. . . . They have

IMMIGRANT TYPES

all been to school—educated people; but just try, for the fun of it, and ask them if they ever read a book. Not on your life. Books have nothing in common with them; Judaism has nothing in common with them; Jewish troubles have nothing in common with them; the whole world has nothing in common with them. They only know one thing—work, eat, and away to the theater. How can they do this? I am asking you; how can one lead a life like that?" And in his voice there was a deep anger. . . .

His voice grew louder and became very angry. "And I—I cannot live like that. I am no machine. I like to think, I like to be in good mood, I want to talk to people, I want to get an answer to my questions. When I live among shoemakers I know that the shoemaker is a blind man; but when I live among educated people, then I expect them to be *Menschen*.

"When I first came here I used to speak and argue with them. But they did not understand me. They would ask: 'Why this and that? This country is not Russia. Here everybody does as he likes.'

"Gradually I realized that they were machines. They make money and live for that purpose. When I grasped this situation a terror possessed me and I did not believe these were my children. I could not stand it to be there; I was being choked; I could not tolerate their behavior and I went away. . . ."[1]

THE CAFFONE

The Italians in America apply the term *caffone* (literary, "simpleton") to a man of their nationality who has the least possible

---
[1] Olgin, *Forward*, February 4, 1917.

association with any group, has no regard for opinion, wears, for example, the same clothes during his whole stay in America, avoids all conversation, ignores his surroundings, and accumulates the sum of money he has in mind as rapidly as possible. We use the term here to designate the pure opportunist, who is unwilling to participate either in the American life or in that of his national group:

82. The *caffoni*, who were in Sicily mostly *villani* [serfs], are looked down upon by their own people and especially by that class of Italians who want to stay here and who feel injured whenever the Italian name is hurt. To this superior class a good name for the Italians is a requisite of their progress. The *caffoni* don't care. All they want is to make money and go back. So we often see the superior class preaching and speaking to the *caffoni* in meetings, in groups and individually, persuading them to uphold the Italian name. The *caffoni* listen, but then they shrug their shoulders and it is all over. "It does not give me any bread whether Italians have a good name in America or not. I am going back soon."[1]

THE INTELLECTUAL

Our documents show that the "educated" immigrant is usually more misadapted to American society than the workman. He

---

[1] Gaspare Cusumano, *Study of the Cinisi Colony in New York City* (manuscript).

IMMIGRANT TYPES

does not, unless he is a technician (chemist, engineer), bring a commodity which we want to buy (as does the laborer), and he must usually make such a place as he can among his fellow immigrants. Document 83 shows the situation of the *intelligentsia* of one group:

83. The characteristic note of the corporate life of Hungarian-America intellectuals is one of utter hopelessness, born of the consciousness of isolation, both from the main currents of American and of old-country life, and of the realization of the doom hanging over the American-Hungarian community. This is the paradox of the immigrant colony—that it is constantly losing its best element, which manifests its superiority just by being able to detach itself and to merge into the larger American life. . . . There are new "movements" every now and then to "organize" American Hungariandom [*"amerikai magyarsag,"* a collective term like *Deutschtum*]. The conscious or avowed purposes of these movements vary; their common unconscious element is to make a showing of some sort, to prove [for themselves] that there *is* such a thing as a Hungarian-American culture and a Hungarian-American future; but these movements invariably collapse or die of sheer inertia. The Hungarian-American socialist press is wont to attack these movements as mere attempts at organized graft, and undoubtedly there is an element among the "leaders" which is trying to exploit these campaigns for personal gain. Nevertheless, it is plain that there is some moral purpose behind them—factors ranging from personal vanity and craving

for prestige to a genuine, though vague, yearning for spiritual achievement. Hungarian-American intellectuals are obsessed by a peculiar megalomania centering about the "mission" and greatness of "Hungarian-Americandom." Nobody ever tried to define what this mission is, but it is constantly spoken of. This megalomania seems to be the converted expression of a manifold inferiority complex— the resultant, perhaps, of the following complexes: (1) The "oppressed race" complex. Magyar chauvinism is just the result of a feeling of inferiority as compared to Austria, of playing the second fiddle within the monarchy, of the fear of being classed by Europeans as a Balkan race. (2) The inferiority complex of the immigrant, the "hunky." (3) The individual inferiority complexes of men who have proved failures at home.

These movements—I am almost tempted to say revivals—are bound to fail chiefly for three reasons: (1) The absence of a clearly defined program, of a nonfictitious moral purpose; (2) the fatal Magyar tendency to dissent, similar to the Polish national disease [in Hungary they call it the "Turanian curse"], unwillingness to self-renunciation and co-ordinated effort; (3) the sameness of the personnel. This last-named is the peculiarly Hungarian-American factor. In the old country there are always reserves to draw upon, there is "fresh blood"; here, especially since the war, it is always the same few dozens of people, in different groupings and alignments, but the same individuals. I aroused against myself the Hungarian intellectuals of Cleveland by saying that Hungarian-American society reminds me of a bunch of gamblers marooned on a desert island and engaged in a desperate, endless game—each trying to live on

IMMIGRANT TYPES

his winnings from the rest, but nobody producing new values.[1]

There is a type of intellectual, the product of a superior and systematic training, who comes rarely but who can contribute particular values to the culture of any nationality. Now, modern progress evidently depends in part on communication in space, on the ability to assemble from all parts of the world values which happen to exist there. Economic efficiency, for example, does not reject any value because it is foreign. But it appears that of all the immigrants who come we are least prepared to receive the foreign intellectual, who is at the same time the type of immigrant best fitted to make a cultural contribution.

Very often the intellectual who comes here has been a failure at home or is a predestined failure anywhere, but will nevertheless attribute his failure here to America's inability to appreciate him. But document 84 is from a really superior man. In addition to the criticism of America, it reveals the psychology of the Polish intellectual:

84. [Was positively influenced in America by the democratic idea, revised my former contempt for

[1] Eugene S. Bagger, *Hungarian Intellectuals and Leaders* (manuscript).

economic considerations, learned to appreciate the social idealism, the active interest in other people's welfare, the willingness to make a sacrifice for a humanitarian cause—oftener met here than in any European society except the Polish—and the free, direct, and sincere attitude toward phenomena which characterizes the good American worker.] In other lines, however, I have hardly come any nearer to American life. Two reasons prevented my "Americanization" in the deeper sense of the term; the divergencies which I began to discover after a longer stay in this country between most of the aspirations actually predominant in American society and certain ideals which, in my cosmopolitan training, I have learned to revere as the best part of the general human civilization, independent of national differences; and—more particularly—the attitude of American society toward foreigners and foreign values. . . .

[Among other things] there is the lack of social freedom, the oppression of the individual by all kinds of traditional or recently created social norms. I have not seen in Europe anything comparable to it except, perhaps, in small and very isolated provincial towns. Since I am not politically active, this social tyranny affects me much more than any amount of political despotism could do, particularly as it extends to the intellectual domain. I feel more bound in the expression of my opinions here than I felt under Russian censorship in Warsaw, in spite of the fact that I am not in the slightest measure inclined toward political, social, moral, or religious revolutionism of any kind, and was considered in Europe, even by the most radical conservatists, a perfectly "inoffensive," mildly progressive intellectualist. . . .

IMMIGRANT TYPES

And yet, I am sincerely interested in America—but in the future rather than in the present America. I could work with real enthusiasm for the progress of American culture in the intellectual line, in which I can be most efficient and in which progress seems most needed; I am sure that I could be really useful to this country, produce some really important cultural values. But my incipient enthusiasm for American cultural development never has any chance to mature, because I realize at every moment that American society does not feel any need of my or any other "foreigner's" co-operation, is in general perfectly satisfied with itself, and perfectly able to manage its own future in accordance with its own desires, to create all the values it wants without having any "imported" values "thrust upon it." In analyzing the evolution of my attitudes toward this country, it seems to me that much of my growing criticism and dissatisfaction with American conditions has been due to the gradual realization of this self-complacency of American society. . . . In France, in Germany, in Italy, in Poland, this attitude manifests itself toward other national *groups*, but not toward individual foreigners when they come to live and work in the country. On the contrary, I have experienced myself, during my travels abroad, and I have seen manifested toward incomers in Poland (unless they were members of the oppressing nation) an attitude which I may call "intellectual hospitality," a tendency to learn, to appreciate, and to utilize whatever values the foreigner may bring with him, unless, of course, he brings nothing but unskilled labor. No European society I know acts as if it possessed and knew everything worth while and had nothing to learn, whereas this is precisely the way

OLD WORLD TRAITS TRANSPLANTED

American society acts toward a foreigner as soon as he ceases to play the role of a passing "curiosity" and wants to take an active part in American life. I do not think most Americans realize how revolting to a more or less educated immigrant is their naïve attitude of superiority, their astonishing self-satisfaction, their inability and unwillingness to look on anything foreign as worth being understood and assimilated. This may work with the peasant who is used in the old country to attitudes of superiority on the part of the higher class, is desirous of imitating them, and finds in this country exactly the same atmosphere, only connected with an unknown language and unknown institution which make real imitation more difficult. But I believe, judging even less by my own experience than by the confidences of others, that the unanimously critical standpoint taken toward this county by all, even if only half educated and socially dependent, immigrants and their universal attachment to and idealization of the "old country" values, are provoked by this "lording it over" the immigrant, his traditions, his ideals, by this implicit or explicit assumption that Americanization necessarily means progress, that the immigrant should simply leave all he brought with him as worthless stuff—worthless, at least, for this country—and instead of trying to introduce the most valuable elements of his culture into American life and select the most valuable elements of Americanism for himself, should merely accept everything American just as it is.

In the same line, and perhaps even more revolting for the reflecting foreigner who comes with the idea of working and settling in this country, is the current tendency of American society to interpret the rela-

IMMIGRANT TYPES

tion between the immigrant and America as that of one-sided benefit and one-sided obligation. This is again an attitude which I have never met in Europe, though European countries are incomparably more crowded than America. . . .

I may have overlooked some important elements of American civilization, but this does not seem to be the main point. No individual can assimilate all the values of a modern civilized society, and I know many Americans for whom American civilization contains and means much less than it does for me. And there is no such thing as an unbiased view of life; the only question is whether a certain bias is due to an uncritical acceptance of locally and temporarily limited social traditions which have no positive significance for general human progress, or to a critical, even if, perhaps, too exclusive, appreciation of certain values reflectively selected from the whole stock of human culture and constituting an important, even if not necessarily the most important, component of every civilization, in all epochs and all societies. Now, my personal bias is certainly no longer a class bias. If there are any specific class attitudes persisting subconsciously in my personality —and I do not think there are—they have nothing to do with the actual problem of my adaptation to American conditions. Nor is my bias in any particular way national. However great may have been the role which Polish national ideals have played in my life, my psychology seems to me less specifically national, contains less particularly racial elements, than that of any individual, Pole, Frenchman, Italian, German, Russian, American, I have ever met. . . . I have, at various times, actively participated in the intellectual life of three different societies besides my own—French, Swiss, and American—using in each case a different language, needing each time only a few months of preparation, and mixing intimately with the respective groups. This fact seems to me a sufficient proof of the lack, on my side, of any racial obstacles to my adaptation. My bias, is, if anything, a professional bias. I certainly have an exalted conception of the function which the scientific profession can and should fulfill in human society—one which entitles it to demand that minimum of favorable social conditions which is absolutely indispensable for intellectual productivity. I also believe that all scientists have an obligation to maintain certain professional ideals, the most important of which are continual perfecting of the standards of theoretic validity in so far as compatible with intellectual efficiency on the given stage of human development; disinterestedness of theoretic pursuit, the only personal reward which the scientist has the right to expect being recognition based exclusively on the objective importance and intrinsic perfection of his work and therefore necessarily slow to come and limited to the most intellectual part of society; freedom of mind and sincerity of expression; enthusiasm for scientific work and for the development of human knowledge in general; and, finally, "true brotherhood" of all scientific workers in the domain of science, manifested in reciprocal interest, serious and thorough criticism, deserved appreciation, encouragement and help in intellectual pursuits. And all this is independent of differences of class, race, religion, etc., which may divide scientists as social individuals, as members of concrete groups, in other fields of cultural life.[1]

---

[1] *Autobiography* (manuscript).

IMMIGRANT TYPES

85. . . . I was naturally deeply interested in the Polish writer's analysis [document 84 above] of phenomena with which I, too, find myself confronted, and on the whole I was inclined to accept his conclusions. . . . I felt, however, that he would have strengthened his case—the case of the European intellectual against intellectual America—by presenting, simultaneously, the case against himself. It is true that European intellectuals are invariably dissatisfied with American life; much of the bitterness with which they criticize American conditions is doubtless justified. But in the interest of fair play the question, "What's the matter with intellectual America?" ought to be supplemented with this other one, "What's the matter with the European intellectual in America?" This implies what the Polish writer has neglected—an analysis of the analyzer.

First among the sources of discontent with which the European intellectual confronts American life is the lowering of his status. . . . An attempt to fix his own place on the social ladder will lead him to the realization that he was better off in aristocratic Europe than in democratic America. For in Europe he belonged—if he achieved any recognition at all— to the upper middle class. Even a moderate degree of literary or artistic eminence secured him admission to the most interesting quarter of a society where money, however important, was never the sole criterion of gentility. In all European capitals there are certain centres of social intercourse where members of the three aristocracies of birth, riches, and intellect meet in a congenial atmosphere and on a basis of full equality. . . .

The European intellectual will then turn to an analysis of his economic status and will find it worse

OLD WORLD TRAITS TRANSPLANTED

than it was in pre-war Europe. Probably he made much less money in dollars and cents, even at the old rate of exchange; but his smaller income insured to him a higher place in the social hierarchy and a much greater amount of comfort. . . . The Sunday afternoon spectacle of thousands upon thousands of automobiles, filled with festive families bound nowhere in particular and beaming with the happiness of dreams come true, serves chiefly to impress him with the meaning of the American slang phrase, "all dressed up and no place to go."

Europe was different. The things he craves for, books, engravings, theatre and concert tickets, good clothes, good home-furnishings, were comparatively much cheaper there. Above all, travel was much cheaper. The fare from Vienna to London, from Budapest to Stockholm, was less than from New York to Cleveland; and why go to Cleveland, anyhow? A Vienna journalist, a Cracow college professor, a Budapest art critic, not the leaders of their profession, just good average, could go for a month's vacation to Switzerland or Belgium or a Baltic resort or Florence, live well, and spend less than at home. For the same class of person in America that sort of thing is about as feasible as spending the week end in the moon. In a word, in America, where he has to work much harder and makes more money, the European intellectual will find that this income leaves him socially an outcast and qualifies him for less substantial material comfort than is enjoyed by his grocer.

One has to be a thoroughbred continental to appreciate another factor which, to an untraveled American, may seem utterly trivial. I mean the absence of the continental type of café. . . . The literary café

IMMIGRANT TYPES

of the continental capital is a place where men of similar tastes and interests may drop in, without any formality, at teatime and after supper, and be sure of finding congenial company, brilliant repartee, interesting gossip, or substantial shop talk, according to what he seeks. . . . The brilliancy of surroundings, the presence of beautiful and well-dressed women, the possibility of meeting new people, often important foreigners—these elements all converge to create an atmosphere of an extraordinarily stimulating character. There is nothing in American life that even remotely corresponds to this stimulus, and the life of literary cafés is missed by the continental intellectual as a drug is missed by its habitué.

But the absence of these easily accessible, standardized meeting places of intellectuals, open to all who have the price of a demitasse, has another, still subtler effect. For the intellectual, constant intercourse with his equals acts not only as a stimulus, but also as a check. It is written that it is not good for a man to be alone. Rubbing up against his compeers is as necessary for the intellectual as gnawing at hard substances is necessary for a squirrel's teeth. Isolation for him results in a sickly overestimation of his importance, a hypertrophied sensitiveness and that notion of omnipotence which comes from the absence of tests. A constant reiteration of "*Hic Rhodus, hic salta*" is a good cure against intellectual megalomania; but for the European litterateur American is not Rhodes. Just as the lack of academic standards favors an individualism that frequently is mere crankiness, the lack of intellectual give-and-take may result in an elephantiasis of self-consciousness. . . .

Here, then, we have the elements of a state of mind

OLD WORLD TRAITS TRANSPLANTED

which inevitably expresses itself in overestimation of self and underestimation of surroundings. The conditions analyzed do not necessarily imply that American culture is inferior to European; but they do determine a feeling in the European intellectual that American life is less exciting, less stimulating, less interesting, less worth while. . . . Out of this maze of factors—the lowering of economic and social status, lack of habitual and easy contact with one's peers, absence of the stimuli of metropolitan life, difficulties of everyday technique, struggle for self-expression through an unyielding idiom, etc.—rises a state of mind for which American conditions are responsible without necessarily being at fault. The characteristic tendency of this mentality is to make "America" a symbol of one's own failures and unfulfilled desires.

The pivot around which this psychology turns is the Canaan-complex—that perennial yearning for the land where everything will be what it is not; the longing for the *tabula rasa*, for the new start. The fuller, the more differentiated the life the European intellectual leaves behind when he comes to America the more probably will he discern the mistakes of that life, and the more certainly will he wish to arrange matters differently in the "new world." The intellectuals of the generation that attained maturity on the eve of the war were afflicted with the disease of æsthetic inertia—*Stimmungsanarchie,* a clever German critic called it. For many who diagnosed the trouble America stood as the symbol of success and energy. What a man of this type expected from America was not political democracy, not even equal economic opportunity—he knew enough of America to discount these catchwords;

IMMIGRANT TYPES

but he hoped for a new milieu, free from the sophistications, the *noblesse oblige*, the hothouse atmosphere of the old world. What he expected, in brief, was the rebirth of personality in and by America. Now the one thing the European intellectual is certain to discover in America is that crossing the ocean does not change a man; that a personality may develop, expand, differentiate by the experience of America, but it will not be reborn. Disappointment in America is determined by the act of embarking for it; arrival reveals the Promised Land as a delusion; the symbol of new life turns into the symbol of discrepancy between dream and reality.

But this disappointment is merely the negative side of a rising new hope; the image of Canaan fades out before the vision of the Golden Age. To the disenchanted, intellectual Europe emerges in a roseate mist of dreams and expectation. That Europe, however, is not the actual Europe, not even pre-war Europe; it is merely a reversed America. Whatever one fails to find here is idealized into what was left behind. For the central fact of the European intellectual's discontent in America is the disparity of his bases of comparison. He contrasts, not America with Europe, but a nightmare of American reality with a non-existent Eldorado which he calls Europe —the Cosmopolis built with the brick of memory and the mortar of hope.

By insisting that criticism of American cultural conditions by European intellectuals be discounted along the suggested lines, I do not mean to belittle the value of such criticism. On the contrary, I believe that its very real and distinctive merit is brought into relief when due allowance has been made for the subjective element in it, the inevitable

OLD WORLD TRAITS TRANSPLANTED

tendency of the critic unconsciously to paraphrase his experience from the category pleasant-unpleasant into the category superior-inferior, to rationalize personal likes and dislikes into absolute standards of value. I believe that the European intellectual not only exercises a right, but discharges a very substantial duty by applying his native standards to a fearless examination of American culture. He may be prone to exaggerate the value of his contribution, and to expect special regard and compensation from a public none too appreciative of intellectual achievement at the best; he may even develop—as did the anonymous Polish author—a redeemer-complex and establish a fixed relation between the recognition meted out to him by Americans and the salvation of the American soul. But this tendency is merely the counterpart of the no less unreasonable assumption of native Americans that foreigners owe a special debt of gratitude to this country for opportunities accorded, as if Americans admitted foreigners and provided them with jobs because they love them, and not because they need them. By helping to pierce the *aes triplex* of American self-complacency and to battle that intolerance of dissent and that glorification of buncombe which are the greatest intellectual dangers of America the educated European may perform a very real service, but he must not forget that his contribution to the growth of American culture is measured by the growth of his own personality.[1]

---

[1] Statement of Eugene S. Bagger (Magyar intellectual) made at our request (manuscript).

VI

IMMIGRANT INSTITUTIONS

THERE is an obvious resemblance between the behavior of a Russian *mir* or a South Slav *zadruga* (see documents 21, 22, 23, p. 31) and that of a pack, flock, or herd of animals. In each case there is some mechanism for securing unanimity—the thing that makes all the sheep follow the leader over the wall. In the animal it is instinctive, predetermined in the nervous system. In the simple community there is, plus the gregarious instinct, a process of defining the situation by discussion (and the latter element is of course the basis of the democratic organization of society). Our discussion of the primary group organization (Chapter II) and of the types of demoralization in America—some of the latter even reaching insanity (see document 56, p. 72)—show that the immigrant does not know how to live except as member of a group.

The situation of the new immigrant would be singularly helpless here if he did not find some points of identity with his previous life, and these he does in fact find among those of his own group or nationality who have preceded him. He almost always comes to friends; frequently they have sent him his ship ticket, and he boards with them until he has found employment and "worked back" the ship ticket. And the different immigrant groups have formed spontaneously in America, organizations that reproduce to some extent the home society or replace it with forms more adapted to the needs of the immigrant here. These organizations are not, in fact, pure heritages, but the products of the immigrants' efforts to adapt their heritages to American conditions. The immigrant, therefore, comes to a society of his own people, and this society, not native American society, is the matrix which gives him his first impression. The character of this society, as we shall see in more detail later, is the primary influence in determining the desire and capacity of the immigrant to participate in American life. The immigrant institutions are not to be commended indiscriminately as means of Americanization. They are primarily devices to make life go on with some success and efficiency, and when they are more than this they often represent the determination to be loyal to the old country rather

IMMIGRANT INSTITUTIONS

than to America, but they are none the less the point of first importance in any study of the individual's transition from one cultural world to another.

FIRST-AID INSTITUTIONS

There are, first of all, certain organizations developed simply as business enterprise, mainly by more instructed and sophisticated members of the various immigrant groups, to meet the practical needs of their countrymen. Among these are boarding houses, banks, steamship agencies, labor and real-estate agencies, the padrone system, etc. The character of these organizations and the abuses connected with them have often been described,[1] and we have given examples of the abuses in documents 47 (p. 56) and 59 (p. 77). The more important point, however, is not the abuses, but the fact that the immigrant must have this aid. These organizations are a practical solution which he must accept; they are the only organization of forces within his reach. The great American banks and steamship agencies are not adapted to his needs. The Jewish woman in New York buys a steamship ticket

---

[1] Grace Abbott, *The Immigrant and the Community*, and *Reports of the U. S. Immigration Commission*, vol. xxxvii.

for her sister in Russia from a ticket peddler, who collects fifty cents a week; the Polish laborer deposits his money with the saloon keeper; and this peddler or saloon keeper will eventually become a joint steamship agent, banker, employment agent, real-estate agent, etc., and may perhaps start a newspaper, or form a coalition with one, to promote his schemes.

86. Strange as it may seem, its very equipment prevents the American bank from entering into a fair competition with the immigrant banker. A Slovak immigrant banker, in apologizing somewhat for the appearance of his banking room, stated that it was necessarily ill kept because the men would come in in their working clothes, often covered with mud, frequently intoxicated, which, together with smoking and spitting, kept the room in a constant state of disorder. Such a condition would not be tolerated by an American bank. Moreover, the average immigrant feels a certain hesitancy in entering in his working clothes a building of the character of some city banks. This informant, who had been a banker for nearly twenty years, stated that he had often been urged to move into more pretentious quarters, but had refrained because he knew he could not keep them clean except at the cost of prestige and business.

These conditions, together with the inconvenient hours maintained by local banks, prevent any widespread patronage of them on the part of the immigrant. . . . .[1]

---

[1] *Reports of the U. S. Immigration Commission*, vol. xxxvii, p. 216.

IMMIGRANT INSTITUTIONS

87. The proprietor's ability to perform the services required comes primarily from his intimate knowledge of foreign conditions, places, languages, and names. His banking hours are made convenient, and in the ignorance and dependence of the immigrant he is looked upon as the safest depository and quickest means of transmission. Moreover, his position is greatly enhanced by racial and sectional prejudices, which are not infrequently encouraged and fostered by the banker to that very end. His business is usually confined to his countrymen or members of allied races. The Sicilian Italians, for example, are divided into five or six groups based upon provincial boundary lines, and a system of mutual patronage has sprung up among the members of each group.[1]

88. Those proprietors, who confine their operations to bank and steamship agencies, as distinguished from those who conduct such in connection with some other business, are usually the most intelligent men of the immigration population of any colony or locality. They are always possessed of considerable influence, and may be political leaders in the older and more established immigrant communities. . . .

Hundreds of saloon keepers and grocers act as bankers without the least fitness or equipment. It is true that they become bankers only as individuals through the fortunate chance of their position as merchants. . . .[2]

89. The most serious charge that is brought against such a coalition of bankers and newspapers is that by constant appeal to the prejudice and patriotism of the immigrant his Americanization is not only retarded, but deliberately combated, in

---
[1] *Reports of U. S. Immigration Commission,* vol. xxxvii, p. 218.
[2] *Ibid.,* 213.

order that he may be held as a source of income to those whom he trusts. An instance in point is the case of a certain Slovak banker, an ex-student of theology, who operates a large, handsomely furnished establishment, with two branch houses. This banker is a national and religious leader among his people, having organized and headed a national Slovak society in this country. He issues a daily, a weekly, a humanistic monthly, a yearly almanac, and from time to time other publications. Although he has renounced allegiance to Hungary, severed all political ties with that country, and become an American citizen, he does not advise his Slovak countrymen to do the same, but instead preaches in all his publications a militant and enthusiastic "Pan-Slovakism." So long as the Slovaks remain Slovaks and can be filled with Slovak patriotism and enthusiasm by such agitation, just so long will they remain a source of profit to the banker. Prior to the recent industrial depression this man was accustomed to transmit abroad, on behalf of his patrons, from $2,000,000 to $2,500,000 annually and to sell 6,000 steamship tickets per year.[1]

MUTUAL AID AND BENEFIT SOCIETIES

There is evidence [2] showing that back of the familial and communal solidarity of the European peasant is the fear of death and of its attendants and preliminaries—hunger, cold, darkness, sickness, solitude, and "mis-

---

[1] *Reports of U. S. Immigration Commission*, vol. xxxvii, p. 229.

[2] Thomas and Znaniecki, *The Polish Peasant*, Introduction to vol. i.

ery." The peasant is strangely indifferent to death, but he fears any irregular features—suddenness, inappropriateness. He wants to die decently, ceremonially, and socially. Since a man's death is usually the most conspicuous incident in his life, attracting the universal attention and interest of the group, since it is the occasion of judgments and speculations on the status of the family—whether they are thereby impoverished, whether they are rich—death and burial are not only the occasion of the natural idealization of the dead, but a means of securing recognition. Immigrant families are notorious for lavish expenditure on funerals.

90. . . . Now I inform you, dearest parents, and you, my brothers, that Konstanty, your son, dearest parents, and your brother and mine, my brothers, is no longer alive. It killed him in the foundry, it tore him in eight parts, it tore his head away and crushed his chest to a mass and broke his arms. But I beg you, dear parents, don't weep and don't grieve, God willed it so and did it so. It killed him on April 20th, in the morning, and he was buried on April 22d. He was buried beautifully. His funeral cost $225, the casket $60. Now when we win some [money] by law from the Company we will buy a place and transfer him, that he may lie quietly. We will surround him with a fence and put a cross, stone, or iron upon his grave. For his work let him at least lie quietly in his own place.[1]

---
[1] Thomas and Znaniecki, *The Polish Peasant*, vol. ii, p. 263.

OLD WORLD TRAITS TRANSPLANTED

Out of this sentiment grows the mutual-aid society, with death, burial, and sickness benefits. The business institutions are formed for the immigrant, but the mutual-aid society is organized by the immigrants. It is the basic institution, out of which grow the numerous lodges, orders, and fraternal organizations.[1]

---

[1] The Jew was an immigrant in Europe before coming to America, and consequently brings the tendency to mutual-aid organization developed there:

"Very little is known outside of the pale of a peculiarly Jewish organization among the artisans and their employees . . . the so-called *khevra*, a word of Hebrew origin, meaning a company, an association. To a certain extent the *khevra* as it exists to-day is analogous to the artisans' guilds and journeymen's guilds of the middle ages in western Europe. Its origin, however, must be sought in the rites of the Jewish religion. Various Hebrew religious functions must be observed in common. In fact, the prayers on certain occasions must be held in the presence of at least ten adults of the Jewish faith. Again, the main accessory of the Hebrew devotional exercises—the *torah* (the Old Testament, written in Hebrew on a long roll of parchment)—is too expensive to be in the possession of any but the richest citizens of the community. Thus, organizations for the express purpose of praying and of owning a *torah* sprang up; and it was easy for these organizations to develop along trade lines, because of the natural leaning of people of the same occupations toward one another. Gradually charitable functions were added to the religious ones; but in the beginning even the charitable acts had a religious basis, such as the execution of the various ceremonies connected with the burying of the dead members of the *khevra*. The members of the *khevra* must not only accompany the body of the dead to its last resting place, but must also assemble daily during the entire month to say the customary prayers. More important from the social-economic point of view is the obligation to stay, in regular turn, with the sick brother throughout the night if necessary.

"The transition from this service to a sick-benefit fund is natural. To make such financial assistance possible, a small

IMMIGRANT INSTITUTIONS

In addition, the more prosperous and responsible members of the immigrant groups who have the burden of providing for the sick and burying the dead of the penniless (for however loose the community ties, these are occasions on which neighborly aid cannot be denied) have evidently had an interest in forming these provident organizations as a matter of self-protection. The obligation is not repudiated, but regulated.

91. Father belonged to a society in which he was an active member. The men often came to our house to talk things over with him and he felt important and often offered our front room for committee meetings. Before they opened the meeting they always assured mother that they would not keep us up any later than ten o'clock. But when the

---

entrance fee and still smaller dues are provided, the first being often as small as one ruble and the latter only four or five kopeck or less per week. If this moderate income still leaves a surplus it may be used in granting the members small loans without any interest. This tendency toward mutual assistance leads to a strong bond among the members of the *khevra* and teaches them the advantages of co-operative activity along broader lines. . . .

"These social tendencies manifest themselves eloquently among the mass of the Jewish workingmen even in this country. The large number of Jewish *khevras*, lodges, clubs, fraternities, brotherhoods, and other organizations—frequently under American names and with the introduction of various rites—that are pursuing religious and partly charitable purposes, and often possessing national organizations, are in reality only an outgrowth of the primitive *khevra*. It was this habit of organization that the labor-union propaganda found such fertile soil among the mass of the Jewish workingmen in New York City."—I. M. Rubinow, "Economic Condition of the Jews in Russia," *U. S. Bureau of Labor, Bulletin 72,* p. 530.

time came they were so deep in discussion that they never even heard the clock strike the hour. I used to sit down in the doorway of the kitchen and front room from where I could see all their faces and listen to their heated arguments. Always it was a piece of burial ground that was the subject of discussion, and when a member, or anyone belonging to his family, died, whether the rest of the members should contribute an extra dollar to cover burial expenses, and whether as a society they should or should not employ a doctor and pay him out of the society fund. At twelve o'clock or even later they would at last break up with the question of the burial ground and the extra dollar and the doctor still unsettled"....[1]

92. The Slovenians have many fraternal organizations. The most important are: the Carniolian Slovenian Catholic Union, organized in Joliet, Illinois, April 2, 1894. It has 17,000 members, capital to the amount of $650,000, and has paid out $1,376,135.32 in benefits. The Slovenian National Benefit Society was organized in 1904, and has its headquarters at Chicago. Its capital is $525,000; it has over 18,000 members and has paid out in benefits $1,029,081. It has 341 branches, distributed in 27 states, and one in Canada. The Slovenian Workingmen's Benefit Association was founded August 16, 1908, in Johnstown, Pennsylvania. Its assets on June 30, 1918, were $158,096.93, of which $45,000 was invested in Liberty Bonds. It has 146 branches, which include 7,299 adult members and 4,500 junior members. It has paid out in benefits $1,000,000. In Cleveland there are 5 branches with a total of 605 members.[2]

---

[1] Rose Cohen, *Out of the Shadow*, p. 196.
[2] E. E. Ledbetter, *Study of the Jugo-Slavs* (manuscript).

IMMIGRANT INSTITUTIONS

93. The Italians of Chicago have 110 mutual-aid societies, representing a population of about 150,000. As the names suggest, the membership is generally from the same Italian province and frequently from the same village. . . . The most popular . . . the *Unione Siciliana*, has 28 lodges. Sick benefits in this order range from $8 to $12 per week, and a death benefit of $1,000 is paid. The monthly fees of these societies run from 30 to 60 cents. There is also, in all societies, a death assessment, making the average cost of membership from $12 to $15 per year. . . . Funeral expenses ranging from $50 to $90 are paid, and every member makes a contribution of $2 to the family of the dead member. During the sickness of a member all other members are obliged to visit and assist him if he lacks a family. . . . All members are obliged to attend the funeral, under penalty for absence. A band of musicians is always provided.[1]

94. . . . The Jewish [fraternal] orders constitute a valuable and important factor in our communal life. The interests of about a million Jews are involved in their existence and welfare. . . . An important phase is that the recipient of benefits from the lodge or order does not lose his self-respect, nor his standing in the organization, as is often the case of recipients of public charity. . . .

The lodges of the various orders have been and still are the most valuable schools through which our immigrated Jews pass. Many have learned their English at their lodge meetings. Others have acquired there their knowledge of parliamentary procedure and decorum at public meetings. Many

---

[1] F. O. Beck "The Italian in Chicago," in *Bulletin of the Department of Public Welfare, Chicago*, p. 23.

of our best-known public men and speakers have begun their careers modestly, in filling an office in their lodge or joining the debates at the meetings. In fact most of our people gain their connection with and knowledge of American Jewish activities, and take an interest in the same, through their affiliation with the Jewish fraternal orders. . . . For organizing, molding and interesting large masses of Jews in the large Jewish problems, they have been found the best means.[1]

95. The prefectural societies [composed of those from the same province in Japan] are very numerous. Of 344 men from whom personal data were obtained 99 had membership in these organizations, the societies of 27 different prefectures being represented among them. The societies indicate the strength of the localities among the Japanese. They serve as centers of social life and give assistance to those who are in need.

The Japanese Benevolent Society was organized in 1901. Its object was to make more complete provisions for the care of the sick, injured, and unfortunate than had been made by the several missions, the Japanese Association, the prefectural societies, and trade associations. . . . This does not indicate the importance of its work, however. . . . One of the more important branches of its work lies in securing reduced rates from the steamship companies for those who are sick or in need, in order that they may return to Japan. As a result of the efforts of this society and of the other institutions to which reference has been made, no Japanese become public charges in San Francisco.[2]

---

[1] Leo Wolfson, *Jewish Communal Register of New York City* (1917–18), p. 859.

[2] *Reports of U. S. Immigration Commission*, vol. xxiii, p. 220.

IMMIGRANT INSTITUTIONS

96. The six [Chinese] companies . . . are commercial guilds. The people from different sections belong to their several companies, analogous to the Hibernian, Saint Andrew's, Slavonian, Italian, German, or New England societies. These societies have their by-laws, their presidents, secretaries, treasurers, interpreters, etc. These officers are chosen by ballot every year and receive their salaries. They are for mutual aid. For certain benefits which are extended to the members they are willing to pay the dues and taxes imposed. The officers of these companies, together with prominent men among the merchants and others connected with the companies, are called together to deliberate and advise on occasions of important events, such as a murder, a riot in the mines or anywhere, a quarrel between members of different companies, the failure of some Chinese firm, or threatened persecutions, or any impending danger, or to make arrangements to receive and do honor to any dignitary. These meetings are simply advisory. They act often as arbitrators in difficulties, so as to prevent their people, if possible, from going to law; or when their countrymen have been robbed or murdered in the mines they take steps to procure through the government officers the apprehension and prosecution of the offenders.

Some of the companies in early Californian times built and supported hospitals for their countrymen. An old building down on what was called Washerwoman's Bay was built and supported by the Chinese for a hospital in early times. These companies do not import coolies; they are not immigrant associations; they are not civil or criminal courts to try and execute offenders; nor are they secret combinations for the purpose of subverting or interfering with the course of justice in the countries to which their people go to sojourn. . . .

One advantage in remaining connected with the six companies, which has weight with most of the Chinese here, is that their bones, wherever buried, will be gathered up and returned to China, and a portion of the dues to each company is for this purpose. . . . Another of the benefits of these companies (in the minds of Chinamen who are in business) is that they help in the collection of debts, or rather oppose barriers to the absconding of debtors. These companies have an arrangement with the different shipping houses by which no Chinamen can get his ticket for his passage unless he brings a stamped permit from his company. If a Chinaman is known to be insolvent, or if there are suspicions that he desires to defraud his creditors, or if a telegram comes from any part of the country saying, "Stop such a man," he will be hindered from going until the case has been investigated and satisfactory arrangements have been made.[1]

NATIONALISTIC ORGANIZATIONS

All the immigrant groups have societies of the character just shown, and the more formal, nation-wide societies are usually made up of these. Nationalistic organizations are readily formed by combining these local units into a city-wide and, eventually, a country-wide organization. Thus the Sons

---

[1] *U. S. Industrial Commission, Report for 1901*, vol. xv, p. 446, (testimony of A. W. Loomis).

IMMIGRANT INSTITUTIONS

of Italy, the most powerful Italian organization in the United States, which has a membership of 125,000, and 887 lodges in 24 states, is a congeries of benefit and insurance societies, but its object is also:

97. To unite fraternally all white males and females of Italian descent residing in the several states of the United States of America . . . in one family, without regard to religious, philosophic, or political faith or belief. . . .

To assist with all its vigor and strength the individual members at all times and to aid any of their relatives in the event of difficulty in obtaining entry into the United States as immigrants, or in case of other distress or difficulty.

To aid in maintaining alive the patriotic spirit and love for the fatherland, by the observance of such holidays as Columbus Day, by providing means for the diffusion of the Italian language, and by adopting the same as the official language at all meetings of this order.[1]

Similarly, the Polish National Alliance is an insurance company and at the same time the largest Polish nationalistic organization, with about 1,700 branches and a membership of about 130,000. (See Map 1, on p. 134). It was founded in Philadelphia, in 1880, as a direct response to the following letter, and up to the present has worked in the spirit of this letter:

---

[1] From the "Certificate of Incorporation" of the Sons of Italy (1905).

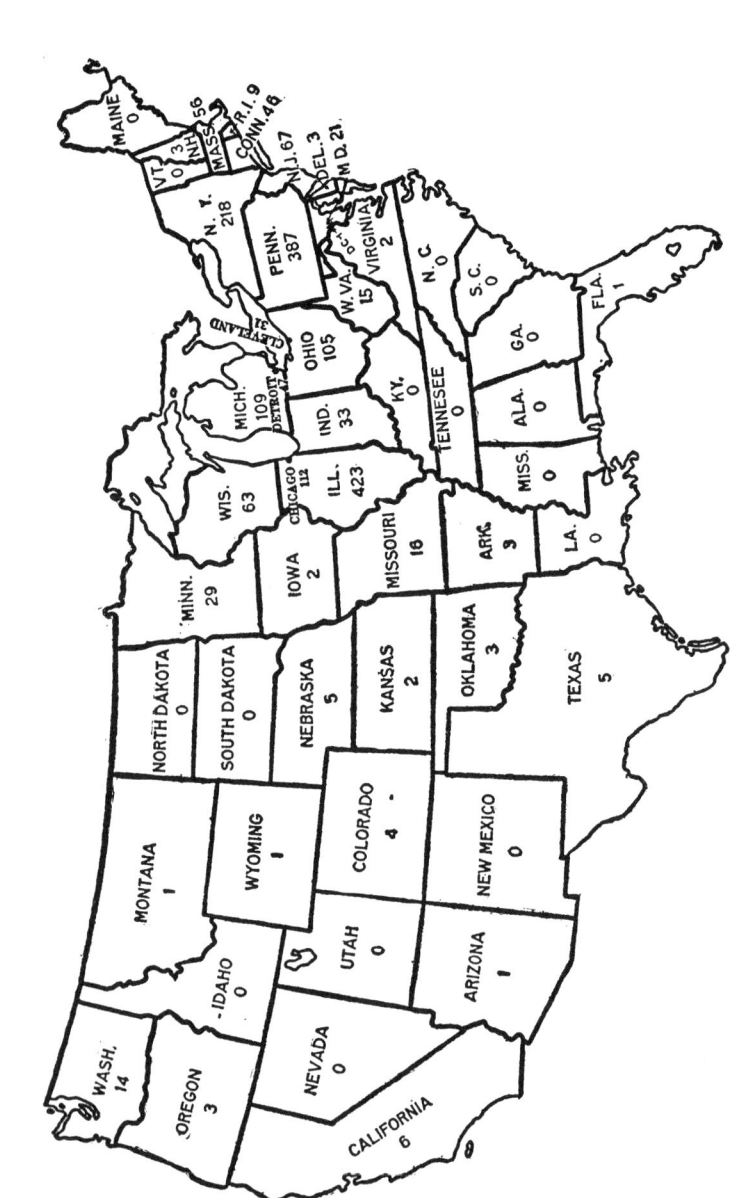

Map 1.—The Polish National Alliance has 1658 Branches Distributed in 33 States

IMMIGRANT INSTITUTIONS

98. Since emigration exists and constitutes a great power—a fact which cannot be denied—it should be the task of a well-understood patriotism to make it as useful as possible for the national cause. This can be done only through organization, which will unify the scattered members and control them in such a way that they will not be wasted but will be preserved for the fatherland. . . .

Every Polish peasant, from whatever Polish province he comes, even from one of those which, like upper Silesia or East Prussia, have been for a long time separated from the national body, when transferred to a strange soil among foreigners develops a Polish sentiment and a consciousness of his national character. This phenomenon is incomprehensible for those who saw the peasant at home without a consciousness of national duties. And yet it is quite natural. National consciousness originates in him spontaneously in a foreign country in consequence of the feeling of the striking difference between his speech, his customs, his conceptions, from those of the people who surround him. . . .

If, after the formation of a conception and sentiment of nationality in him, there is some one capable of explaining to him the meaning of this national character and of making him understand the duties resulting from this character, then this plain man, formerly ignorant and passive for the national cause, will become an individual consciously and actively serving the idea which rests upon nationality. . . . There is, therefore, no doubt that if a national intellectual class is formed in America the numerous masses can and must be changed into an active human group useful for the national cause; and in order to give them the possibility of becoming useful and at the same time surround them with conditions which will prevent them from losing their nationality, it is indispensable to unite the isolated individuals into more or less numerous associations and communities and bind these together in such a way that the resulting organization, while serving the purposes of the Polish cause, will be not only useful, but indispensable for the private interests of every one of its members. . . .

When the mass of Poles in America is morally and nationally raised by the fact of being unified and is economically prosperous—which should be also one of the tasks of the organization—it will render great services to Poland, even by the mere fact of representing the Polish name well in America. These services can gradually become very considerable, when the Poles begin to exercise an influence upon the public life of the United States, when they spread among Americans adequate conceptions about the Polish cause and information about the history, literature, and art of our nation, when finally they become intermediaries between Poland and the powerful Republic so as to foster sympathy with our efforts for liberation and develop it into an enthusiasm which will express itself in action.

Then only can happen that which is most desirable—*i.e.*, the emigrants who have acquired training in practical lines and wealth in America will begin to return to their fatherland to be useful citizens. . . . We do not need to put forward those benefits which a large organization of Poles in America could bring at the decisive moment when the future

IMMIGRANT INSTITUTIONS

of our fatherland will be at stake, for this is easy to see.[1]

Another Polish nationalistic organization composed more exclusively of intellectuals, is the Alliance of Polish Socialists. Like the Polish National Alliance, it has worked, up to the present, mainly to establish a Polish nation in America as a substitute and center of influence for a Polish state in Europe. The Polish socialists, however, have had more definitely the program of preparing in America leaders for Poland when her "day" should come. This principle was formulated, for instance, in a letter of Kozakiewicz, one of the founders of the Alliance, which was read and indorsed at the general meeting of delegates in 1917:

99. "In view of our weak direct participation in the political life of this country . . . we should direct all our work to the aim of training active, independently thinking socialists, educated men, and conscious citizens, ready to sacrifice themselves for our idea. . . . Let us form men everyone of whom will be able in any locality, without help, spontaneously to create and—more than this—to lead an organization." The ultimate aim has been up to

[1] Extract from a letter from Agaton Giller, former member of the Polish national government of 1863, written in 1879 from Rapperwil, Switzerland, to the *Gazeta Polska* of Chicago. Reprinted in Stanislaw Osada, *History of the Polish National Alliance* (in Polish), p. 102.

the present, as we have seen above, realization of the socialistic ideal in Poland rather than in America. When the time comes for our companions to return to Poland, may we be able to say with pride, "These are men from the American school, trained by the Polish organizations." [1]

While among some of the immigrant groups (the Poles, for example) interest in the nationalistic movement has tended to dominate all other interests, the Zionism of the Jews is merely one expression of the general organization and growing self-consciousness of this group:

100. The nationalist Jew . . . is the product of two historic movements. The *Haskallah* (enlightenment) movement in Russia during the middle of the last century caused many Jewish students to forsake the Talmudical halls of learning and . . . to devote their energies to the creation of a new literature in Hebrew, expressive of the facts of modern life and of the new orientation of the Jews in the modern world. The ideal of this movement, the *Haskil* (the enlightened), is one who is acquainted with science, literature, and art, and who knows thoroughly the literature of his people, both ancient and modern, even to the extent of being able to contribute to it. With the *Haskallah* movement another force combined in creating the nationalist Jew. This force was Zionism. Modern Zionism originated in Russia as a "Love of Palestine" movement, and spread

---

[1] Florian Znaniecki, *Study of Polish Organizations in America* (manuscript).

IMMIGRANT INSTITUTIONS

throughout the world under the leadership of Dr. Theodore Herzl. . . . It is simply a modern formulation of the age-long yearning of the Jew for Zion. It looks to the establishment of a "publicity secured, legally assured homeland for the Jews in Palestine," and to the "fostering of Jewish consciousness throughout the world." [1]

Similar motives—the desire to serve the mother country in and from America—have inspired the representatives of other "oppressed and dependent" European and Asiatic nationalities (see documents 71, 72, 73, p. 98). The Chinese nationalistic activities, for example, are carried on largely by university students and commercial clubs, and have the sympathy and participation of American friends of China.

The Japanese Association of America is nationalistic only in the sense that it regulates the life of the Japanese in America and promotes their efficiency. It is really a bureau of information both for the home government and for the Japanese in America. It advises the Japanese government as to the policy to be pursued, how many and what kind of Japanese shall be permitted to come, whether the practice of sending "picture brides" leads to disorder, and so forth. (See document 109, p. 169.)

[1] Alexander M. Duskin, *Jewish Education in New York City*, p. 36.

There is in America a body of about 1,100,000 French Canadians, settled mainly in the New England states, who are carrying on a struggle for the perpetuation of their culture along the same lines as the French in Canada. As a consequence our New England mill towns have the French language, French parishes and parochial schools, French nationalistic societies (*St. Jean de Baptiste d'Amérique, Canado-Américan*), and a French nationalist press. (See Map 2, on p. 141.)

101. The French Canadians of Quebec have increased in population from 60,000 in 1763 to 3,000,000 scattered through the United States and Canada. Wherever in New England these have settled in numbers, that community is gradually ceasing to be English. Lewiston, Maine, is an example which has not only ceased to be a "Yankee" city and is losing its American characteristics, but is gradually assuming a French aspect. The parish with its organizations has successfully prevented its parishioners from coming under native influences and is driving the English language from the business sections. . . . The French Canadian population of Biddeford is nearly 70 per cent. . . . This population is fairly well distributed over the whole city. A Yankee section exists rather than a French section. . . . Three thousand young French Americans are annually sent to the colleges of French Canadian nationalism in the province of Quebec. . . . Probably the most important and most popular newspaper among the New England Franco-Americans is *La Presse*, of

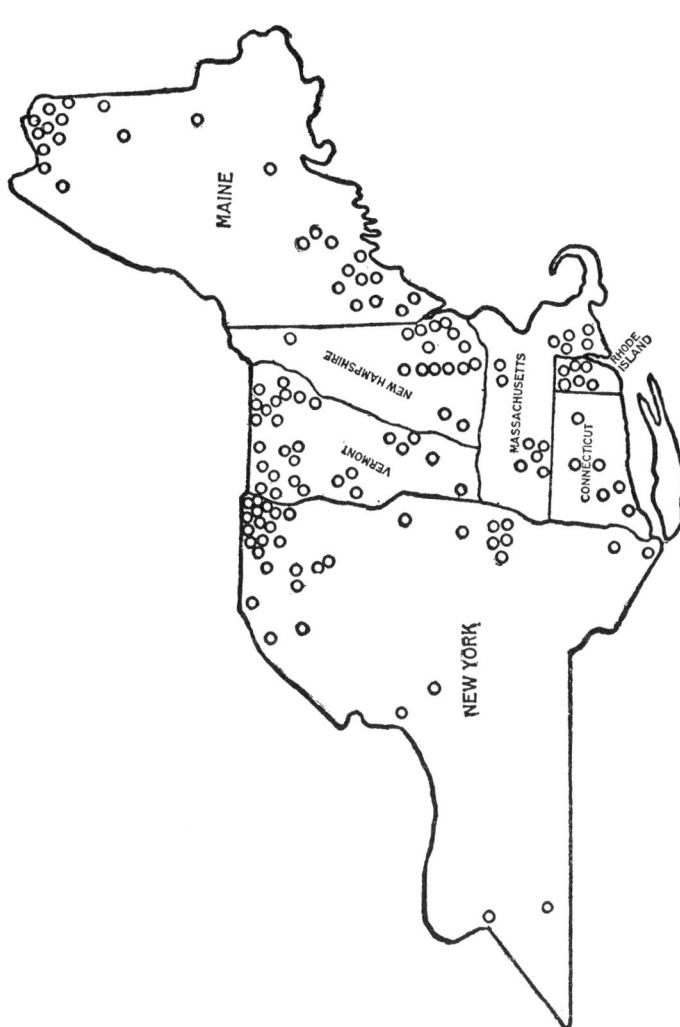

Map 2.—French Canadian Parishes of New England and New York

Montreal. . . . An examination of *Who's Who in America* fails to reveal the name of any one of the 110,000 Frenchmen of the state of Maine.[1]

Nevertheless, the French Americans recognize that this is a transitory situation. Some of their organizations—*e.g.*, St. Jean de Baptiste—have been obliged to allow proceedings to be conducted in English to prevent young people from joining American societies. (See document 163, p. 290.)

A number of elements enter into the nationalistic sentiments of the immigrant: (1) the idealization of home conditions, natural in one who is absent; (2) the desire to aid the struggle for self-determination going on at home; (3) the desire to gain recognition at home, preparatory to a return; (4) the wish to improve his status in the eyes of the American public by improving the status of the national group; (5) the feeling of non-participation in American life which leads to the attempt to create here a situation in which he can participate. All these sentiments stimulate participation in public life, some of them participation in American life. The form taken by the movement in the different groups depends on the character of their historical expe-

---

[1] H. L. Harper, *The French Canadians of New England* (manuscript).

riences. When, for example, the superior member of a foreign group compares his community with the larger American community, and particularly when he is humiliated in the latter because of his connection with the former, he may wish to repudiate his native group, try to lose the marks of identification with it, because he is ashamed of it. Thus, the cultured Italian may find it impossible to identify himself with a Sicilian group containing the *caffone* and black-hand elements, and may avoid the Italian group altogether. Similarly, the Jew may wish to lose his identity as Jew because of the popular prejudice against his race. But this effort usually fails because the individual cannot completely lose the marks of identity with his native group; he is betrayed by some sign—his speech or gestures, or sentiments. He consequently finds himself out of his old society without being completely in a new one and in a painful position—without recognition from any group whatever. We find, therefore, that the men who begin by deserting their groups end by attempting to improve the status of these groups—seeking to make them something with which a man may be proud to identify himself. The fact that the individual will not be respected unless his group is respected becomes thus, perhaps, the most sincere source of the nationalistic movements in America. To this extent the nationalistic movements represent an effort to participate in American life.

CULTURAL INSTITUTIONS

There remain certain cultural institutions of the immigrant, the press, the theater, the school, the church, etc. The press and the school are treated in other volumes of this series, and in Chapters VII and VIII we mention these institutions, especially the church and synagogue, in characterizing the immigrant community.

VII

THE IMMIGRANT COMMUNITY

THE community comprised of a number of families is the simplest form which society has assumed in the universal struggle against death. All the primary human needs can be satisfied in the community. Polish peasant communities, before 1860, lived as practically self-sufficient groups. They knew by report that there was a great world, and they had some relations with it, through Jews and manor owners; they had a priest and the religious-magical traditions of Christendom. But practically the extent of their world was the "*okolica*," "the neighborhood round about," and their definition of this was, "as far as a man is talked about." Their life was culturally poor, and they showed no tendency either to progress or to retrograde, but *they lived*. The peasant did not know he was a Pole; he even denied it. The lord was a Pole; he was a peasant. We have records showing that members of other immigrant groups realize first in America that they are members of a nationality: "I had never realized I was an Albanian until my brother came from America in 1909. He belonged to an Albanian society over here."[1]

The immigrants here tend to reproduce spontaneously the home community and to live in it. Letters show that they frequently reply to inquiries from home for a description of America, "I have not yet been able to see America." There are immigrants on the lower East Side of New York who have been here for twenty years and have never been up town. Even the intellectual immigrants feel painfully the failure to meet cultivated Americans. (See document 33, p. 46.)

THE ITALIANS

Among the more important immigrant groups the Italians show perhaps the strongest *wish* to remain in solitary communities. They settle here by villages and even by streets, neighbors in Italy tending to become neighbors here. Map 3 shows the concentration of immigrants from different Italian provinces and Sicilian towns in a section of lower New York.

---

[1] Menas Laukas, *Life History*, recorded by Winifred Rauschenbusch (manuscript).

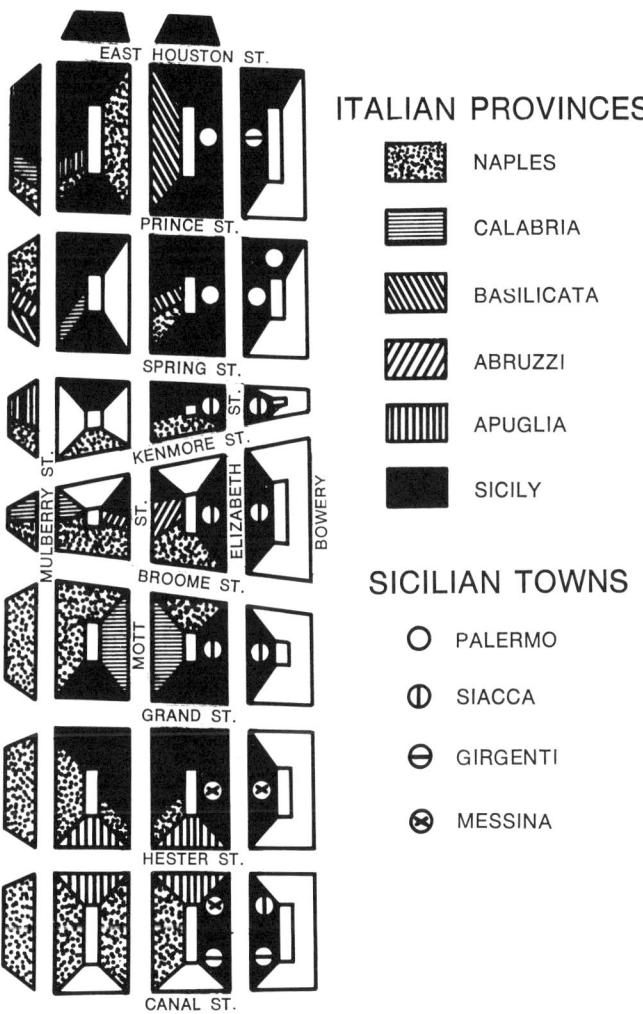

Map 3.—Bowery Colony of Italians Showing Settlements According to Native Provinces and Towns

THE IMMIGRANT COMMUNITY

The colony, from the village of Cinisi, Sicily, in the vicinity of East Sixty-ninth Street and Avenue A, New York, may be taken as typical. There are more than 200 families at this point, and there are other groups from Cinisi in Brooklyn, Harlem, and on Bleecker Street. (See Map 10, p. 242.)

102. The colony is held together by the force of custom. People do exactly as they did in Cinisi. If some one varies, he or she will be criticized. If many vary—then that will become the custom. It is by the group, collectively, that they progress. They do not wish the members of the colony to improve their economic conditions or to withdraw. If a woman is able to buy a fine dress, they say: "Look at that *villana* [serf]! In the old country she used to carry baskets of tomatoes on her head and now she carries a hat on it." "Gee! look at the daughter of so and so. In Cinisi she worked in the field and sunburnt her black. Here she dares to carry a parasol."

So strong is this influence that people hesitate to wear anything except what was customary in Cinisi. Everywhere there is fear of being "*sparlata*"— talked badly of. A woman bought a pair of silk stockings and the neighbors talked so much about her that her husband ordered her to take them off. . . . To dress poorly is criticized and to dress sportily is criticized. In this way one had to conform or be ostracized.

A number of families moved from the central group of Brooklyn. There they have combined and rent a whole two-story house. They are living better than those in the other groups and I often hear the East Sixty-ninth Street people say: "Look at those *paesani* in Brooklyn. When they were here they were in financial straits. One of them had to flee from the criticism here. He did not have the money to pay his moving van and crowded all his furniture into a small one-horse wagon. He even put his wife on to save car fare. He left a pile of debts and now he dares come around here with a horse and buggy."

If a wife is spied by another Cinisaro talking to a man who is known as a stranger—that is, who is not a relative—she is gossiped about: she has the latent willingness to become a prostitute. They say: "So and so's wife was talking with an American. Eh! She has the capacity to do wrong."

Nothing in the American women surprises them. They have already made an unfavorable judgment. My mother, for instance, was about to say that my wife, who is an American, was an exception to the rule, but when my wife went to Central Park with the baby she said, "They are all alike."

The colony has no newspapers, except one woman who is known as the "*Giornale di Sicilia*," or the "Journal of Sicily." She carries the news and spreads it as soon as said. She has now gone to Italy and the one who takes her place is a gossiper who is known as a "*too-too*"—referring to the "tooting" of a town-crier's horn. She is, moreover, malicious, and gives a version of a story calculated to produce ridicule. She not only talks about the breakers of customs, but about those who are financially low. To be financially low is looked down upon, and the *Giornale di Sicilia* warns people to look out for such and such a person, as he may ask

THE IMMIGRANT COMMUNITY

for a loan. To be willing to lend means that one has accumulated money and thus the secret of the lender is out. So this is the reason they refuse to lend to one another and if one is down and out he would rather get money from a Jew than from a *paesano*. So deceptive are they as to their financial standing (partly through fear of blackmail) that it is customary to figure out a Cinisarian's fortune not by what he says, but by how many sons and daughters are working.

Now and then some Cinisarian takes his chances in the business world. He writes to his relatives in Cinisi, has oil, wine, and figs, lemons, nuts, etc., sent to him, and then he goes from house to house. He does not enter in a business way, but goes to visit some family, talks about Cinisi, then informs them that he has received some produce from the home town. And sure enough, the people will say, "You will let us get some, eh?"

"Of course. Tell your relatives. I can get all you want."

In this way the business man makes his sales. He progresses until he gets a place opened and then come his worries. He must forever show that he is poor, that he is barely making a living, for fear of some attempt to extort money from him.

Not many men of the Cinisi group are in business in New York, the reason being that one Cinisarian will not compete with another in the same line of business.

The central group is closely united and there is little possibility that they will adopt any customs of the neighboring peoples, who are mostly Irish and Bohemians. The Irishwomen are considered wives of drunkards and, as all of the husband's salary goes to the bartender, the wives are believed to earn a living in prostituting themselves. The Bohemians are libertines; the girls are free; and, moreover, Bohemians and Hungarians are looked upon as bastard peoples.

In the Cinisi colony there are no political parties. The group has not been interested in citizenship. Of 250, one or two were citizens before the war and now all those who returned from the war are also citizens. These young men sell their votes for favors. The average Cinisaro, like all foreigners, has the opinion that a vote means $5. The Cinisaro knows of corruption at home. In Cinisi there is very much of it. Money is raised to build a water system for Cinisi year after year, and it gets away without a water system coming in exchange.

The Cinisi group are more interested in Cinisarian politics than in American. They talk of the parties of the artisans, of the gentlemen, of the *villani*, of the hunters, in Cinisi.

Most of the Cinisari in the Sixty-ninth Street group intend to return to Sicily. The town of Cinisi is forever in their minds: "I wonder if I can get back in time for the next crop?"—"I hope I can get back in time for the festa"—"I hope I can reach Cinisi in time to get a full stomach of Indian figs," etc. They receive mail keeping them informed as to the most minute details, and about all the gossip that goes on in Cinisi in addition; they keep the home town informed as to what is going on here. They write home of people here who have transgressed some custom: "So-and-so married an American girl. The American girls are libertines. The boy is very disobedient." "So-and-so who failed to succeed at college in Palermo, is here. He has

THE IMMIGRANT COMMUNITY

married a stranger"—that is, an Italian of another town. In this way they blacken a man's name in Cinisi, so that a bad reputation awaits him on his return.

The reputation given them in Cinisi by report from here means much to them, because they expect to return. Whole families have the date fixed. Those who express openly their intention of remaining here are the young Americanized men.

When the festival of Santa Fara, the patron saint of Cinisi, was planned (partly as a reproduction of the home custom, partly as an expression of gratitude to Santa Fara for the miracle of ending the war), there was some opposition on the ground that all funds should be sent to Cinisi for the festival there. The festival was held (April 26 and 27, 1919), but was so disappointing that it is said to have increased the desire to return to Cinisi and see the original.[1]

103. Until 1914 the Sicilian colony in Chicago was an absolutely foreign community. The immigrants were mostly from villages near Palermo, though nearly all of the Sicilian provinces are represented. The most important of the village groups are those from Alta Villa Milicia, Bagheria Vicari, Cimmina, Termini-Imarezi, Monreali, and the city of Palermo. These groups retained their identity, living together as far as possible, intermarrying and celebrating the traditional feasts. Immigrants who settled in Louisiana came up to join their village colony. Those who had been leaders in Sicily retained their power here and, having greater force and intelligence, made contracts with local politicians, police officials, labor agents, and real estate dealers, and

[1] Gaspare Cusumano, *Study of the Colony of Cinisi in New York City* (manuscript).

OLD WORLD TRAITS TRANSPLANTED

became the go-betweens for their colony and the outside-world labor agents.

Women continued to live as they had in Sicily, never leaving their homes except to make ceremonial visits or to attend mass. The presence of several garment factories in the district made it possible for them to earn by doing finishing at home. In later years hundreds of women went into the garment factories to work, some taking the street cars out of the district; but they went to and from work in groups, their shawls carefully wrapped about them.

In the entire district there was no food for sale that was not distinctly foreign; it was impossible to buy butter, American cheese, sweet potatoes, pumpkin, green corn, etc., but in season artichokes, cactus fruit (*fichi d'India*), pomegranates, cocozella, and various herbs and greens never sold in other parts of town were plentiful. There were no bookstores. Italian newspapers had a limited circulation, and the Chicago daily papers were sold at only two transfer points on the edge of the district. There were no evidences of taste in dress or house decoration. This group seemed to have had no folk music, but took great pleasure in band concerts when spirited marches and melodies from Verdi's operas were played. There was no educational standard; the older people were almost all illiterate; they accepted this as natural and explained it by saying, "We are *contadini*, and our heads are too thick to learn letters." Some of the younger ones had had a little elementary training, but with very few exceptions no one in the colony had gone beyond the "*quarto elementario.*" Few had seen military service or learned trades except, of course, the tailors, barbers, and shoemakers. One heard of an occasional cabinet maker, harness

THE IMMIGRANT COMMUNITY

maker, solderer, carpenter, or mason, but none followed his trade here, as the training did not fit him to American methods. Many who had worked in the orchards in Sicily found their way to South Water Street and worked as truckers and fruit packers and, becoming familiar with the way produce was handled, started their friends out as fruit and vegetable peddlers, thus establishing a wholesale business for themselves. Most of the men, however, were sent by their leaders to the railroads and building contractors as laborers. . . .

Individually, Sicilians seem to vary as much in their manner and ideals as Americans, but as a group they have certain very marked characteristics—reserve, suspicion, susceptibility to gossip, timidity, and the desire to "*fa figura*." Intense family pride, however, is the outstanding characteristic, and as the family unit not only includes those related by blood, but those related by ritual bonds as well (the *commare* and *compare*), and as intermarriage in the village groups is a common practice, this family pride becomes really a clan pride.

The extent to which family loyalty goes is almost beyond belief; no matter how disgraced or how disgraceful a member may be, he is never cast off, the unsuccessful are assisted, the selfish are indulged, the erratic patiently born with. Old age is respected and babies are objects of adoration. The self-respect of a man can be gauged by the number of his children, and the women seem to accept the yearly bearing of a child as a privilege. Both children and adults seem satisfied with the social opportunities offered within the family itself. The births, baptisms, chrisms, betrothals, marriages, and deaths furnish the occasion for ceremonial visits and festivities.

OLD WORLD TRAITS TRANSPLANTED

Traditional religious forms and superstitions are observed on these occasions, but the church and the priest seem adjuncts rather than the center of the various rites.

The leaders of the village groups organize brotherhoods for the purpose of perpetuating the feast of the patron saint and to arrange the elaborate funerals with which they honor the dead. The societies meet each month, collect dues, have endless and excited discussions over the petty business that is transacted, with, however, most serious regard for rules of order. Some of the *fratellanza* have women's auxiliaries, but they are directed entirely by the men, and the women seem to have no voice in the conduct of affairs; they pay dues and march in the processions. The annual feast is the great event of the year, exceeded in importance by Easter only. The group responsible for a feast put up posters announcing the day and the program, and through committees arrange for all of the details of the celebration; electric-light festoons are strung across the streets, concessions for street booths are sold, bands are hired, band stands are erected, and the church is paid for a special mass and for the services of the priest who leads the procession. The whole community participates to some extent, but those from the village whose patron is being honored make the most elaborate preparation in their homes. . . . Those who have been ill or suffered physical injury during the year buy wax figures of the part that was affected—legs, hands, breasts, etc., to carry in procession; others carry long candles with ribbon streamers to which money is affixed by a member of the brotherhood who rides on the shrine and exhorts the crowds to make their offering.

THE IMMIGRANT COMMUNITY

The shrine is lowered to the street every hundred feet or so and little children are undressed, their clothes left as an offering, and they are lifted to kiss the lips of the saint. Sometimes a blind or lame child is carried about on the shrine in the hope of a miraculous cure. The climax is the flight of the angels. The shrine is set in the middle of the street in front of the church, and two children, dressed as angels and bearing armfuls of flowers, are lowered by strong ropes so that they are suspended just over the figure of the saint, where they sway while chanting a long prayer.

The offerings made during the most important of these feasts amount to from four to six thousand dollars. This money goes into the treasury of the *fratellanza* and is used for the expense incurred by the *festa* and for the death benefit. There are those who say that tribute is paid to certain individuals as well.

These feasts are not approved by the priest, and people say that trouble is started by the jealousy aroused when one village tries to outdo the other. It certainly is true that at these *festas* there is often a shooting.

The position of women in the Sicilian homes in this district is hard to define. The general impression is that women are slaves to their husbands, but this is far from true except in the cases of very ignorant and primitive types. The head of the family takes the responsibility of protecting the women and girls very seriously, and for this reason women have little life outside their homes. It is a mark of good breeding for a man to show "*la gelosia*" regarding his wife and daughters, and it would be a sign of disrespect to them if he did not guard them carefully. Within the home, however, the wife directs the household and it is not unusual for her to take the lead in family affairs, such as the expenditure of money, plans for the children, or the choice of friends.

When a girl reaches the age of twelve her freedom comes to an end; she is considered old enough to put away childish things. Until she is married she is not supposed to have any interest outside her home except school or work, and with these two exceptions she is not supposed to be out of her mother's sight. A family that fails to observe this rule is subject to criticism.

A marriage is arranged by the parents as soon as a suitable young man of their village presents himself. The girl is not consulted and often does not even know whom she is to marry until the matter is all settled. After a girl is promised her fiancé must be consulted before she can go out, and she never appears in public without her mother or father in attendance. It has become the custom to have a civil ceremony performed shortly after the betrothal. This does not constitute a marriage and often it is several months or even a year or two before the actual marriage takes place. Meanwhile the engaged couple meet only in the presence of their parents or attend various family ceremonies together, always suitably chaperoned.

Sometimes a girl is coveted by a man considered undesirable by her parents, or by one who did not know her before she was engaged. In such a case the man may try to force his attentions on her in the hope of attracting her in spite of her parents or her promise. If she does not respond and will not elope voluntarily, it is not unusual for him to try to

THE IMMIGRANT COMMUNITY

take her by force, either carrying her off himself or getting his friends to kidnap her and bring her to some secret place. When a girl becomes engaged her family is on the lookout for just such occurrences, and if they have any suspicion that she is being pursued she is kept a prisoner until she is safely married. If the man is known he is dealt with in no uncertain way—told to stop or take the consequences.

If a girl permits herself to be kidnaped the affair is usually ended with the blessings of all concerned, though the jilted one sometimes makes it necessary for the couple to move to another part of town, at least until he consoles himself with another wife. If a girl is carried away entirely against her will there may be bloodshed as a result.

Not all kidnapings occur in this way; often impatient men, tiring of the long and ceremonious period of betrothal and failing to persuade the fiancée to elope, try to carry her away. A well-bred girl will put up a good fight to escape, and if she succeeds the engagement is broken; but if she is forced to submit the family accept the situation and all is forgiven. There are, of course, many voluntary elopements by young people who are attracted by one another and who, because of family differences, could never get the consent of their parents.

Seduction is an almost unheard-of thing among the foreign people and in the few instances where a girl has been wronged it has meant certain death to her betrayer. Not long ago a man seduced a young girl and left town when he discovered that she was pregnant. Her family moved from the district and after a few months the man, Piazza, returned. The girl's brothers met him and seemed friendly, so he agreed to visit their new home. Shots were heard by neighbors, and when the police arrived they found Piazza and the girl's oldest brother dead. The bodies were seated on opposite sides of the table and it is supposed that both drew and fired their revolvers simultaneously.

During the last four years there has been a great change, the colony is slowly disintegrating, old customs are giving way. Contacts with the outside world, through work and school, have given boys and girls a vision of freedom and new opportunity. They are going to night schools and making their friends outside the old circle. They are out of patience with the petty interests and quarrels of the older group and refuse to have their lives ordered by their parents, whom they know to be ignorant and inexperienced. Families are not being broken up, the deep affections still persist, and though the old folks have misgivings, in their indulgent way they are letting the new generation take the lead and are proud of their progressive sons and daughters. Young married couples are making their homes north of the old district, within easy reach of their parents, but away from the old associations. Evidences of refinement are seen in their homes and in their manner, and their children are dressed and fed according to most modern standards.[1]

It appears from these statements: (1) that the Sicilian heritages are so different from the American that the members of this group feel no original interest in participating in American life; (2) that this dif-

---
[1] Marie Leavitt, *Report on the Sicilian Colony in Chicago* (manuscript).

THE IMMIGRANT COMMUNITY

ference is accepted in America as a natural fact, somewhat as an outlying herd of animals would be accepted and tolerated or exploited, without thought of its social incorporation; (3) that this solitary group is almost as inaccessible to superior individuals of its own nationality who might be its leaders as to American influence (see document 82, p. 104); and (4) that, nevertheless, the mass begins to dissolve and change, owing to informal contacts with American life, made especially by the younger generation, and certainly largely through the public school, which is the one point at which contact is formal and inevitable.

THE CHINESE

The personality of the individual is always more impenetrable to the student than are the institutions which represent him. While it is difficult, for example, to understand a Chinese, there is nothing mysterious about Chinese institutions. The more data we secure on them, the more we are impressed with their resemblance to our own.

The Chinese are pre-eminently a democratic and a village people. The different provinces are only loosely bound to the central government, and the people have made many local alliances. There are in China (1) about 450 clans, the general purpose of which is defense against the central government, mutual aid in business and other affairs; (2) trade organizations, or guilds, with objects similar to those in Europe; (3) town and district councils, resembling the peasant communes and town councils of Europe and America.

In America the Chinese is even more helpless than the European immigrant. He finds more strangeness and prejudice, and the Chinese do not bring their families, and consequently cannot live in complete colonies. The result is the formation of communities of men. The Six Companies and the various *tongs* represent the form taken by the community when not based directly on the family. The following document, if read with reference to its provision and prohibitions, illustrates the character which Chinese community life tends to assume under these conditions:

104. . . . People of the three districts of Heangshan, Tung-yuen, and Tsang-shing are required to report themselves at the company's room; otherwise the company will exercise no care for them in their concerns.

The entrance fee shall be ten dollars; if not paid within six months, interest will be expected. . . .

THE IMMIGRANT COMMUNITY

No fees will be required from those proved to be invalids or from transient persons. . . . Disputes will not be settled between persons who have not paid the entrance fee. Members purposing to return to China must make the fact known to the agents, when their accounts will be examined, and measures will be taken to prevent it if the entrance fee or other debts remain unpaid. Strangers to the agents of the company must obtain security of persons who will be responsible for their character and debts. Members leaving clandestinely shall be liable to a fine of fifty dollars; and the security for a debt, for helping one thus to abscond, shall be fined one hundred dollars.

In the company's house there must be no concealment of stolen goods; no strangers brought to lodge; no gunpowder or other combustible material; no gambling; no drunkenness; no cooking (except in the proper quarters); no burning of sacrificial papers; no accumulation of baggage; no filth; no bathing; no filching of oil; no heaps of rags and trash; no wrangling and noise; no injury of the property of the company; no goods belonging to thieves; no slops of victuals. For the heavier of these offenses complaint shall be made to the police of the city; for the lighter, persons shall be expelled from the company. Baggage will not be allowed to remain longer than three years, when it must be removed; nor more than one chest to each person.

Invalids that cannot labor, are poor and without relatives, may be returned to China at the expense of the company for their passage money; but provisions and fuel and other expenses must be obtained by subscriptions. Coffins may be furnished for the poor, but of such a careful record shall be kept.

OLD WORLD TRAITS TRANSPLANTED

Quarrels and troubles about claims in the mines should be referred to the company, where they shall be duly considered. If any should refuse to abide by the decision of the company, it will nevertheless assist the injured and defend them from violence. If, when foreigners do injury, a complaint is made and the company exerts itself to have justice done without avail, it ought to be submitted to. Whatever is referred for settlement to the assembly of the five companies conjointly, cannot be brought before this company alone.

Where a man is killed a reward shall be offered by the company for apprehension and trial, the money being paid only when he shall have been seized; the members of the company shall subscribe each according to what is just. If more than the anticipated amount is required, the friends of the deceased shall make up the deficiency. Complaint shall be made of offenders to the civil courts, and proclamations for their arrest shall be placarded in the principal towns; but anyone found guilty of concealing them shall pay all the expenses to which the company has been put. Difficulties with members of other companies shall be reported to the agents of this company, and, if justice demand, shall be referred for the judgment of the five companies conjointly. Offenses committed on shipboard, upon the sea, shall be referred to the five companies conjointly. Difficulties brought upon men by their own vices and follies will not receive attention. Thievery and receiving of stolen goods will not be protected; nor will troubles in bawdy houses nor those in gambling houses; nor debts to such; nor extortions of secret associations; nor the quarrels of such associations; nor those who are injured in

THE IMMIGRANT COMMUNITY

consequence of refusal to pay their licenses; nor smuggling; nor any violation of American laws. The company will not consider complaints from a distance, of a doubtful character, or without sufficient proof. No reply will be made to anonymous letters, or those without date and a specification of the true origin and nature of difficulties. Names must be carefully given in all complaints from the interior. No payments of money will be made in the settlement of cases where the rules of the company are not complied with. Where the conduct of an individual is such as to bring disgrace on the company and upon his countrymen, he shall be expelled, and a notice to that effect be placarded in each of the five companies' houses; nor will the company be responsible for any of his subsequent villainies, or even make any investigation should he meet with any violent death. Costs connected with the settlement of disputes shall be borne by the party decided to be in the wrong. In difficulties of a pressing and important character in the mines a messenger shall be sent thence, and a judicious person shall at once accompany him to the place. In any quarrel where men are killed or wounded the person who originated it shall be held accountable. Any defensive weapons belonging to the company shall be given to individuals only after joint consultation, and the registry of their names. Those requiring such weapons of defense shall give security for their return. If any shall take them on their own responsibility they shall be held accountable for any consequences.[1]

105. The Chinaman only knows the company

---

[1] Translation of portions of the rules of the *Yeung-Wo Ui-Kun* (one of the Chinese Six Companies) by E. B. Speer, "Democracy of the Chinese," *Harper's Magazine*, vol. xxxvii, p. 845.

which brings him here. He does not know what he could do. He looks to his company for the food he eats when he lands here; he is taken care of by them; he is sent to the country by them here and there in the reclamation of swamp and submerged land.[1]

In addition, the Chinese have formed various more intimate associations or *tongs*, The word *"tong"* means "a society," but in China the term was restricted to the kinship group. Here it has become a term of general application. Thus the Hong Tuck Tong is the cigar makers' union, the Hong Wo Tong, the gold and silver workers' union. Three facts—(1) the absence of the family as a factor in community life; (2) the method of immigration (document 105), which is not arranged, in general, by correspondence with relatives and friends already in this country, and so does not result in the formation of settlements here based on kinship and acquaintance, as in the case of the European immigrants; and (3) the lack of all participation and prospect of participation in American life—have contributed to the formation of certain notorious and positively antisocial Chinese associations. Thus, the Hip Ye Tong and the Po Sang

---

[1] Testimony of Clinton Hastings, *U. S. Industrial Commission, Report for 1901*, vol. xv, p. 593.

THE IMMIGRANT COMMUNITY

Tong have been connected with gambling and traffic in women, and the "highbinders," the Chi Kung Tong, have a general resemblance to the Italian Black Hand. We see here, as we shall see later in studying the Black Hand activities, that when the attitudes of a group are so far different from ours that it is neither willing nor able to participate in our society, its members tend to become a predatory element.

106. In general the highbinders . . . exist on blackmail, on pay for protecting gambling houses and disreputable places in general. I know that they take it upon themselves to try cases, to review judgments of our courts with utter disregard for our laws. I know that they nullify our decisions. For instance, if an American court had rendered a decision, they would intimidate the witnesses so that when the cases go into a higher court everything would be changed. They defy our courts by ways and means of their own. I know that they impose their own sentences upon offenders from their own standpoint. They levy fines in some cases and death in others. I know that they have in their service paid men to do the killing, and so long have they had this service that the men have a particular name; they are called "hatchet men." I know they control our judicial oaths; that they can say an oath shall or shall not be taken. I know them as organized societies of crime. . . . They distribute revolvers to their members . . . and I know they use our courts, if necessary, to enforce their decisions . . . by laying a charge against a certain

Chinaman and having our judge pronounce the sentence. I know that these highbinders furnish witnesses for anything wanted at so much a head. I have had cases in which men have come forward to testify, and when the time came they were spirited away. I know that the headquarters of these societies are in San Francisco, but they have branches in Canada. Speaking approximately, I would say that there are as many as from 1,500 to 2,000 highbinders in San Francisco.[1]

107. To Lum Hip, *salaried soldier:*
It has been said that to plan schemes and devise methods and to hold the seal is the work of the literary class, while to oppose foes, fight battles, and plant firm government is the work of the military.

Now, this *tong* appoints salaried soldiers, to be ready to protect ourselves and assist others. This is our object.

All, therefore, who undertake the military service of this *tong* must obey orders and without orders you must not dare to act. If any of our brethren are suddenly molested, it will be necessary for you to act with resolute will.

You shall always work to the interest of the *tong* and never make your office a means of private revenge.

When orders are given you shall advance valiantly to your assigned task. Never shrink or turn your back upon the battlefield.

When a ship arrives in port with prostitutes on board and the grand master issues an order for you to go down and receive them, you must be punctual and use all your ability for the good of the commonwealth [or state].

---

[1] Testimony of J. Endicott Gardner, *U. S. Industrial Commission, Report for 1901,* vol. xv, pp. 769–770.

THE IMMIGRANT COMMUNITY

If in the discharge of your duty you are slain, we will undertake to pay $500 sympathy money to your friends.

If you are wounded, a doctor will be engaged to heal your wounds, and if you are laid up for any length of time you will receive $10 per month.

If you are maimed for life and incapacitated for work, $250 shall be paid to you and a subscription taken to defray costs of your journey home to China.

This paper is given as proof, as word of mouth may not be believed.

Furthermore, whenever you exert your strength to kill or wound enemies of this *tong* and in so doing you are arrested and imprisoned, $100 a year shall be paid to your friends during your imprisonment.

Dated 13th day of 5th month of 14th year of Kwong Sui, Victoria, B. C.

(Seal of Ches Kong Tong).[1]

THE JAPANESE

The Japanese in America have been treated by their home country as colonists here. The Japanese Empire has the bureaucratic type of efficiency, and the Japanese Association in America, with its various branches, is practically a department of the Japanese government. The accompanying map shows the cities in California having Japanese associations. It acts as a bureau of

---

[1] Letter of instructions to a highbinder, attached to the statement of J. Endicott Gardner, *U. S. Industrial Commission, Report for 1901*, vol. xv, p. 771.

information for the Japanese immigrants, registers and regulates them, and advises the home government as to problems arising

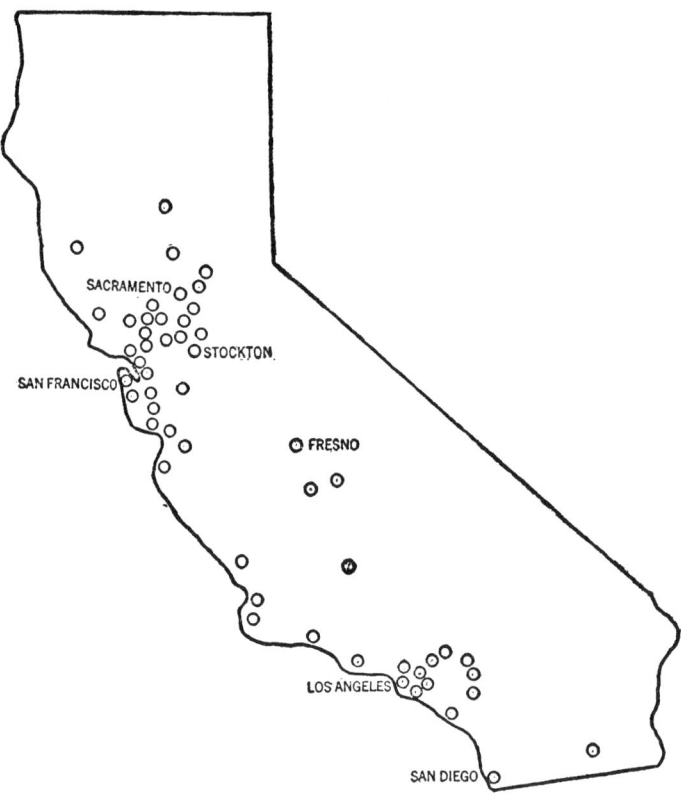

MAP 4.—CALIFORNIA BRANCHES OF THE JAPANESE ASSOCIATION

here. The Japanese are consequently the most efficiently and completely organized among the immigrant groups.

THE IMMIGRANT COMMUNITY

108. The Japanese government has evinced an unusual interest in the whereabouts and activities of its subjects. The immigration companies developed out of it; emigrants have been treated, it would appear, almost as colonists. Certain obligations were laid upon the emigration companies to care for those emigrating through them, and under certain circumstances to provide for their return to the native land. Appeals to the government at home have been frequent and the response has been quickly made. The closeness of the relation between the government and its subjects, and the solicitude of one for the rights and welfare of the other, have been important in explaining the situation which has developed in the West.[1]

109. The Japanese Association was organized in 1900, at the time of the threatened outbreak of bubonic plague, when the Japanese and Chinese, being Asiatic races, were dealt with in a different manner from other races. The organization was effected to protect the "rights" of the Japanese. When the crisis due to the fear of bubonic plague ended, the Japanese organization was continued in existence, because of the strong anti-Japanese movement which had sprung up in San Francisco. Upon the renewal of this agitation in 1905 the association was reorganized and extended its activity to the entire state of California. Local associations were soon organized in no fewer than thirty-three different places. The general nature of the association is indicated by these details relating to its organization and reorganization. Its objects, as set forth in its constitution, are: (1) to elevate the character of the Japanese immigrants; (2) to promote association

[1] H. A. Millis, *The Japanese Problem in the United States*, p. 249.

between Japanese and Americans; (3) to promote commerce, agriculture, and other industries; and (4) to further Japanese interests. The indefiniteness of this shows the general and elastic character of the association. It interests itself in whatever concerns the Japanese. In addition to this, the association has recently received recognition from the Japanese consulate, and has become an administrative organ of the consulate in issuing certificates of various kinds and in related matters.[1]

110. In every community with which we are here concerned the Japanese have been well organized under so-called bosses. At Rialto four camps of Japanese were found, numbering about 100 in all. At Highgrove there were 110 under one boss. At Riverside there were some 700 Japanese under 7 bosses, one of them controlling 160, another 174 men, at the time of the agent's visit. At Redlands there were 175 Japanese in four camps. They were similarly organized at Colton and various other places.

The camps of Japanese are assembled by the boss or contractor from Los Angeles's lodging houses, Fresno, and other places where work is slack, and are made available for any kind of work on the most convenient terms. The offices are provided with telephones, by means of which orders are taken. Each day the required number of men is sent out to fill such orders as were received the night before. The ranch owner (and sometimes packer) pays the contractor for the work done and is not put to the inconvenience of paying each man employed as the work is completed or his employment ends. In some cases the employer receives at the end of the month

[1] *Report of the U. S. Immigration Commission*, vol. xxiii, p. 220.

THE IMMIGRANT COMMUNITY

a statement not unlike that submitted by a grocer or butcher.

This organization is very convenient for the small rancher, whose need for men varies greatly from week to week or even from day to day, and in the absence of which he must go to a village or elsewhere to hire the number of men required. It goes far in explaining the real preference of the small rancher or packer in many communities for Japanese laborers.

Another advantage in employing Japanese is that the majority of the pickers of that race own bicycles, so that they can easily reach work at a distance from their camps and can be transferred from one grove to another at a distance with little loss of time. The agent of the commission met several gangs of about fifty Japanese, all riding bicycles, in process of transfer from one place to another a mile or more away. Very few white pickers own bicycles, and so must walk to work or be provided with transportation.[1]

In the cities of the Pacific Coast the organization of the Japanese communities is much like that of an American community, as is indicated by document 111, showing the organization of business in Seattle, and the map showing the location of business and residence quarters in San Francisco. (Map 5, on p. 172.)

111. (1) Forty public and social institutions (*e.g.*, Japanese Commercial Union, Tea Dealers Union,

---
[1] *Report of the U. S. Immigration Commission,* vol. xxiv, p. 226.

OLD WORLD TRAITS TRANSPLANTED

12 Prefectural Societies); (2) 14 schools and religious organizations; (3) 13 newspapers and magazines; (4) 5 banks; (5) 5 shipping corporations; (6) 40

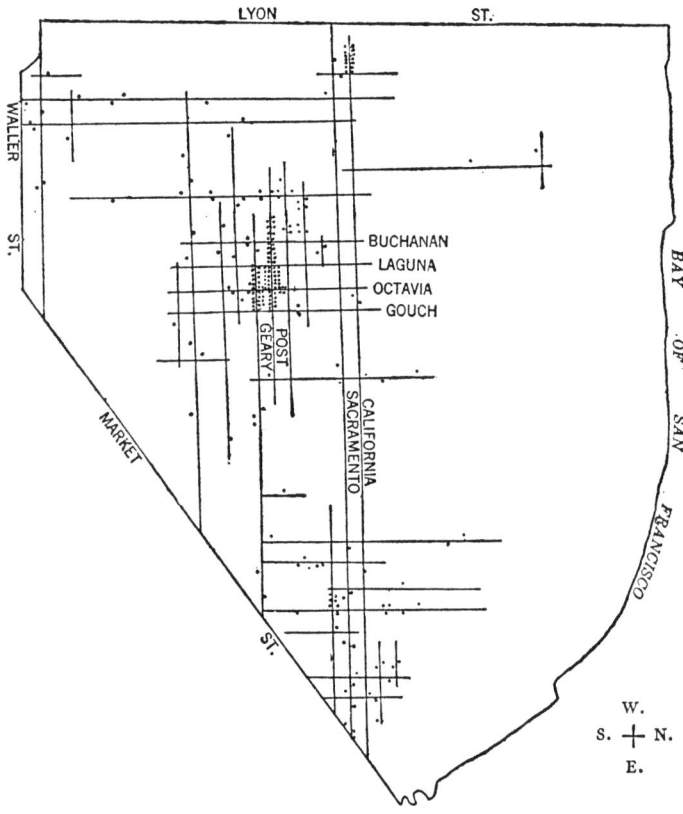

MAP 5.—LOCATION OF JAPANESE BUSINESS IN SAN FRANCISCO

trading companies; (7) 6 book dealers and printing houses; (8) 12 physicians and 1 hospital; (9) 8 dentists; (10) 11 midwives; (11) 6 masseurs; (12) 10 drug stores; (13) 18 contracting and commission

THE IMMIGRANT COMMUNITY

agencies; (14) 9 interpreting insurance and general agencies; (15) 13 provision dealers; (16) 12 dealers in watches and phonographs; (17) 9 photograph, sign, artists' and sculptors' studios; (18) 5 manufacturers; (19) 22 general merchandise stores; (20) 7 ten-cent stores; (21) 31 tailors and dressmakers; (22) 138 hotels; (23) 4 moving picture theaters; (24) 40 grocers; (25) 33 fruit dealers; (26) 52 restaurants; (27) 22 shoe stores; (28) 5 furniture stores; (29) 24 express and taxi offices; (30) 74 barbers, etc.[1]

The map on page 174 shows the number and location of the Japanese cultural institutions in San Francisco. The latter include 27 provincial societies, 4 Buddhist churches, 2 consulates, 4 branches of the Japanese association, 1 manufacturers' association, 4 associations of business proprietors, 3 associations of agriculturists, 16 trade unions, 3 associations of professional men, 18 schools, 8 clubs, 7 newspapers, and the following branches of American organizations: 11 religious organizations, 1 boy scouts, 2 women's patriotic societies.[2]

The thrift, cleanliness, quickness, sobriety, industry, adaptability, eagerness to learn, of the Japanese are everywhere recognized.

112. In all cities of the West with more than a few hundred Japanese, there are schools the primary

[1] From the *Japanese Directory* of Seattle, Washington.
[2] *Japanese-American Directory* of San Francisco.

object of which is to teach adult Japanese the English language. The number of these institutions and the many Japanese who attended them at an earlier

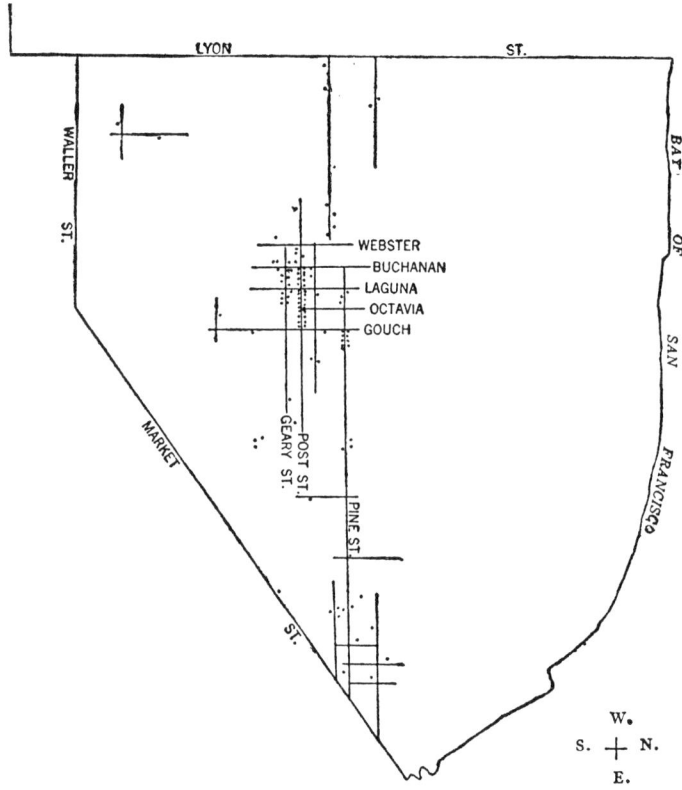

MAP 6.—ORGANIZATIONS IN THE JAPANESE COMMUNITY IN SAN FRANCISCO

time when many immigrants were arriving, are the best evidence of the ambition and eagerness of the members of this race to learn Western civilization. No adult immigrants in the West, unless it is the

THE IMMIGRANT COMMUNITY

Hebrews, show as great desire to learn the English language.[1]

113. Mr. —— came to this country eleven years ago. Nine years ago he purchased a farm and was joined by his wife and two small daughters. He now owns a walnut and fig ranch of thirty-six acres, which was bearing when he purchased it, and leases a vineyard besides. He occupies a cottage of five rooms; the house is in good repair, and it and the premises are well kept. The floors are well carpeted and as a part of the furnishings of the living room are four leather-seated oak chairs and a few well-framed lithographed pictures—all American. In the back parlor is a piano, and among the conveniences in the kitchen is found a standard washing machine. The two daughters had just begun to take music lessons from an American teacher. One of the girls was in the eighth grade, the other in the sixth. Both are thoroughly American in every respect save that they are more gracious and more polite than the average native child. Their Americanism had extended even to insisting upon having American dolls with blond hair and blue eyes.[2]

The efficiency of the Japanese is directly connected with the type of organization at home. We have pointed out that they had developed the principle of allegiance to an extraordinary and even fantastic degree. In the feudal period, for example, men committed suicide when the fortunes of their political leaders fell, and at one time this

---

[1] *Report of U S. Immigration Commission,* vol. xxiii, p. 153.
[2] H. A. Millis, *The Japanese Problem in the United States,* p. 195.

practice became so prevalent that tne government could counteract it only by decreeing that the wife and children of a man committing harakiri should be crucified. In this connection was developed that subordination of the individual to authority and that capacity for organized action which still distinguishes the Japanese, particularly in war. At the same time the treachery developed toward enemies in their local wars was as extreme as the allegiance within the group. There are many incidents in the wars between the Japanese clans which for treachery read like chapters from the life of Cæsar Borgia.[1]

When, eventually, the isolation of the Japanese was broken down and they entered into commercial relations with the larger world, they showed the same bad faith and treachery in foreign business that they had used toward their domestic enemies. If, for example, a cargo of pig iron was ordered from England by a Japanese firm and the price of pig iron declined before the boat landed, the firm refused to accept the shipment. They had had none of that trading experience which makes the Chinese so notable for business integrity.

The Japanese displayed this same attitude in their first American contacts:

[1] See, *e.g.*, Murdock and Yamagata, *A History of Japan*.

THE IMMIGRANT COMMUNITY

114. The Chinese are entirely honest in all contractual relations. The confidence in them is so great that they usually pay no rent until the crops are harvested. The fruit-shipping houses frequently make loans to them on their personal unsecured notes. They do not abandon their leases. The standing of the Japanese, on the other hand, is much lower. They are usually required to pay a part of the cash rent in advance, the loans made by fruit shippers are secured by mortgages on the crops, and the loans are limited in amount to the value of the work done. In rather numerous cases they have abandoned their leases, with the result that in some instances there are two or more outstanding leases for the same land covering the same period, the land being leased to new parties as abandoned by others.

There is widespread complaint that the Japanese are unsatisfactory in other respects. It is commonly said that they neglect the orchards and teams furnished them and that farms leased to them are permitted to deteriorate rapidly. That there is some foundation for these complaints is shown by the very general preference shown for Chinese and the fact that leases are made to them for less rent than required of Japanese.[1]

115. The Mexicans were employed in thinning along with the Japanese, and worked on the same wage basis of so many cents per 1,000 feet, the rate varying according to the difficulty of the work. At first the Mexicans worked carefully and were content to make $1.50 a day. The Japanese, on the other hand, were able, by much less careful work, to make from $2.50 to $3 per day under

---
[1] *Report of the U. S. Immigration Commission*, vol. xxiv, p. 428.

advantageous conditions. The favor with which the growers naturally regarded the Mexicans alarmed the Japanese. Their leaders accordingly went to the Mexicans, it is said, and told them that they were foolish to be so careful with their work, pointing out the fact that they were making only $1.50 a day, while the Japanese "boys" were making twice as much. The Mexicans accepted the suggestion and are now regarded in this community with as little favor as the Japanese.[1]

116. The question as to whether a contract shall be kept or broken is apparently, in these cases, a commercial one, the answer depending upon the amount of money involved. If the contract prices, less advances already made by the growers, is greater than the expense of completing the work the contract will be fulfilled; if it is less, the contract will be broken. One instance is reported where a bond was required from the contractor for the faithful performance of his agreement.[2]

But precisely because of their historical traits of allegiance and organization the Japanese are capable of transforming their lives and practices more rapidly than any other immigrant group, and under the direction of the Japanese Association they are acquiring a reputation for business integrity. Because of their historical trait of allegiance also they are inclined to make more far-going concessions than any other group in

[1] *Report of the U. S. Immigration Commission*, vol. xxiv, p. 106.
[2] *Ibid.*, p. 108.

THE IMMIGRANT COMMUNITY

order to overcome American prejudice and secure status here. Like other immigrants, they had the very natural practice of sending home for wives (called "picture brides"), but in response to American sentiment they have abandoned this practice. They have even gone so far as to undertake to limit their efficiency here in order not to provoke the resentment of Americans:

117. It is the sense of the Board of Directors of the Japanese Association that the so-called "picture marriage" which has been practiced among certain classes of Japanese residing in this country should be abolished because it is not only in contravention of the accepted American conception of marriage, but is also out of harmony with the growing ideals of the Japanese themselves. With this belief in mind the Board of Directors will make the utmost efforts to carry out this resolution. . . .[1]

118. . . . The majority of these Japanese [criticized for working long hours] lacked educational opportunities at home. Recognizing this, it impels them to work very hard so that they can give their children a chance to get education. It is a well-known fact that the Japanese will do anything to get an education or to enable their children to obtain it. . . . We are advising them, as best we know how, not to work so hard as to cause their neighbors to criticize them, and to create some leisure for self-development. At the same time, it appears rather strange even to

---
[1] Statement issued (at San Francisco) October 28, 1919.

us that the Americans should complain of Japanese industry. . . .[1]

While these opportunistic concessions are not to be praised, they nevertheless indicate that the Japanese are making extraordinary efforts to be assimilated. They are not citizens, but their children are and they wish them to be. They are anxious to break up their own colonies, to engage in all sorts of occupations, to acquire American manners, and to get education—all with the motive of adapting themselves to this country. Whether we like them or not, no other foreign-language group is so completely and intelligently organized to control its members, and no other group has at all equaled them in the work of accommodating themselves to alien conditions.

THE MEXICANS

There is an undetermined quantity of immigration from Mexico to the United States. The total Mexican population within our borders may be as much as 600,000,[2] and contains two elements:

(1) The old colonists in New Mexico,

---

[1] Address of the Japanese Association of America to President Wilson (mimeographed copy, undated), p. 21.
[2] *U. S. Bureau of Labor*, Bulletin 78, p. 520.

southern California, and Texas, representing the population settled there before the Americans arrived. These retain their original culture and are still powerful in politics. The present governor at New Mexico is of Spanish-American descent.

(2) The immigrant labor coming in at present. About 50,000 Mexicans come northward annually, and perhaps 20,000 of these remain. There are Mexican colonies of recent origin in Austin, San Antonio, and Los Angeles. Documents 119 and 120 are characterizations of this element, by a trackmaster who has worked various kinds of labor in southern Kansas and by a railroad official, respectively:

119. Mexicans are better than Greeks or Italians, and next to the American hobo. They must be well fed, and want fresh beef and mutton, but don't eat so much pork. They don't have feuds and disorders like the Italians, who are always fighting unless the whole gang is from the same town in Italy. We send a man every spring to the Rio Grande to get our men for the summer. We have to keep our engagements with them or we can't get any men the next year. Though they are used to low pay at home, they want as much as anybody when they get to this country.[1]

120. We have worked Mexicans out of El Paso for several years, and since 1903 have substituted

---
[1] *U. S. Bureau of Labor*, Bulletin 78, p. 477.

them for Italians, who were disorderly, and for negroes in northern Texas, nearly to Texarkana. They suit us better than any other immigrant labor we can get. They are better than negroes at ballasting, laying ties, and ordinary trackwork; but the negroes can beat them laying rails, and will work better long hours or at rush jobs, as in case of washouts or getting a track around a wreck. Our chief difficulties are due to ignorance of the language and to the rough ways of our foremen, who sometimes frighten the Mexicans so they won't work. Mexicans are not very regular, and we have to carry about 50 men on a payroll to be sure of 30 to 35 men working every day.[1]

The Mexicans are the least organized of all the groups. At the same time they show an easy adaptability to American habits and a surprising interest in education:

121. If Mexicans are an inferior people how is it that thousands of them are leaving their country where the booze flows freely and coming to a foreign country where it flows not at all? Isn't it a sign that the Mexican wants a chance to prosper where prosperity is for all? . . . They come to Texas, to Arizona, New Mexico, and California; they work, they buy red and blue clothes, they eat, they smoke, they drink coffee and tea, and chew ice-cream cones, they invest in large white hats, nickel cigars, and other unwonted luxuries. In short, they emerge promptly on a higher plane of living than they ever before experienced. Furthermore, they obey the

---

[1] *U. S. Bureau of Labor*, Bulletin 78, p. 477.

THE IMMIGRANT COMMUNITY

laws, respect authority, and prosper according to their capacity.[1]

122. ... Since childhood, I have always had a peculiar affection and a profound admiration for those who impart instruction—those who, by shaping the intelligence, brighten up the future, and allow a clear background for life's struggle; but since I have become a mother I realize the magnitude of so difficult a task, and even more than ever hold these privileged ones in love and veneration. With such a concept, is it any wonder that I feel moved, that I admire, that I hold to-day more than ever, unlimited gratitude toward this blessed institution in which I receive, in company with many other mothers and young women, the incalculable benefit of its instruction to us? By this instruction we are allowed to take another step toward progress and an open future for ourselves and our children. Where can we find wise counsel in perfecting our intelligence so that we may be able to develop and cultivate that of our beloved children, and how else can we discover a worthy and honorable means of aiding and advising our families when necessary?

I do not know how to express the thousand thoughts which crowd my mind and echo from the bottom of my heart! Words fail me—this subject which concerns me is so great, so beautiful and so sublime—KNOWLEDGE! A magic word which, with its few letters, embraces a world of happiness; a glorious word which, as "Let there be light" to the uncreated, scatters the shadows of this horrible darkness which

---

[1] *Dallas News*, quoted by Vera L. Sturges, "The Progress of Adjustment in Mexican and United States Life"; a paper read at the National Conference of Social Workers, 1920 (manuscript).

abandons us without a guide on the edge of a precipice. . . .[1]

In transmitting the address of which document 122 is an extract, the secretary for non-English-speaking women, Southwestern Field Committee of the Y. W. C. A., says:

123. These sentiments are quite typical for hundreds of Mexican women in Texas. Now and then our workers have to win the support of their husbands, but for the most part the men are eager to have their wives study. We do not use our efforts on the very poor peon-class women, unless they come to us or stay by the things we start. The middle class is very much more worth while, and Mexico's greatest need is the development of this class as rapidly as possible. The aristocrats are most in need of socializing, but, as with the peon class, the effort spent is too great, considering the scarcity of qualified workers, unless they come fairly easily. Our hands are full helping those who crave—we simply cannot keep up with the demand for English, American cookery, home nursing, etc.[2]

There is in the state of New Mexico a Mexican community about three hundred years old, of peculiar interest to our study because it shows how long an alien group

[1] Talk by Señora Maria Teresa Palafox de Pina in the International Institute, Laredo, Texas, February 5, 1920, at a party in honor of the arrival of the director of the institute.
[2] Letter from Vera L. Sturges.

THE IMMIGRANT COMMUNITY

may remain on American soil without change or improvement if it brings a low level of culture, no leaders, no institutions for preserving and developing its characteristic culture or appropriating the surrounding American culture, no channels of communication with the culture of the mother country, which in this case is also low. These conditions and a particular geographic and psychic isolation characterize the Spanish-Americans of New Mexico.

We have selected the county of Taos and the towns of San Juan and Chamita for special investigation.

124. In New Mexico the Mexican is less industrious and less thrifty than the Indian. Every self-respecting Indian has good clothes put away which he can don on occasion, but the Mexican, if he has good clothes, cannot resist the temptation to wear them. Both gamble, but the Mexican far more than the Indian. Of the two, the Indian is more likely to have a bank account. The Indian is less likely to run in debt and the storekeeper, who has been here fifty years, says he has never lost an account with an Indian, even though he has had to wait many years, but he cannot trust a Mexican very far. A Mexican is disposed to consider that an account liquidates itself by long standing. . . .[1]

125. About 20 per cent of the Mexicans at Chamita can read their own language. Less than 5

[1] Mary Austin, *The Indian-Mexican Settlements of San Juan and Chamita* (manuscript).

OLD WORLD TRAITS TRANSPLANTED

per cent can read or speak English (in other districts the percentage is much higher, in some lower). They have no knowledge of politics outside their own locality and have strong Mexican sympathies. They are inordinately ignorant and superstitious about common things. Though less prejudiced than Indians, they are even less provided with the means of production and add nothing to the country's wealth. The literary and musical instincts are strong in them, but so little known to the public that I can name but one collection of their songs, half a dozen, translated and published by Charles Lummis in *The Land of Poco Tiempo*. Naturally handicraftsmen, all their crafts are in abeyance.[1]

126. Of the 13,000 present population of Taos County, it is estimated that 10,000 speak Spanish by preference. There is one county high school in Taos County with nineteen pupils enrolled. There are forty-four school districts, employing eighty-three teachers. The names of all these teachers except twelve are Spanish. . . . Only four of the twelve are, to my personal knowledge, without any Spanish strain, and two of these four are Sisters of the Order of Loretto—Sister May McGinnes, and Sister Ann Gartin (French). . . .

None of the public schools in Taos County have libraries. Aside from the books on the teacher's desk, there is not a book available to school children in the whole county. There are no town libraries, and it is possible to travel the whole day in some districts, visiting every house en route, and not find any book of any description other than a mail-order catalogue or an occasional Spanish prayer book. . . .

---

[1] Mary Austin, *The Indian-Mexican Settlements of San Juan and Chamita* (manuscript).

THE IMMIGRANT COMMUNITY

The Mexican is not really an agriculturist, but a handicraftsman. He is patient in craft and a shrewd and ready trader in things. But he has never learned to manage money. . . . The chief economic reasons for the discontinuance of the handicrafts among them is their inability to take the measure of their work in money. Curio dealers and others lie in wait to purchase their beautiful things at the moment of their greatest need. They have no way of finding out what these hand-made things are worth. All they know is that the Americans give them less for the things than they can live on. They begin to feel that these things are of no value because the Americans always cheapened them to the utmost. . . . That is one reason why certain of their old crafts survive only among the convicts. I have seen a convict take half a silver dollar and spend three or four hours working it into a bracelet such as would sell at Tiffany's for three or four dollars, and then some passing tourist will beat the convict down to selling his work for sixty or seventy cents. But a convict's time is not worth anything. I have seen some American who has "spotted" a blanket, or a beautiful old hand-carved chest, wait until sickness or want forces its sale for less than the purchaser could buy a "store" blanket or new lumber to make another chest. Then the Americans rail against the shiftlessness of the Mexican. . . .

One of the reasons why few Mexicans grow rich is the ineradicable spirit of communism. If a man kills a sheep and his neighbor has no sheep to kill, still the neighbor has a piece of mutton. If a man knows a good wild pasture, or a woman a nice thicket of wild plums, they tell the others. The idea of personal advantage is of very little effect among them.

OLD WORLD TRAITS TRANSPLANTED

In the old days, if a Mexican found a silver mine, all his friends went along and dug out a little bag of ore apiece. This sort of communism is now principally confined to the family. There is scarcely such a thing as a rich relation, because the thrifty relation seldom has enough, after dividing with the other members, to be called rich. This economic interest probably has something to do with the importance attached to kinship, and particularly to the parental relationship. There is no doubt that family claims prevent private ambition. Many Mexican men have told me this. They wished to go to school, to go away into other towns, to big cities or more prosperous places to live, but they have yielded to the plea of their parents, especially of the mother, to keep the family intact. . . .

The great lack in the life of the Spanish-speaking New Mexican is imaginative literature. During the Spanish pioneer period this lack was supplied partly by the last wash of that wave of creative literature which was sweeping through Spain at the time, Calderon, Lope de Vega, and the great Spanish romanticists. It was supplied in part by the dramatic and stimulating history of their own achievement in New Spain. There are traces, too, in the folklore of New Mexico, of the rich, and at that time unsubmerged, field of native Mexican literature. By the time of the American occupation all these streams of imaginative life had been attenuated, if not actually dried up, and *nothing has been done since* to remedy the situation.

The County Superintendent of Schools told me that 50 per cent of the adult Spanish-speaking population of New Mexico *ought*, in view of the history of public school education in this locality, to be able

THE IMMIGRANT COMMUNITY

to read the local Spanish newspaper. I hardly think this is actually the case. I have seen groups of men listening to one of their number reading the paper aloud, and the reader was almost always a young man. Of the two Spanish newspapers published in Taos, *El Bulletin* has a circulation of about 800, and *La Revista* has about 3,000, one-third of which are out of the county. *La Revista* was once the leading Spanish newspaper in America, and still has exchanges all over the world. . . . But even if they could read Spanish, very little reading matter finds its way here. The church is exceedingly negligent in this matter. A little literature from Old Mexico finds its way here, but is naturally expensive. The better-class Spanish families all read English and have no books in Spanish in their houses.

When it comes to English reading matter the case is scarcely better. At this time there is probably not a Spanish-speaking family which has not some member with enough English to read the newspaper, the mail-order catalogue, and such practical necessities. But the number who would be able to read and understand English literature is even less than the number who can appreciate Spanish literature. A glance at the school reading explains this. There is nothing whatever in any Taos County school to read except the textbooks. There is nothing whatever in any textbook which would create in any child's mind the least suspicion that reading is a method of coming into touch with its environment. This country has a beautiful and dramatic mythology, but there is only Greek mythology in the school readers. On his way to school the child is confronted with an abundant and beautiful flora, but the references in the reader are to English daffodils and New

England Mayflowers. He reads about Bunker Hill, but nothing about Black Mesa. Fray Marcos and De Vargas are not even names to him. . . .

The most outstanding conclusion from all this is that in our handling of our Spanish-speaking population we have violated all the fundamentals of folk growth. First of all, the best thing in the Spanish-American peoples is their pride of race. It is the one thing more than another by which we could have laid hold of and awakened their pride of citizenship. Instead of which we needlessly wounded and poisoned it at every step. Through our earliest representatives we made a mock of their love of ritual, of dignity and ceremony in personal relations. "Americans," said Don Amado Chaves to me, "think dignity and ceremony belong only to the rich."

We have ignored their racial contribution of fine deeds—the early history of New Mexico is crammed with gallant and adventurous exploits—and overlaid them with the achievements of the Anglo Saxon strain, thus destroying all the power of their past over their ideals of conduct. And even if it were possible to substitute the past of one people for the past of another, we have made an utterly inadequate attempt to do so, for we have hardly so much as succeeded in interesting them in the facts of our Anglo-Saxon past. It is not a paradox to say that a people with no past is a people without a future, it is a simple statement of fact, like saying that a tree with no roots produces no fruit. . . .

Not the slightest attempt was ever made to find a market for the sort of thing that is being constantly imported from Italy and Spain. There were no fairs, exhibitions, prizes, honors, none of the things that we know very well are the medium in which artistry

THE IMMIGRANT COMMUNITY

flourishes. And on the other hand, there have been all sorts of mean trickery used to buy their products for less than their worth, smuggle them out of the country, and sell them for many times what they cost. An American woman in Taos who insists on paying something like a reasonable price for handmade products is accused of "spoiling" the trade of the other people.

That has been one end of the process. At the other end is the destruction of the source of art in the suppression of their native stock of myth and symbol from which their designs were derived. More and more, as I study New Mexican, Indian, and Spanish groups, I discover design to be a language of profound experience.

The way in which certain beautiful things are shown to be peculiar to certain localities or even to certain families, the way in which these designs sink out of sight and reappear after generations in times of spiritual distress, indicates that the things themselves have grown up out of experience as an expression of that experience, and perish with it. . . .

These people do not need missionaries. All they need is to have the burden of their isolation lifted, to have the stopped currents of their imaginative life freed on the one side by giving them access to their own history and traditions, and on the other by giving them markets for the products of imagination and industry.[1]

127. The organization known as *Los Hermanos Penitentes* (The Penitent Brotherhood) is the most important society of the Spanish-speaking population of the Southwest, and the only organization

---

[1] Mary Austin, *Social Survey of Taos County, State of New Mexico* (manuscript).

discoverable among the Mexican population of San Juan. It has some 50,000 members in the state of New Mexico, and spreads into Colorado and Old Mexico. Although a religious organization, it exercises great influence in politics and in the social life of the communities where it is found. . . . [Discountenanced by the Catholic Church in 1896,] the society continued to flourish, applied for and obtained a charter from the legislature, which permitted it to exist on the same footing as other secret organizations. As late as thirty years ago it is estimated that 95 per cent of the adult male population of New Mexico belonged to it. . . .

The avowed object of the society is to keep alive the "passion and sufferings of Our Lord." Special saints' days, the first and second days of May, and funerals of brother members, are celebrated with penitential exercises. The whole of Lent is kept with prayers and lashings, and Holy Week is celebrated with all manner of penitential practices, including crucifixion. Formerly the crucifixion was actual, and deaths as a result were not uncommon. But since 1886 it has become the custom simply to tie the victim to the cross, instead of using nails. And lately the practice of using an effigy, life size, has been general. Even where the brother is still tied to the cross the time has been reduced from three hours to about forty-five minutes.

Among the penitential practices are the carrying of heavy crosses in procession, walking on trails strewn with cactus, carrying heads of cactus on the bare back or clasped to the bare breast, hugging a post wrapped with cactus, cutting the back and lashing it with braided whips of yucca fiber. Penitential pilgrimages made on hands and knees are

THE IMMIGRANT COMMUNITY

also a favorite mode of expression. Formerly these practices were all as public as possible, but the attitude of the Church and unfavorable comment in the non-Catholic press have led to secrecy. The crucifixions still take place at the prescribed afternoon hour, but whipping is done in the lodge or at night, when most of the processions take place. . . .

Besides the special services for saints' days, the processions begin with the first Friday in Lent. These are whipping processions, when the heavy crosses, weighing several hundred pounds, are dragged to and from the Calvarios by men half naked and wearing crowns of the wild-rose brier. Every penitent is accompanied by a brother who eases him to the ground at each one of the fourteen stations. But when a man staggers and faints he is whipped to his feet. . . . Aid is furnished to sick members and funeral expenses are borne when necessary. . . . Political aid and legal aid in difficulties are also rendered, but not openly or officially. Formerly the solidarity of the *Penitentes* made the society a refuge for outlaws of every description, and aided the Spanish-speaking population to maintain its isolation from the American régime. As nearly every adult male is a member, it is natural that the whole community should be more or less involved. . . . Brotherly service in sickness and affliction is rendered, and the rules of the order act occasionally as a social corrective. . . . A married man was expelled from the order for misbehavior with a young woman. These are offenses against the families of brother *Penitentes*. When the offense is against the law of the state, however, there seems still to be a disposition to regard the offender as simply unfortunate.

OLD WORLD TRAITS TRANSPLANTED

Commenting on the small number of civil cases in one of the communities where 90 per cent of the population was Spanish-speaking, I was told: "You see, they are all *Penitentes* up there." On inquiry, I learned that most disputes between *Penitentes* came before the *Hermanos Mayor* and that there was seldom any exception to his decisions. The following was a partial list of the matters that had come before him: (1) damages caused by a cow in neighbor's garden; (2) quarrel about wood purchased; (3) several cases of small debts; (4) young man forbidden to marry a girl by her father on account of personal prejudice, settled in the young man's favor; (5) widower with small children reproved for neglect of them; (6) mother whose son was in France (a Penitent) helped to get her allowance which she was too ignorant to apply for.

In spite of the alien attitude toward the law, and the fact that that no Penitent on a jury will convict another Penitent, there was a large percentage of voluntary enlistments among them, and at the Holy Week celebrations this year, in the processions, were numbers of young men in uniform with foreign-service stripes. . . .

Thus the *Penitentes*, with its religious fervors, its ritual and mystery, its friendly offices for the dead, its annual processions and dramatic performance of Holy Week, has grown deep into the life of the people.[1]

There are old and cultivated Spanish-American families in New Mexico, still powerful in politics (the present Governor is a Spanish-American), and the state has

---

[1] Mary Austin, *The Penitentes at Chamita de San Juan* (manuscript).

THE IMMIGRANT COMMUNITY

modern schools, industries, political administration, but these institutions mean that the country is being settled by Americans. The mass of the Mexican population remains as little adapted to these institutions as the Indians of the state.

The whole situation shows what may happen to an immigrant group when it neither participates in American life nor continues to draw its culture from the mother country. We shall notice later that even when an immigrant community does keep up its cultural intercourse with the home country, if it does not participate in American life, its level of culture tends to fall below the level of culture of the home country.

At present the situation in New Mexico is ripe for a nationalistic movement, if the leaders appear.

THE JEWS

The Jews tend even more than other immigrant groups to settle in cities. It is estimated that there are 3,320,000 Jews in America, and of these 1,500,000 are in New York City.[1] The accompanying diagram compares the number of Jews in New York

---

[1] *Jewish Communal Register of New York City* (1917-18), p. 82 *American Jewish Yearbook* (Oppenheim reprint), p. 66.

OLD WORLD TRAITS TRANSPLANTED

with those in other countries. If we include Newark, New Rochelle, and other near-by towns, then within a district equivalent in size to thirty square miles will be found fully one-half of the Jews in the United States.

- NEW YORK CITY 1,500,000
- GERMANY-615,000
- GREAT BRITAIN 257,000
- SOUTH AMERICA-117,000
- HOLLAND-106,000
- PALESTINE-100,000
- FRANCE 100,000
- CANADA 75,000
- ITALY 44,000
- SWITZERLAND-19,000
- BELGIUM-15,000

DIAGRAM 1.—COMPARISON OF THE JEWISH POPULATION OF NEW YORK CITY WITH THAT OF OTHER COUNTRIES. (JEWISH COMMUNAL REGISTER, 1917–18, FRONTISPIECE.)

THE IMMIGRANT COMMUNITY

128. No doubt this figure will cause astonishment to many. One million and a half Jews is an extraordinary community. The next largest Jewish community in the world—that of the city of Warsaw—is estimated to have been between 300,000 and 330,000 Jews, about one-fifth as many as we estimate for New York. All of the countries of western Europe, together with the countries of South America, Canada, and Palestine combined, do not have as many Jews as live in this city. If we accept the estimate of the number of Jews in the world as about 14,000,000, one Jew out of every ten resides in New York.[1]

It costs the Jews of New York $3,120,000 a year to eat kosher meat, over and above the normal cost of meat,[2] and they spend annually on Yiddish newspapers alone, $2,097,453.[3]

129. This estimated 1,500,000 constitutes over 25 per cent of the whole population of New York City. This is by far the largest proportionate group among any of the 10 largest American cities; in the 9 next largest cities, the average proportion which the Jewish group constitutes of the general populaion is slightly under 10 per cent. In the 62 remaining cities which have a population over 100,000, the respective Jewish populations average 4.5 per cent of the total group. For cities of the second class (those having a population between 50,000 and

---

[1] Alexander M. Dushkin, *Jewish Communal Register* (1917-18), p. 82.
[2] *Jewish Communal Register*, p. 320.
[3] *Ibid*, p. 614.

OLD WORLD TRAITS TRANSPLANTED

100,000) the average proportion of Jewish inhabitants is shown to decline quite evenly as the population figures for the respective cities are ranged in decreasing order, from 3.3 per cent for cities of from 90,000 to 100,000 each, to 2.4 per cent for those of from 50,000 to 60,000 each. Continuing this curve, the average percentage of Jewish population in cities of between 20,000 and 50,000 falls to a trifle over 2 per cent, in still smaller localities to a little over 1 per cent, and in places having less than 1,000 inhabitants to ½ to ¼ of 1 per cent.[1]

The Jews come to this country more definitely as settlers than any other group, but they come from many countries: Russia, Rumania, Poland, Galicia, Germany, Turkey, etc. Most of them speak Yiddish in addition to the language of the country from which they come (Russian, Polish, Rumanian, Hungarian, and so forth), but there are various dialects of Yiddish, and the Jews from the Near East do not know Yiddish, but speak Greek, Ladino (Judæo-Spanish), Turkish, Arabic, and so forth. In their religious ritual they may be orthodox, conservative, or reform. There are among them members of the pietistic, mystical, magical Chassidic sect; and at the other extreme are the freethinkers. Consequently the differences and mutual prejudices between

---

[1] Renee Darmstadter, *The Jewish Community in New York City* (manuscript).

THE IMMIGRANT COMMUNITY

different groups of Jews may be as great as those between members of different nationalities, and these inner divisions affect both their institutional life and their personal relations:

130. The Spanish and the Portuguese Jews found it difficult in the first half of the last century to admit whole-heartedly the German Jew to a close kinship with them—a difficulty which the German Jews experienced almost half a century later with the Jews hailing from Russia, and the Russian Jews in their turn only a decade later with the Jews coming from Galicia and Rumania. Because of this clannishness, several Jewish communities sprang up practically side by side in New York City; a Spanish-Portuguese community, a German community, a Russian community, an Oriental community, and a Galician, a Hungarian and a Rumanian community. Almost every one of these communities was self-sufficient, with its own synagogues, charitable and educational institutions, and, what was inevitable, with its own politics. Under such conditions, the least untoward act, fancied or real, on the part of one group, led inevitably to strong separatistic tendencies in other groups. So, for instance, did the ascendancy of the German community result in the struggle of the so-called Downtown against Uptown, a struggle in which the combatants were mainly Russian and German Jews. In the same way did the sense of grievance which the Galician, Rumanian, Russian-Polish, and Bessarabian Jews felt against the ascendancy of the Russian Jewish community find its outlet in the formation of separate Verbands. For the Verbands, in spite of their voluble protestations of good intentions, were invariably organized as

offensive and defensive alliances, a sort of *Verein zur Abwehr des Anti-Galizianerismus* or *Anti-Rumanierismus*, as the case might be. Only subsequent conditions changed their original plans and induced a new course of development.[1]

131. The Levantine Jews are very much isolated from the great Yiddish-speaking mass of Jews all about them. According to one of their spokesmen, Joseph Zedalicia, president of the Federation of Oriental Jews, the Levantine Jews "feel more discrimination from the other wings of the Jews than they do from the non-Jews." Part of the problem is that the Jews themselves, especially those of the lower East Side communities—at least up until recently—did not actually realize that these very new immigrants were also Jewish. They looked on these "Spanioles" among them as "dagoes." Instances of street disturbances and neighborhood disputes and complaints have been numerous. Some years ago a group of residents in one section petitioned the mayor at the time, Mr. Gaynor, to remove the "Turks" in their midst. When they found that these people were Jews they hastened to settle the matter "among themselves." [2]

132. I am a Galician Jew and . . . God destined me to have a Russian [Jewish] wife and it is a misfortune for me—not because she feeds me with their Russian dishes, which are not bad, but the Russian company she brings up to our house is unbearable . . . [detailed complaint].[3]

---

[1] S. Margoshes, *Jewish Communal Register*, p. 1286.
[2] Renee Darmstadter, *The Jewish Community* (manuscript).
[3] Letter to *Forward*, December 6, 1914. The editor replies humoristically, and advises him to thank God his wife is not a Rumanian.

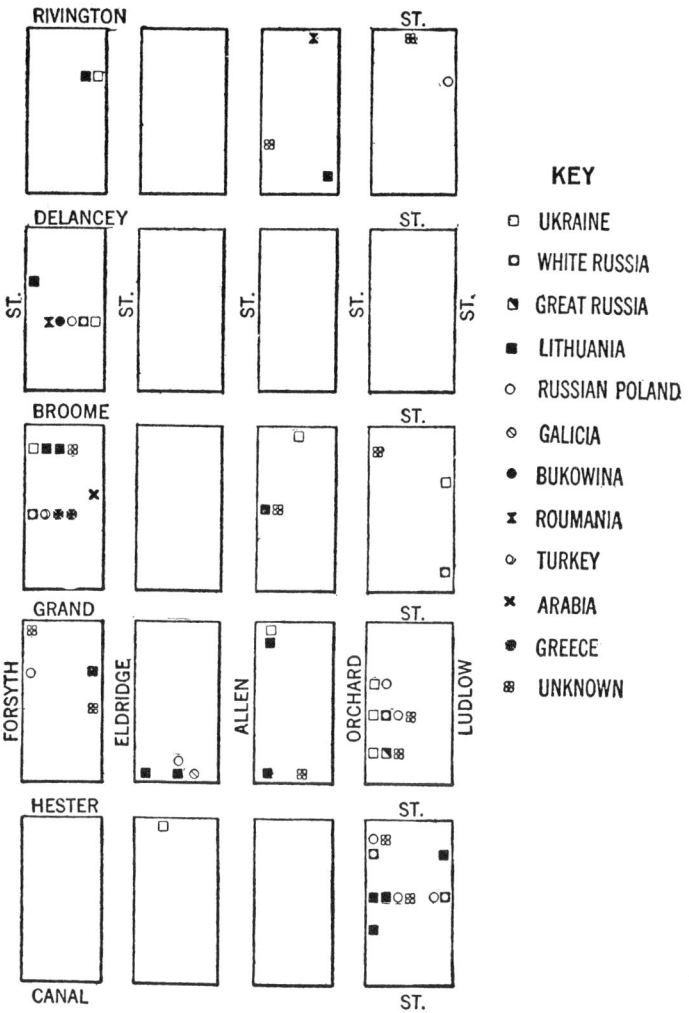

MAP 7.—BIRTHPLACE OF THE FOUNDERS OF THE JEWISH SYNAGOGUES IN A CONGESTED NEW YORK DISTRICT

OLD WORLD TRAITS TRANSPLANTED

The preceding map indicates the Jewish synagogues in a section of New York, showing the wide diversity in origin of their founders. Only the Jews themselves appreciate how profound are these differences. While their spiritual life is based on the same historical traditions, the different groups have lived in different ghettos as separate, self-governing communities, suspicious of any intrusion whatever into their affairs. The group of Jewish leaders who organized the Kehillah, of which we shall speak later, have recorded this separatist attitude:

133. . . . Quite a number of societies actually succeeded in withholding the information from us. The history of this huge canvass is full of episodes which are of great interest to the communal student. Here is a typical case. A congregation in Williamsburg is written to for information. No answer. It is written to again, with the same result. A canvasser is detailed to the job. He finds the beadle and states his errand. This dignitary is noncommittal. An inquiry for the home address of the president elicits the doubtful information that he, the beadle, does not know it. The card is then returned to the office with the brief narrative. A special investigator is sent. He uses strategy, spends an hour in fraternizing with the disgruntled old beadle, treats him to an extra-fine brand of tobacco, and finally obtains the address of the president. This gentleman is too conscientious to impart any information

THE IMMIGRANT COMMUNITY

whatsoever without the consent of his fellow-members. After the next meeting the information will be forthcoming. But it does not. The congregation fears a trap. You may fool some people, but you cannot fool them. The congregation is ultimately listed among those marked "no information available...."[1]

The Jew, like the peasant, first settled here in a colony, the ghetto. This is not a new experience. Indeed he may have lived in several ghettos, Vilna, Budapest, London, before he makes his way to America. We call the territories in which the Jews and other immigrants first settle here areas of first settlement. The lower East Side, the upper East Side, in the neighborhood of 110th Street and Central Park, Brooklyn, Brownsville, East New York, are such areas for the Jews.

134. Within an area of first settlement are found the customs and institutions of the home country; language and social ritual, dress and food habits, the familiar notions of neighborly relations, the traditional sanctions in family and personal conduct. Here are set up in their essential forms the patterns of community and family organization under which the individuals of the group lived in their European homes; the synagogue as it exists in the towns of the Pale, the primitive forms of burial and mutual aid societies, unmodified by the transplanting to a new geographical environment. Spiritually, the old

---
[1] Meir Isaacs, *Jewish Community Register*, p. 96.

OLD WORLD TRAITS TRANSPLANTED

environment itself is transplanted. The greater number of the synagogue and benefit society groups, among all of the several divisions of the Jews of the East Side, are organized on the basis of common origins in Europe. The name of such a synagogue or aid society indicates that it has been formed by a group of persons who emigrated from the same village or city in the Old World; its purpose and organization is the same as it would be in the home village; coming together to pray, visiting the sick, caring for the burial of a member who has died, etc. The pattern of action is the same as it would be in the home village, and the feelings which keep it alive are those traditional sentiments of neighborly kinship and religious responsibility to which the same organization in Europe answered.[1]

As the Jews become more prosperous they begin to move to better quarters of the city, and the neighborhoods of Fourteenth Street and Second Avenue, the Bronx, are areas of second settlement. Finally the Jew may separate himself completely from his original colony and repudiate it. The contempt of the ghetto Jew for the *allrightnick* (see documents 44 and 81, pp. 52 and 102), is connected with this movement.

135. ... I visited a friend of mine in Riverside Drive—a Russian-English Jew who spent the last few years in Palestine. We took the bus. He ... began to talk to me in Jewish and in a loud voice. ...

---

[1] Renee Darmstadter, *The Jewish Community of New York City* (manuscript).

THE IMMIGRANT COMMUNITY

At Thirty-fourth Street and Fifth Avenue we changed busses. My friend continued his loud conversation in Jewish. "Please, do not speak Jewish around here," we heard a voice behind us. . . . It was the transfer agent of the bus company. . . . And he repeats his request in Jewish this time. "Why?" my friend asks him. "Just so. They won't have it." "Who won't have it?" "These people," and he points to the great crowd who daily pass this corner in the afternoon. . . . But *they* consist of many Jews. . . .[1]

Although it has lost its hold upon great numbers, the synagogue, including the activities associated with it, remains the most important feature in the life of the Jewish community as a whole, with the possible exception of the newspaper. The "synagogue Jew" is passing away. He has become a descriptive phrase and a literary type, but the attitudes created by the synagogue remain. The character of the Jew is the joint production of the hostility of the Gentile world and the communal life of which the synagogue was the center. The fact that the Jews pay the amount mentioned above for kosher meat is proof that the old attitudes are alive.

136. The function of the synagogue was not limited to that of defense. Like the moated mediæval

---

[1] P. Hirschbein, "Impressions," *The Day* (Yiddish newspaper), January 6, 1917.

OLD WORLD TRAITS TRANSPLANTED

castles, which outwardly with their bastions and moats have all the appearance of fortresses, but which from the inner courts present the aspect of palaces intended to house and enrich a life of peace, so the synagogue not only protected the Jewish faith from a hostile world, but was also for the Jew a home for the development of his strivings and ideals. It was a house of prayer, a "*beth tephillah,*" a house of study, a "*beth ha'midrash,*" and a meeting house, where communal undertakings were formulated, and where all plans for the communal good were discussed and adopted. The synagogue rendered possible the cultivation of the spiritual life in the Diaspora, and thus gave point to the truth that wherever the Jewish people went it was accompanied by the "*shekhina,*" or Divine Presence.

Establishing a synagogue or being affiliated with one was not considered a matter of option. It was an accepted principle that wherever there were ten Jews they were in duty bound to form themselves into a congregation, and to carry on all the customary Jewish communal activities. While the Jew is in a position to discharge most of his religious duties by himself, it was realized that detachment from communal life could not but eventually lead to complete severance from the faith. Hence the designation of "evil neighbor" for one who, though living near a synagogue, kept aloof from it. That accepted principle it was which, enforced by the sanction of public sentiment, brought every Jew within the influence of the synagogue.[1]

137. The total number of permanent synagogues in Manhattan, by actual count from the list given in the *Communal Register* (pp. 544 ff.), is 597; the

---
[1] M. M. Kaplan, *Jewish Communal Register*, p. 117.

THE IMMIGRANT COMMUNITY

total count for all the boroughs of Greater New York, from the same list, is 843, those of Manhattan constituting, therefore, about 70 per cent of the number in the greater city.

The area within which the synagogues in lower Manhattan are concentrated falls within the boundaries of three conjoined Kehillah Districts—the Tompkins Square District (Dist. VII of the New York Kehillah), the Delancey District (Dist. VIII), and the East Broadway District (Dist. IX). Within these districts fall also the areas of greatest density of Jewish population [see Map No. 7 p. 201]. This is also the region of greatest concentration of the mutual aid societies. Out of the 968 organizations of this character listed in the *Communal Register*, 823 are located in these three districts of the lower East Side. The next largest number, 83, belong to the West Side and Harlem District. East Harlem has 28, Central Manhattan, 19; Yorkville, 9. Only 7 are given for the two districts of the Bronx. Among all the districts the East Broadway District makes second largest provision of synagogues—12.2 per 10,000 of population; the Delancey District, which has the largest population, making also largest synagogue provision—*i.e.*, 15.3 per 10,000 of population.[1]

138. The synagogue has lost hold on more than one-half of the largest Jewish community in the world. The estimated Jewish population of this city is about 1,500,000, which is a very conservative figure. But taking into consideration the 30 per cent who constitute the child population up to the

---

[1] Renee Darmstadter, *The Jewish Community of New York City* (manuscript).

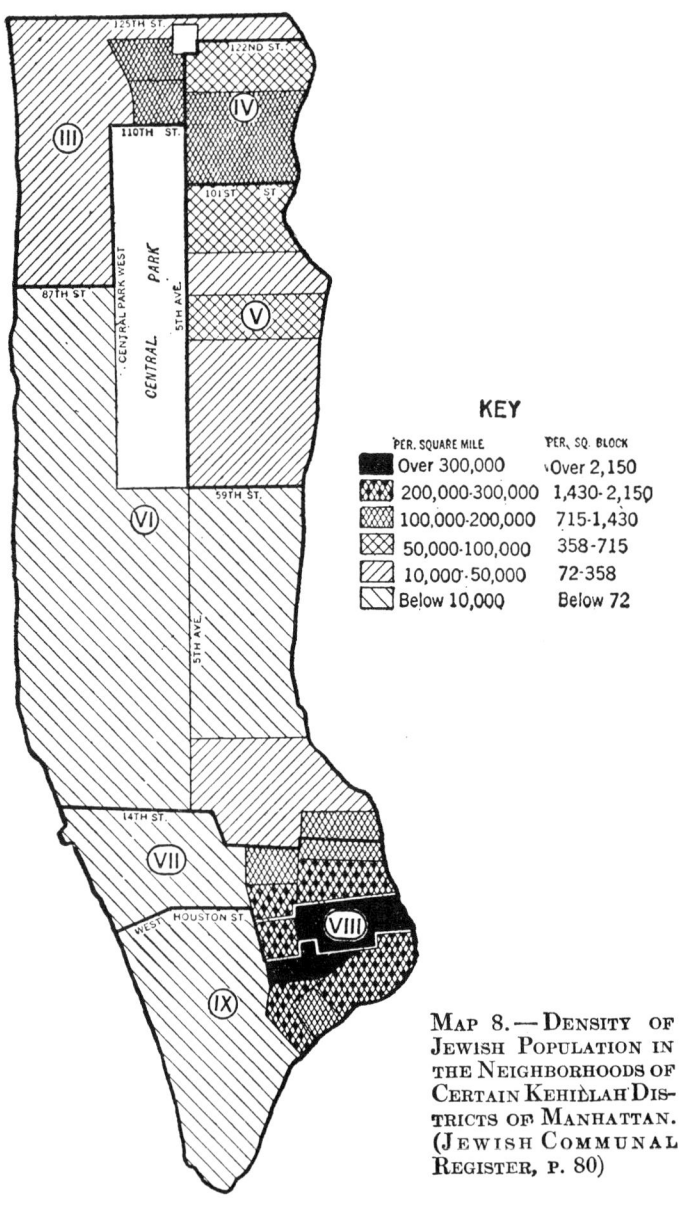

Map 8. — Density of Jewish Population in the Neighborhoods of Certain Kehillah Districts of Manhattan. (Jewish Communal Register, p. 80)

THE IMMIGRANT COMMUNITY

age of fourteen, and allowing 10 per cent for adolescent Jewish girls, who, unfortunately, have hardly any place in the synagogue, we should expect at least 900,000 seats to accommodate Jewish worshipers on the high holidays, when the maximum attendance is reached. We find, however, the total seating capacity to be 381,000. If we add to that the 30,000 to 35,000 seats to be found in the 120 small synagogues not yet investigated, we see that out of 900,000 Jews only about 415,000 are synagogue Jews.

Secondly, we observe the remarkable unevenness in the per cent of the population affiliated with the synagogues, when judged by districts. Whereas in the Delancey District 44 per cent are synagogue Jews, in Bushwick and in Richmond only 7 per cent, in West Queens only 2 per cent, worship in synagogues. It is evident that the density of population, economic conditions, and length of stay in this country have so rapid an effect upon synagogue affiliation that we cannot but infer that the synagogue owes its existence more to the momentum of the past than to any new forces created in this country that make for its conservation and development.[1]

In 1908 the more self-conscious Jews of New York, recognizing that the old community agencies were no longer adequate to control the moral life of the vast Jewish population, that the various Jewish communities and agencies in New York did not know one another and were not known by

[1] M. M. Kaplan, *Jewish Communal Register*, p. 120.

OLD WORLD TRAITS TRANSPLANTED

the Americans, realizing the value of organization both for the regulation of their community life and as a power for influencing American opinion, and aroused by a statement of Commissioner Bingham that the Jews contributed 50 per cent of the criminals of New York City,[1] undertook to unite all the Jewish communities and organizations into one Kehillah, or Jewish community. The first step was to make an inventory and an impartial interpretation of all Jewish community activities in New York City, and the result was published in 1918 as the *Jewish Communal Register*. This volume of 1,536 pages lists and describes 3,637 organizations: synagogues, burial societies, immigrant aid societies, employment bureaus, loan societies, mutual aid societies, lodges, relief societies, day nurseries, child-caring agencies, hospitals and convalescent homes, old-age homes, institutions for defectives, correctional agencies (prevention of delinquency, after-care of inmates of prisons), research bureaus, technical, religious, and private schools, and so forth. The total amount spent annually by the Jewish communal agencies in New York City for Jewish purposes is approximately $17,657,000, not

---

[1] This statement was afterward retracted. See *Communal Register*, p. 49.

THE IMMIGRANT COMMUNITY

including social clubs and theaters, but including the Yiddish newspapers.

THE POLES

In Polish-American society the parish is the center of community life, but the formation of the colony precedes the formation of the parish. Wherever Poles are collected for work, other Poles join them from the old country, and the colony grows spontaneously. The first organization is a mutual aid society. It is only when the colony has grown in numbers that a priest is called. But when the parish is established in America, it has a much larger social function than it has in Poland. It assumes, to a degree, the character of a commune.

139. Just as the benefit society is much more than a mutual insurance company, so the Polish-American parish is much more than a religious association for common worship under the leadership of a priest. The unique power of the parish in Polish-American life, much greater than in even the most conservative peasant communities in Poland, cannot be explained by the predominance of religious interests, which, like all other traditional social attitudes, are weakened by emigration, though they seem to be the last to disappear completely. The parish is, indeed, simply the old primary community reorganized and concentrated. In its concrete totality it is a substitute for both the narrower but more coherent village

group and the wider but more diffuse and vaguely outlined *okolica*. In its institutional organization it performs the functions which in Poland are fulfilled by both the parish and the commune. It does not control the life of its members as efficiently as did the old community, for, first of all, it seldom covers a given territory entirely and is unable to compel everyone living within this territory to belong to it; secondly, its stock of socially recognized rules and forms of behavior is much poorer; thirdly, the attitudes of its members evolve too rapidly in the new conditions; finally, it has no backing for its coercive measures in the wider society of which it is a part. But its activities are much broader and more complex than those of a parish or of a commune in the old country.[1]

The priest and the parish committee are careful to select a site for the church as close as possible to the centers where Poles work, and in a locality where rent is low and land is cheap. There follows a further territorial concentration of Poles. The original population—Italians, Germans, Irish—slowly moves out as the neighborhood becomes predominantly Polish. The parish thus becomes the community. Polish business is developed, associations of the type enumerated in document 140 are formed, affording their members economic advantages, social entertainment, a field for

---

[1] Florian Znaniecki, *Study of Polish Institutions in America* (manuscript).

THE IMMIGRANT COMMUNITY

economic co-operation, educational opportunities, help in expressing and realizing their political ideals, and a congenial social milieu in which the desires for recognition and response are satisfied. Even Poles who are not religious are thus drawn into the parish institutions.

The following document, 140, is an enumeration of the organizations connected with the largest Polish parish in America—St. Stanislaw Kostka, in Chicago; document 141 characterizes one of these organizations.

140. Zuaves of St. Stanislaw Kostka; Society of the Virgins of the Holy Rosary; Brotherhood of the Young Men of St. Joseph; Citizens' Club of Thaddeus Kosciuszko; Theater and Dramatic Club; the Parochial School; the Parish Committee; the Association of Altar Boys; the Marshals of the Upper Church; the Marshals of the Lower Church; the Arch-sorority of the Immaculate Heart of Mary (two groups); the Women of the Holy Rosary (four groups) the Arch-brotherhood of the Saints; the Third Order of St. Francis; the Choirs of the Upper Church; the Choirs of the Lower Church; the Club of Ladies of Queen Labrowska; the Society of the Alumni of the Parish School; the Musical and Literary Society of Leo XIII; the Needlework Club of St. Rose of Lima; the Polish Roman Catholic Union (central office); the Society of St. Cecilia (No. 14 of the R. C. Union); the Society of King John III Sobieski under the patronage of the Most Holy Virgin Mary; Queen of the Polish Crown (No. 16 of the R. C. Union);

the Society of the Most Holy Name of Mary (No. 2 of the R. C. Union); the Society of St. Stanislaw the Bishop (No. 31 of the R. C. Union); the Society of St. Walenty (No. 847 of the R. C. Union); the Society of the Heart of Jesus (No. 32 of the R. C. Union); the Society of St. Stefan (No. 318 of the R. C. Union); the Society of St. Nicholas (No. 42 of the R. C. Union); the Society of Polish Women of God's Mother of Czestochowa (No. 53 of the R. C. Union); the Society of Priest Wincenty Barzynski (No. 91 of the R. C. Union); the Society of Polish Women of St. Cecilia (No. 219 of the R. C. Union); the Society of St. Bernard the Abbot (No. 320 of the R. C. Union); the Society of St. Andrew the Apostle (No. 233 of the R. C. Union); the Society of Polish Women of St. Agnes (No. 256 of the R. C. Union); the Society of the Polish Crown (No. 296 of the R. C. Union); the Society of Polish Women of St. Lucia (No. 378 of the R. C. Union); the Society of Polish Women of St. Anna (No. 480 of the R. C. Union); the Society of Polish Women of St. Apolonia (No. 482 of the R. C. Union); the Society of St. Helena (No. 924 of the R. C. Union); the Society of Polish Women of Queen Wanda (No. 525 of the R. C. Union); the Polish Alma Mater (central office); the Branch of St. Kazimierz the King's Son (No. 1 of the Alma Mater); the Branch of St. Kinga (No. 12 of the Alma Mater); the Branch of St. Monica (No. 25 of the Alma Mater); the Branch of St. Clara (No. 26 of the Alma Mater); the Branch of St. Cecilia (No. 92 of the Alma Mater); the Branch of St. Joseph (No. 49 of the Alma Mater); the Court of Pulaski (No. 482 of the Union of Catholic Foresters); the Court of God's Mother of Good Advice (No. 91 of Catholic Foresters); the Court of St.

THE IMMIGRANT COMMUNITY

Vincent of Ferrara (No. 174 of Catholic Foresters); the Court of St. Stanislaw Kostka (No. 255 of Catholic Foresters); the Court of Priest Barzynski (No. 995 of Catholic Foresters); the Court of St. Walenty (No. 1,001 of Catholic Foresters); the Court of St. Irene (No. 445 of Catholic Foresters); the Court of Frederic Chopin (No. 1,391 of Catholic Foresters); the Court of St. John (No. 864 of Catholic Foresters); the Court of Leo XIII (No. [?] of the Catholic Foresters); the Court of St. Martin the Pope (No. 1,143 of the Catholic Foresters); the Society of the Guardianship of St. Joseph (Group 115 of the Polish Association in America); the Society of St. George the Martyr (Group 96 of the Polish Association); the Society of St. Roch (Group 71 of the Polish Association); the Society of St. John of Nepomuk (Group 26 of the Polish Association); the Society of the Heart of Jesus (Group 124 of the Polish Association); the Society Pearl of Mary (Group 152 of the Polish Association); the Society of St. Wojciech (Group 104 of the Polish Association); the Society of Young Men of St. Kazimierz (Independent Mutual Help Association); the Society of Ladies of Queen Jadwiga (Mutual Help Association); the Loan and Savings Association of St. Joseph No. 3; the Building Loan and Savings Association of Pulaski; the Building Loan and Savings Association of St. Francis; the Press Committee; the College of St. Stanislaw Kostka; the Novice's Convent of the Resurrectionists; the Convent of the Sisters of St. Francis; the Chicago *Daily News* (Polish)—74 in all.[1]

---

[1] Listed and described in *Album Pamiątkowe z Okazyi Złotego Jubileuszu Parafii Św. Stanisława Kostka* (Memorial Album of the Celebration of the Golden Jubilee of the Parish of St. Stanislaus Kostka).

OLD WORLD TRAITS TRANSPLANTED

141. *Zuaves of St. Stanislaus Kostka.* The Zuaves were organized into an association May 1, 1915, by Rev. Franciszek Dembinski, the present rector of the parish. They wear uniforms, helmets, and swords on the model of the Papal Guard in the Vatican. These little knights participate in large celebrations like New Year's, the Forty Hours' Divine Service, Pentecost, Christmas, the first communion of the school children; they stand on guard at the grave of Lord Jesus (before Easter), take part in the processions on Easter and Corpus Christi. The Zuaves drill in the school courtyard. The drill is taught by the well-known captain of the cavalry of Stanislaw, Mr. Franciszek Gorzynski. The Zuaves are composed of thirty members chosen from the Society of Altar Boys. . . . They are sons of parents who have belonged to the parish for many years and have been educated in the parochial school. They are obliged to shine as models of devotion, to partake regularly of the Holy Sacraments and thereby to be good sons of their dear parents, to know the history of their ancestors, the great men of Poland, to talk Polish among themselves and at home. In a word, the Zuaves are expected to be the guardians of everything that is divine and Polish in order to grow to be real Polish patriots and defenders of the Christian faith. [Picture of the group and names of members given.] [1]

Document 142 illustrates the formation of a small parish, and document 143 shows the condition of the same parish after twenty-five years, under the leadership of an exceptionally energetic priest.

---
[1] Album of the Parish of St. Stanislaus Kostka, p. 95.

THE IMMIGRANT COMMUNITY

142. The first Pole who came to New Britain was Mr. Tomasz Ostrowski. After him others began to arrive and in September, 1889, a mutual help society under the patronage of St. Michael the Archangel was established. [All the officers enumerated. . . .] In 1894 Priest Dr. Misicki, rector of the parish in Meriden, Connecticut, came every Sunday to celebrate the holy mass in New Britain in the old Irish church on Myrtle Street, at a yearly salary of $500. Then the society, together with other noble-minded Poles, began to think about establishing a Polish parish, which was organized under the patronage of St. Kazimierz. . . .

In September, 1895, Rev. Lucyan Bójnowski . . . was appointed rector of the parish . . . and a wooden church was built under the patronage of the Sweetest Heart of Jesus. . . . First of all Priest Bójnowski made efforts to turn the people from drink, from getting married in court, from indecent dress, from holding balls on Saturdays and nightly revelries, from playing cards, loafing in saloons, fighting in their homes, immoral life, conjugal infidelity, theft, bad education of children, indecent behavior on the street, and disorderly conduct at weddings and christenings. Instead, he encouraged them to go to confession and communion, to participate in various divine services, to belong to fraternities, etc. . . .[1]

143. (1) The old church now contains schoolrooms and the rectorate. It is worth $25,000. (2) The new church (the largest in New Britain) cost $150,000 when built, and is now worth $300,000. (3) The new school was built in 1904 at the cost of

---

[1] From a history of the parish of New Britain, written by Priest Bójnowski, and published in 1902.

OLD WORLD TRAITS TRANSPLANTED

$150,000. It is now worth twice as much. (4) A house for the teaching nuns is worth $15,000. (5) The parish has a cemetery worth $25,000. There are no debts on all of these buildings and lots. (6) In 1889 a co-operative bakery was established with an original capital of $6,000 contributed by 5 associations. At present its property is worth $60,000. (7) In 1904 a Polish orphanage was founded. It owns now 4 houses, 146 acres within the limits of the town, 107 acres outside the limits, 30 head of cattle, 7 horses, 70 hogs, 500 hens; total value over $200,000. No debts. (8) There is a parochial printing office. The lot, the building, and the machinery are worth $35,000. There is a debt of $5,000. (9) The Polish Loan and Industrial Corporation, founded in 1915, has a capitalization of $50,000, and owns $45,000 worth of houses. (10) The Polish Investment and Loan Corporation, founded in 1915, has a capitalization of $75,000 and real estate worth $10,000. (11) The People's Savings Bank, founded in December, 1916, has $496,000 deposited. (12) The New Britain Clothing Corporation, founded in 1919, capitalized at $50,000, has merchandise worth $100,000 and real estate worth $140,000. (13) The White Eagle Factory, established in 1919, capitalized at $25,000, produces cutlery. All of the above are co-operative organizations. (14) We gave 750 solbiers to the American army and 301 to the Polish army. (15) We have contributed to the Polish Relief Fund and to the Polish Army Fund, up to this moment, $110,672.36. (16) The parish counts now nearly 9,000 souls, including children. In 1894 there were only 700, counting Lithuanians, Slovaks, and Poles. (17) The

THE IMMIGRANT COMMUNITY

parochial school has 35 teachers and an attendance of 1,736 children.[1]

THE BOHEMIANS

In contrast with the Poles, who, as we have seen, are very difficult from the standpoint of assimilation, the Bohemians are almost ideal material. They are democratic in their tendencies, have the settler psychology, own a larger percentage of their homes here than any other immigrant group, bring the smallest amount of illiteracy and the largest amount of skilled labor of any group from the former dual empire, not excepting the Germans.[2]

The feature of Bohemian life in America which has attracted most attention and caused most criticism is their freethinking organizations. They are a deeply moral people and every Bohemian has in him a bit of John Hus, but in America there has been a movement away from the Catholic religion toward rationalism. Their morality is here formulated in terms of the negation of religion. Perhaps half of the Bohemians in America are freethinkers:

---

[1] Letter of Priest Bójnowski to Florian Znaniecki. We know from other sources that most of the institutions of the parish are due to the initiative of Priest Bójnowski himself.

[2] See, e.g., Thomas Čapek, *The Čechs in America* (Introduction).

144. Professor Steiner in an article on the Bohemians in America in the *Outlook* for April 25, 1903, says that they are the most irreligious of all our immigrants and quotes Mr. Geringer, editor of the *Svornost*, "that there are in Chicago alone three hundred societies that teach infidelity, that carry on propaganda for their unbelief, and that maintain Sunday-schools in which the attendance varies from thirty to three thousand." This must count as one, each branch of all the organizations, in which case that cannot be far from correct. It must be borne in mind, however, that many of these organizations are aiming at something else, and in some cases directly prohibit discussion of religious subjects, but the sympathy of the members is such that they come to be recognized as free-thought societies by the members and by outsiders. . . . Probably the best articulated organization which openly advocates freethinking is the Bohemian-Slavonian Benevolent Society, generally known by the initials of the Bohemian name, C. S. P. S. This was founded in St. Louis in 1854, and now has 25,000 members. At first it was Catholic and for benevolent purposes. In September, 1909, it declared absolutely for free thought. This does not mean that all the members are interested in the propaganda of freethinking, but no one is a member who is not in sympathy with it, and through the official monthly paper, which each member must take, a great influence is exerted.

The object of the brotherhood, as expressed in its constitution, is "to endeavor to perpetuate the Bohemian language in this country and secure for both sexes the moral as well as the intellectual and material elevation of our countrymen; to foster

THE IMMIGRANT COMMUNITY

brotherly love and *intellectual freedom* among the members; and to give mutual aid in sickness and death as well as in public life." Observation shows that this purpose is kept rather consistently, though there are many members whose only interest is the sickness and death benefit. The organization has the form of lodges, and in many towns in the country they have good halls. An interesting tendency which shows a reaction from the Church is the gradual dropping of forms and secrecy. Formerly it had three degrees, but now only the password, and many of the members object to even retaining that. Again, formerly they had elaborate badges, but these have become more and more simple, and the button which is worn as an insignia is very plain.[1]

THE SCANDINAVIANS

The Scandinavians bring a psychology which presents no particular obstacles to assimilation. They are not carrying on a nationalistic struggle here; they are not possessed of a mania of grandeur as representatives of states that are great, have been great, or will to be great. They are not the objects of exploitation by their own leaders. They are usually settlers, or have the settler psychology, represented in document 62, p. 84. In general, the Church is the center of their cultural activities, and they read and print much religious literature. They

---
[1] Herbert A. Miller, *The Bohemians in America* (manuscript).

have also a tender sentiment for their home country and language:

145. The Synod expresses its appreciation of the loyalty of our people toward our country and our government, its willing sacrifice of men and means for all governmental purposes, and the work which is being done in the army and navy by our chaplains, the National Lutheran Commission and the Lutheran Brotherhood; and reaffirms its fidelity toward our country, its constitution, laws, and government, and its purposes to place property and life, in the future as hitherto, at the disposal of our country and our government. The Synod is also gratefully cognizant of the fact that our Lutheran people of Swedish parentage in Canada, with great readiness, have placed men and means at the disposal of the British government in the present war.

In all our school activities—as well as in all other branches of our church work—it is incumbent upon us to meet existing linguistic needs. Our immigrants and our children must learn the English, the official language of the country, but the Swedish should also be retained as a valuable cultural heritage, as far as possible. The Synod is of the opinion that limitation in the study of foreign languages is a lowering of national educational ideals, and that the prohibition of the use of other languages than the English is at variance with American principles of liberty for which the nation has bled and is bleeding.[1]

The map on page 223 shows the distribution of Norwegian Lutheran churches in Minnesota.

[1] *Augustana Synodens Referat* (1918), p. 29.

THE IMMIGRANT COMMUNITY

We shall speak later of the pauperization of culture which an immigrant group in America suffers when it fails to use the

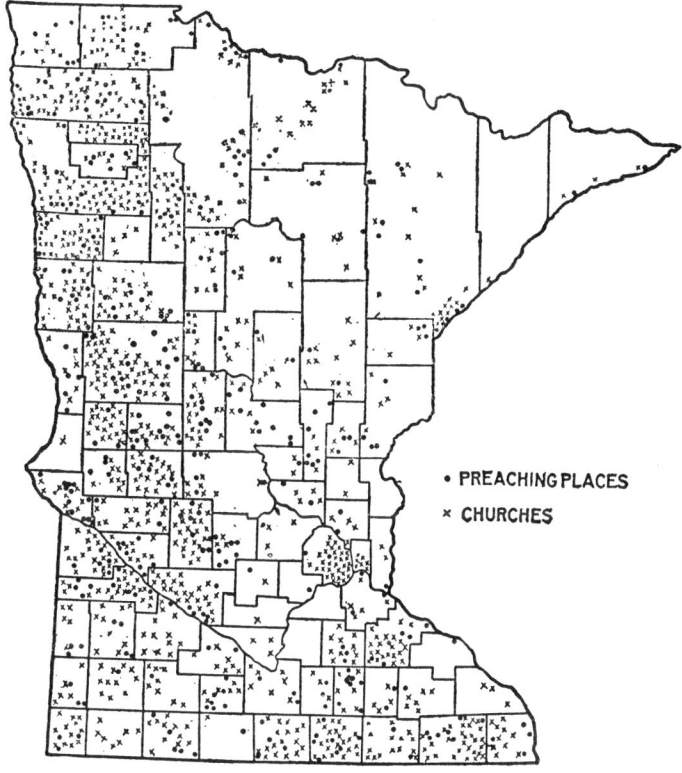

MAP 9.—NORWEGIAN LUTHERAN CHURCHES IN MINNESOTA [1]

general values provided by the larger American society (see p. 304 and document 168.) This has happened, in some measure, to the Scandinavians.

[1] Drawn from map in *Norsk Lutherske Menigheter i Amerika*, 1916.

OLD WORLD TRAITS TRANSPLANTED

146. In higher education the Scandinavians have allowed their denominational zeal to outrun their judgment. They have founded numerous seminaries and so-called colleges, but almost invariably as a part of the necessary equipment of a religious denomination, for how could a self-respecting sect, no matter how young or how slightly differentiated from its older brethren, permit its children to attend the schools of those whose denominational beliefs or practices had become objectionable enough to warrant a schism in the church? A few of these institutions, like Luther College, at Deborah, Iowa, Gustavus Adolphus College, at St. Peter, Minnesota, Augustana College at Rock Island, Illinois, and Bethany College at Lindsborg, Kansas, have maintained an excellent standard of work and exercised a wide and beneficent influence. The great majority, however, have simply wasted resources by the multiplication of ambitious, struggling, poorly equipped, so-called colleges, with little or no endowment, and often dependent upon the congregations of the denomination which gave them birth.

One of the results of the excessive splitting up of the Scandinavian churches is that the energies which ought to be concentrated are frittered away on unnecessary schools. A separate denominational school and a family paper seem to be indispensable parts of the machinery of every newly organized sect, no matter how young or how small or how poor it may be.[1]

---

[1] C. H. Babcock, *The Scandinavian Element in the United States*, p. 111.

VIII

TYPES OF COMMUNITY INFLUENCE

IN the preceding chapters we have implicitly or explicitly characterized the influence of certain immigrant communities on their members. In the present chapter we compare the preparation that the largest three groups of the so-called new immigration—the Poles, the Jews, and the Italians—give their members for engaging in American activities. These groups are numerically about equal, the Poles numbering about 3,000,000, the Jews, 3,300,000, the Italians about 3,200,000.

THE POLISH COMMUNITY

Polish leaders in Europe have done a unique work for the improvement of the condition of the people. After many bloody and futile revolutions, the nobility realized that its strength was spent and turned to the people—particularly the peasants. After 1863 a "movement for enlightenment" was begun whose object was to make the peasant self-conscious, nationally conscious, and materially prosperous. Men and women of the nobility, students, young girls, priests, all the Polish intelligentsia, participated seriously and ceaselessly. Newspapers were developed appealing to the peasant, agricultural societies were formed, banks were established for the peasant, some enthusiasts married peasant women. At first the peasants viewed all this with suspicion, but in the end they realized that the motives of the other classes were unselfish, and began to respond and participate. They wrote to the newspapers, asked information about soils and bee keeping, reported successes, organized co-operative societies.

The results of this movement were very real and practical. One of them was the complete economic defeat of the Prussians in German Poland. In their attempts to Germanize this region the Prussians spent $140,000,000 in colonizing it with Germans from the Rhine provinces. To resist them, the Poles, under the leadership of Maximilian Jackowski (a noble), organized 330 peasant societies; a powerful prelate, Wawrzyniak, organized a system of peasant banks; any Pole who outbid the Germans on land and saved it for Poland was lauded in more than

300 newspapers and periodicals; all German goods were boycotted. In the end the Poles had more land than when Bismarck inaugurated the German colonization movement, after the war with France. In Prussian Poland the movement was mainly economic and political. Bernhard's important book, *Die Polenfrage* (1909), was a semiofficial report on the situation, informing the Prussian government that it was defeated and advising it to expropriate Polish land. The movement in Russian Poland was rather along educational and co-operative lines and is recorded in **Volume IV** of *The Polish Peasant*.

As a result of this social experiment, the Poles learned to regard the individual member of the community as a supreme value and thus benefited Poland immensely, in spite of the fact that Poland was not a state and was surrounded by states ready to destroy her values as fast as she created them. Having this in mind, it is remarkable that the Polish communities in America have conspicuously neglected those of their members who are not successful.

147. The social attitude manifested with reference to questions of public charity and social work in general are interesting. It has been noticed that as compared, for instance, with the Jewish charitable

institutions, the Poles in America have little to show in this line. Care for orphans and care for the old and incurable are practically the only problems which are more or less seriously dealt with; in other fields initiative is rare and realization insufficient. The few charitable institutions are due to the personal efforts of a few leading members of Polish-American society acting through the Church and influenced by Christian principles, rather than to the recognition of altruistic obligations by the society at large. In a word, no social need to take care of the weak seems to be felt by Polish-American communities. . . .

The moral reason by which the Polish-American community justifies its apparent egotism is found in the very basis of its organization. The latter is socially and economically an organization for self-help; its first purpose is to prevent the individual from becoming a burden to the community, and the individual who does not choose to avail himself of the opportunities which this organization offers, voluntarily resigns all claims to the help of the group. If the latter still feels obliged to assist in some measure the orphans, the old, and the incurables, it is only in so far as it feels that the system of mutual insurance is not yet efficient enough to cover these cases adequately.

Of course since the Polish-American community tends to ignore even the merely inefficient, we cannot expect it to take any care of the demoralized. The contrast is striking between the intense reformatory work in this country. Individual demoralization is either ignored or the demoralized individual is simply dropped at once. No one bothers about the innumerable cases of family decay, juvenile delinquency, alcoholism, vagabondage, crime. Few know

TYPES OF COMMUNITY INFLUENCE

the full extent of the demoralization going on among American Poles.[1]

This means that while the Poles have been carrying on a struggle here to preserve their members from Americanization and save them for Poland, or for a *Polonia Americana*, they have at the same time abandoned their unfit and misadapted members to the ministrations of our charity organizations, legal aid societies, and juvenile courts. The cases with Polish names cited in the documents in Chapter IV are examples.[2]

American social workers who handle Polish cases feel that the Polish organizations are often inclined to avoid their responsibilities toward those who are legally entitled to benefits, as shown in document 148 below:

148. Plaintiff, Sigmund Stecki, belonged to the Polish National Alliance, group 565, paid his dues regularly and was in good standing. According to the by-laws a sick member unable to support his

---

[1] Thomas and Znaniecki, *The Polish Peasant*, vol. v (in press).

[2] The Polish-American organizations have imitated the organization of the historical Polish *state*, not the *peasant community* in Poland. The peasant community was absolutely democratic, while the Polish state was formerly a "nobility-nation," aristocratic and hierarchic to an almost unparalleled degree. And it was the latter spirit which Polish leaders introduced into their organizations here. All of their organizations select their members carefully (see document 147). Even the one corresponding to the American Boy Scouts (document 141, p. 216) selects its members for their good breeding, piety, "knightly" qualities, etc., whereas the American Boy Scouts convert even the worst characters.

family is entitled to a sick benefit of $5 a week for three months, and $3 a week for six months thereafter, if he is sick more than a week and reports his sickness.

Plaintiff was sick from May 23 to July 3, 1912—eight weeks. He reported his sickness. The secretary of the lodge (his cousin) came to see him, and said he would rather pay from his own money than from the lodge, because he had recommended plaintiff to the lodge and would be disgraced by plaintiff's sickness. Plaintiff had a swelling in his right leg from eczema. Doctor Golembianski from the lodge did not call on plaintiff until the end of his sickness. Plaintiff called at his office once the following week. That was all the care he got. No help came from the lodge. When plaintiff was well, he attended a meeting of the lodge, and when he noticed no movement to pay his claim he rose and asked why they had forgotten him. The lodge said he had failed to notify them. He assured them his wife had notified the secretary, the secretary had called, and also the doctor who had reported to the lodge. Then they gave him $10 only; the balance of $25 they never paid.

[Plaintiff acutely sick three times later without aid.] The fourth time Horn Brothers (his employers) wrote to [the proper group of] the Polish National Alliance, suggesting they were getting money under false pretenses. He got no answer and turned case over to the Legal Aid Society.

At first they paid no attention to us. Then [their attorney] wrote that his society had decided to pay plaintiff nothing for five reasons: (1) he did not belong to the group; (2) he did not pay according to the constitution; (3) he did not go to their doctor

TYPES OF COMMUNITY INFLUENCE

to be treated; (4) he indulged in intoxicating liquors during his illness, preventing recovery; (5) this society had paid him twice and according to the constitution once is required [in cases of chronic sickness].

[Their attorney] told our attorney when they met in court that plaintiff was "no good," beats his wife, gets "dead drunk," fights, was brought into court and fined for fighting, had been expelled from numerous lodges for "crookedness," that plaintiff's cousin, first secretary, did not notify the lodge of plaintiff's first illness as the rules required, etc.

As to the reasons for not paying: (1) he did belong to the lodge at the time, but dropped out later when they continually refused to pay him; (2) he did pay dues, and paid $12 in all for dues; (3) he did go to their doctor whenever notified; (4) he never drank to excess; (5) the disease was always acute, not chronic. Investigation by his employers showed that all the stories against his character were false. He was honest, steady, reliable, kind to wife, and Horn Brothers thought highly of him.

The judge gave judgment for plaintiff for $75. But the lodge then moved to set aside judgment, showing they were not a corporation as sued.

The Legal Aid Society could not find whom to sue and has done nothing. The case dragged so long in court that everybody, even Horn Brothers, lost interest. The last letter from Horn Brothers, dated October 30, 1914, says:

"[The attorney] in this case, met Mr. Stecki about two weeks ago, and claimed they would fight the case and spend $200 or $400 in defeating his claim. It seems from all we can gather that there has been a fight among themselves and that it is a band of saloon keepers who are running this for their mutual advantage. If this is a fact, it should be wiped out, and we trust you will do what you can to accomplish this end."[1]

Another defect of the Polish community is the failure to provide various types of organizations which would assist their members in adjusting themselves to the complex American life. Practically all of their organizations have the same function—mutual aid, social recognition, and cultivation of the Polish spirit. The Polish National Alliance, for example, is merely a federation of about 1,700 such societies.

149. By multiplying indefinitely associations and circles, and by a very active propaganda exercised through all possible mediums, nearly all the members of the parish—men, women, and young people— even those who for some reason or other have not yet joined the parish, or have dropped out, can become in some way connected with the system and thus acquire a minimum of public character. This public character grows whenever an individual is, even if only momentarily, connected as public functionary with some scheme for common action— religious ceremony, entertainment, meeting, bazaar, collection for a social purpose, etc.—and this increased public importance is every year attained by large proportion of the community. The highest degree of public dignity is, of course, the share of those who are elected officers in associations or become mem-

[1] *Records of the Chicago Legal Aid Society.*

TYPES OF COMMUNITY INFLUENCE

bers of permanent committees, or directors of institutions; and if we realize that every association has from 6 to 20 officials, that every committee numbers on the average 10 members, and that some large parishes have more than 70 associations and committees, while even a small parish has at least a dozen of them, we see that every active and fairly intelligent individual, whatever his sex and age, is sure of becoming some time a public dignitary; and even if the existing organization does not give him enough opportunities, he can always initiate a new institution and gain recognition as organizer and charter member.[1]

By thus multiplying "dignities" and providing opportunities for public appearance —in theatrical representations, concerts, balls, and recitals—the Polish community has succeeded in institutionalizing a large part of the activities of its members, and subjecting them to control. But with the exception of the Alliance of Polish Socialists (a numerically small body appealing to the specialized city workman) every Polish institution here attempts to meet *all* the needs of the individual member. The result is that the Polish immigrant is arrested within his community. He shows little tendency to participate in American life and institutions, is hardly ever seen in our colleges and universities, shows notably little public

---
[1] Thomas and Znaniecki, *The Polish Peasant,* vol. v (in press).

OLD WORLD TRAITS TRANSPLANTED

spirit, remains on a relatively low level of efficiency, and contributes heavily through crime and poverty to the burden of the American state.

THE JEWISH COMMUNITY

Although the Jew has always been obliged to organize his community life in a separate and self-sufficient way in the different European states, and consequently brings to this country the habits of organization, the conditions of industry in Europe were so different, the American melting-pot has so powerful an effect on the old ritualistic and communistic attitudes, the mass of Jews is so great in New York City, the Jews so strange to one another, that the problem of organization has been as great for the Jews as for the other groups. The Jews, however, have the settler psychology. They bring their intellectuals, professionals, business men, as well as their revolutionists and workers, and have, more than other groups, the elements for a complete society.

Other immigrant groups are usually defective in leadership and creative individuals; few intellectuals come, and those who do come are usually only intelligent enough to exploit the simpler members of their own

TYPES OF COMMUNITY INFLUENCE

groups, not to compete with intellectual Americans. Consequently it is in general true that the immigrant leader is able and willing to organize his people just sufficiently for his own good, but not sufficiently for their good.

The Jews, on the contrary, are conspicuous as creators and organizers in different fields—economic, scientific, artistic, etc.—and their superior members not only live without exploiting their own people, but sincerely devote their abilities and resources to the improvement of the mass of their race. Furthermore, for the first time since the dispersion the Jews have found in America a toleration which has made it possible for them to show an open interest in their own welfare and to discuss openly the improvement of their status and the realization of their ideals.[1]

For these reasons, the Jews, far more than any other immigrant group, are resorting to reflective social activity and supplementing the old social forms, spontaneously

[1] "For centuries Jews had been forced by circumstances to abandon their own traditions of democracy inherited from their fathers and expressed in the Hebrew commonwealth, and to seek protection, not through the methods of free and open discussion, and the development of public opinion, but by secret and indirect means, through the efforts of individuals who had or were supposed to have influence."—Louis D. Brandeis, *Jewish Rights and the Congress*, address, Carnegie Hall, January 24, 1916.

OLD WORLD TRAITS TRANSPLANTED

reproduced, with new, conscious organizations. The organization of the Kehillah in New York City was, in fact, the beginning of a scientific study of the Jews by themselves. Their primary aim was:

150. (1) To secure exact, systematic, comprehensive knowledge concerning the Jewish community of New York City, and the Jewish problem in all its phases; (2) to engage upon as many experiments as possible through first-hand experience of the various phases of the problem; and (3) to point out paths along which the community might develop in order to become in fact a conscious, organized, united community.[1]

Beside taking action to meet a large number of specific needs, emergencies and abuses, the Kehillah has established a number of co-ordinating, standardizing, and research institutions. Among them are: a Bureau of Jewish Education ("for the purpose of standardizing the methods of Jewish education; . . . to find ways and means of providing Jewish training for all the Jewish children of school age in this city"); a Bureau of Industry (" . . . to direct vocational training, to provide employment for the handicapped, as well as for the highly skilled, and to work out methods for the maintenance of peace in industries where

[1] *Communal Register*, p. 55.

TYPES OF COMMUNITY INFLUENCE

Jews preponderate"); a School for Communal Work, a Bureau of Philanthropic Research, etc.[1]

From the standpoint of organization the Jews are the most interesting of the immigrant groups. There is among them, indeed, a great variety of disorder and personal demoralization—gambling, extortion, vagabondage, family desertion, white slavery, ordinary and extraordinary crime—as a consequence of the rapid decay in America of the Jewish traditions and attitudes;[2] there are divisions and animosities among them, and quarrels about opinions—the mere statement that the Jews are a national rather than a religious community was sufficient to convulse the recent Jewish congress at Philadelphia for more than an hour —and Jewish leaders realize that the sys-

---
[1] *Communal Register*, pp. 49–55, 1139–1155.

[2] The American born Jew may become totally and unreflectively bad, but usually the Jew shows a survival of his ritualistic-communistic morality in his scrupulous approach to any act of wrong-doing. He always seeks some show of *sanction* for the unsocial act. Thus, if he wishes to repudiate a marriage engagement he persuades himself that the girl is anæmic or that he has heart disease and that the children will consequently be unsound, and seeks a confirmation of this opinion. A considerable number of the " Bintel-Brief " in the newspaper *Forward* seek the editor's sanction of an unsocial wish. The writer knows his motive is bad, but is not sure the editor will know it. In the issue of February 20, 1920, for example, a writer represents that his *blind* wife wishes to separate from him in order to allow him to pursue a happy existence, and seeks the editor's approval of a divorce.

OLD WORLD TRAITS TRANSPLANTED

tematic activities we have mentioned have had as yet little effect on the great mass of Jewish life. But in our examination of the Jewish type of organization we gain an impression that the experiments of this community upon its own problems contain an interest not limited to the Jewish community, but extending to American society as a whole. Our interest in the organization of other immigrant communities is limited to the possible discovery of devices which may assist these groups until they are able to enjoy the benefits of American institutions. In the case of the Jewish group, we find spontaneous, intelligent, and highly organized experiments in democratic control which may assume the character of permanent contributions to the organization of the American state. In this respect the Jewish organization differs completely from the Japanese (see Chapter VIII), which is the most efficient organization among the immigrant groups, but one based on the military principle of ordering and forbidding.

THE ITALIAN COMMUNITY

Italian leaders frequently point out that the power of the Italian community both to

TYPES OF COMMUNITY INFLUENCE

organize for itself and to use American organizations is limited.

151. The Italians in America may be compared to a man who is starving in the midst of an abundant supply of excellent food to which he has no access, either because it is locked away from him or because he is too ill to assimilate it, or because he feels a strong repugnance toward the receptacle that contains it.[1]

152. If the Italians would do as the Jews do we should be better off. The Italian institutions here are very few and very poor, and most of the big organizations do nothing to help them. . . . I should like to open the eyes of the public to the fact that very little is done here for Italians by Italian organizations. Such organizations as the Sons of Italy do not use their money as they should. They may spend it in Italy for private needs and things. They should spend it here for American institutions for Italians. We should all unite as the Jewish people do.[2]

153. Do we not see all the giant strides which the Hebrew element is making in the conquest of this country? It is true. They are owners of business, banks, and affairs. Israelites are the lawyers, judges, doctors, professors, teachers, managers of theaters, the monopolists of arts. The most perfect institutions of mutual aid and providence are Israelite. The biggest settlement in New York is Israelite. Their clubs, social, political, artistic, and professional, are the best of their kind. Their schools are the most frequented and most active. What wonder

---

[1] Joseph Giardina, *Winning the Italians for Christ* (manuscript).
[2] Father Bassi, St. Lucy's Church, New York City (interview).

if they audaciously proclaim themselves the owners, the conquerers of this country! Those who can emulate them in this method of intellectual and social invasion are the Italian element, which has much affinity of intellect and artistic sensibility with the old and refined Jewish race. But we must do as they do; we must thus invade the schools, teach ourselves, have our children taught, open to them the social paths by means of the hatchet of knowledge and genius. We must organize our forces as the Jews do, persist in exhausting that which constitutes gain for our race over the Anglo-Saxon race. . . .

But instead of this, what a contrast! The schools where the Italian language is taught are deserted. The Italian families falsify even the ages of their children in order to send them to the factories, instead of to the schools, showing thus an avarice more sordid than that of the traditional Shylock. There is not a young Italian girl who knows how to typewrite in both languages and our men of affairs must employ Jewish girls or Americans for lack of Italians.

Without being niggardly and egoistic as the Jew sometimes is, let us try to imitate him in his ardor for conquest and in the discipline and knowledge with which he knows how to organize his admirable institutions, which put him in a position to raise a high voice and command respect for the name of the race.

This is the reason we have put at the head of this article the exhortation, "Let us do as the Jews."[1]

[1] Editorial, *Bolletino della Sera*, November 30, 1907. Incidentally this statement is typical of the Italian attitude toward success in America: that this is to be gained not by constructive work in co-operation with the American public, but in some way *at the expense* of this public. It corresponds to the predatory economic theory which preceded Adam Smith.

TYPES OF COMMUNITY INFLUENCE

On the other hand the Italians retain longer than many other nationalities the virtues of the primary-group organization. Their family and community life has a very affectionate and intimate character, and its ties usually remain strong enough to prevent that demoralization of the second generation which characterizes the Poles and, to some extent, the Jews. The Italian family tends to remain solidary long enough to secure the result which Mrs. Leavitt indicates at the end of document 103, p. 151. Map 10 on the following page indicates the location of Italian colonies in New York.

It is certainly true that the spirit of *mafia*, *camorra*, and vendetta, the most notorious of the Italian heritages, which developed here into the Black Hand activities, has had a paralyzing effect on the development of Italian life. Before 1905, in New York, Chicago, New Orleans, Pennsylvania, Ohio, wherever Italians were congregated, systematic blackmail and murder produced a feeling of insecurity and terror unfavorable to all constructive activity:

154. Here in the land of liberty, of labor, of the boldest steps in human progress, there has originated and extended through the Italian colonies such an air of mystery and terror that it disturbs the peace of families, hampers the profitable development of

all the industries, dishonors the Italian name, and tends to prolong that state of moral degradation from which the lowest social strain of certain unhappy regions of Italy are just now beginning to emerge. . . .

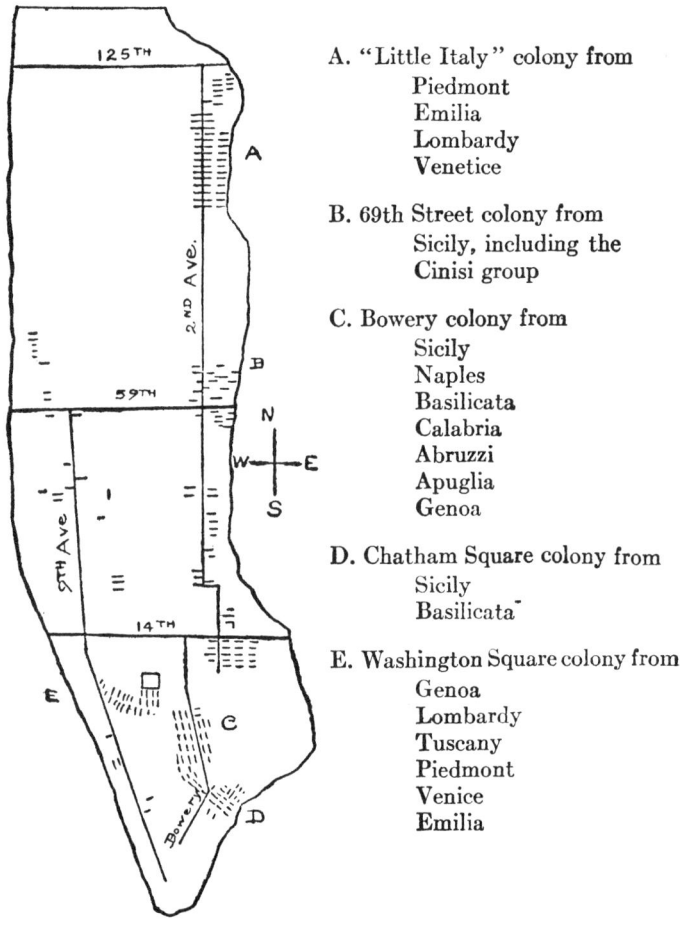

A. "Little Italy" colony from
　Piedmont
　Emilia
　Lombardy
　Venetice

B. 69th Street colony from
　Sicily, including the
　Cinisi group

C. Bowery colony from
　Sicily
　Naples
　Basilicata
　Calabria
　Abruzzi
　Apuglia
　Genoa

D. Chatham Square colony from
　Sicily
　Basilicata

E. Washington Square colony from
　Genoa
　Lombardy
　Tuscany
　Piedmont
　Venice
　Emilia

MAP 10.—LOCATION OF ITALIAN COLONIES IN NEW YORK CITY WITH SOURCES OF EMIGRATION IN ITALY.

TYPES OF COMMUNITY INFLUENCE

Whole Italian families, in which a blackmailing letter or a threat in another form has been received from the Black Hand, live in continued anxiety and fear of the vague, unknown, but always terrible danger which hangs over them, and nobody knows whom it will fall upon, the father, one of the children, a relative, or all together, in the destruction of the house or little store, demolished and set on fire by the explosion of a dynamite bomb. . . . Even business men of conspicuously strong character, and professional men of unusual ability, frankly admit that, after a threatening letter, a certain time has to pass before they are able to attend to their business with all the composure and energy required. . . .[1]

155. In these last few years the number of threatening letters has been increasing at an appalling rate, and the field of victims has been enlarged to include all: the poor laborer who by means of great sacrifices has succeeded in putting aside a few dollars, or, perhaps, bought a wretched little property not yet entirely paid for; the small merchant who, with others of his family, is his own clerk in his little store, and barely manages to make a living from it; the proprietor who has retired from business and would enjoy in peace the fruit of his toil; the wholesale merchant; the professional man; and even the representative of the Italian government in Chicago.

The letter in its classic form is short, written in an unassuming and sometimes friendly tone. It contains the request for money, with an indication of the place where it is to be delivered, and a threat, sometimes veiled by mysterious allusions, and sometimes expressed with a brutal lack of reserve.

---

[1] *La Mano Bianca*, p. 18. A report issued by the Italian White Hand Society, Chicago, 1908.

OLD WORLD TRAITS TRANSPLANTED

At the place designated the victim does not find anybody; but at the house he finds, a few days later, a second letter, in which the request is repeated, also the threat, in an aggravated form. And thus at brief intervals comes a third and a fourth letter, each containing more violent threats than the preceding, expressed either in words or symbols, such as drawings of pierced hearts, of pistols, daggers, crosses, skulls and crossbones, bombs, etc. All these letters are prepared with a system of progression which shows in the author a mind by no means crude and untrained, but shows, rather, a consummate skill acquired by practice in this class of crime.

In this manner the victim is intimidated to such a point that there is not left in his veins another drop of blood beyond that needed to nourish his fear, and to enable him, in such a depressed condition of mind, to lay hold on the anchor of salvation which is pointed out to him in one of the letters, that is, to apply to "friends." Some phrase in the letter hints vaguely at so-called friends; suggests that whoever seeks will find; gives to understand, in short, that somebody might intervene between the victim and the mysterious and terrible god that has made the demand, and is threatening with all the thunderbolts in his possession, so that the matter might be adjusted in some way. In one letter in the possession of the "White Hand," this "friend" who is to be the intermediary, and who in reality is the accomplice if not the author of the blackmail, is indicated with sufficient precision. He must be a Terminese from Termini, says the letter, meaning from the town of Termini, not from the country, and must live in the same street as the victim, which is a very short street. . . .

TYPES OF COMMUNITY INFLUENCE

So the unfortunate victim finally looks for the "friend" who can save him from the threatening peril, and has no difficulty whatever in finding him. For some time there has been continually at his side somebody who has shown himself more solicitous than ever before, if known for a considerable time; obliging and exceedingly friendly, if of recent acquaintance. This man sometimes guesses, sometimes induces the other to tell him the trouble which has destroyed his peace of mind, and curses the assassins who blackmail poor people and who ought to be hung or put in the penitentiary. He knows some mysterious people, banded together, who live and have a good time with money extorted from honest, industrious people. . . .

The trial of Schiro before Judge H. N. Chetlain of the Chicago court, furnishes very eloquent proof of the means by which the conscience of poor people is depraved, and the terror of mysterious societies of villains is strengthened and spread by tyrannical power.

Antonio Schiro, offering his services to Giovanni Gastello as a "friend" for a transaction with the authors of a blackmailing letter, suggested that he accompany the offer of a smaller sum with a letter which would cause it to be accepted. He would write the letter himself for Castello, and in fact did write it and deposited it, together with the money, at the place designated by the mysterious blackmailers. Found when he was caught, it was offered in evidence at the trial. It ran as follows:

"My dear children, I answer your dear letter which stated that you wanted this flower. So, my dear children, I cannot. I can only give you this flower of two hundred because I am not a person like you, gentlemen, believe. You must excuse me if I cannot make you content because I am a laborer and have nothing else to say, but salute you friendly and sign. Your friend Giovanni. You come and get this letter in the place you know, because I cannot go there. Good-by, good-by and make a good life." . . .

The White Hand, which had studied all phases of those cases which had come to its knowledge, finding it extremely difficult to reach the principal actor, directed all its attention toward this so-called friend whose conduct and explanations gave some clue which might furnish a more or less substantial proof of his participation in the crime. Then the tactics of these criminals were changed, and to the common "friend" of the blackmailed and the blackmailer was assigned the role of enemy of the latter, under the necessity of submitting to a humiliation, the humiliation of being obliged himself to carry to the feet of the powerful and mysterious god the tribute of the money extorted and the homage of his own obedience.

In this way every weapon of the prosecution is broken. The go-between did not offer himself, he was appealed to; he always advised against yielding to the imposition; he refused to intervene; they begged him to, entreated, implored; he yielded out of consideration for his friend, being himself a victim of the oppression of the same mysterious enemy. And in the face of this evidence, in fact, no jury can find him guilty. . . .[1]

156. This type of crime has been carried on to such an extent that, though the majority of those in the colony are honest and industrious laborers,

---

[1] *La Mano Blanco*, pp. 11–16, *passim*.

TYPES OF COMMUNITY INFLUENCE

nearly every one seems to feel that he is in constant danger of either becoming the victim of a plot or of being forced to involve himself with the gang.

Continental Italians and those of other nationalities who live in the district may own well-stocked stores or acquire a reputation for wealth, but are never molested or threatened, but a Sicilian who shows any sign of prosperity almost invariably begins to receive threatening letters and, though a love of display is a national characteristic, few have the courage to raise their standard of living as long as they continue to live in the district. The streets lying in the heart of the colony are thought to be centers of danger, so there has been a tendency to move toward the boundaries, or a few blocks beyond, and families that have done so have a sense of security, though they still live within easy walking distance and return daily to visit friends, attend church, patronize the shops, etc.

In the district itself it is considered very bad form to discuss these affairs. No one alludes to them voluntarily, or in plain terms speaks of a murder. A murdered man is spoken of as the "poor disgraced one," and the murders or persecutions as "trouble." Certain men are called "*mafiosi*," but this generally means only that they are domineering, swaggering, and fearless, and no one would think of making a direct accusation. There are men who are said to be "unwilling to work for their bread," and certain names are never mentioned without a significant raising of eyebrows. The term Black Hand is never used except jokingly, nor does one hear the words vendetta, *omertà* or *feudo*, though every one is imbued with the sentiments for which they stand. In the whole colony there is no one so despised as an informer, nor is it thought desirable to show an interest in another's private affairs. There is a general belief that men who are murdered usually deserve their fate. Murdered men are not buried from the church unless a large sum is paid for a special mass.

The American press and police attribute all these "Italian killings" to the Black Hand and consider them inevitable. Every so often the newspapers print an interview with a police official in which a certain number of murders are prophesied to occur in this district, and the public are given to understand that the situation is hopeless. When a murder is committed it is either reported as a minor occurrence in a single paragraph, or absurdly elaborated in highly romantic style. A few years ago the chief of police, on being urged to have a careful study made of the situation, dismissed the matter by saying, "Oh, we've always had trouble up there; they never bother anyone but each other."[1]

The Italian community had no power of organization to combat a practice which was traditional and operated like one of the laws of nature. The Italian press got as much news value as possible out of the situation, and threw the blame on the Americans, claiming that they admitted too many Italian criminals, and that the American police and court systems were defective in comparison with the Italian.[2] But grad-

---
[1] Marie Leavitt, *Report on the Sicilian Colony in Chicago* (manuscript).

[2] Both of these claims were in fact true. The majority of Sicilian criminals have probably been at one time or another in

TYPES OF COMMUNITY INFLUENCE

ually as the practice became epidemic, affecting all classes of Italians, and involving Americans also, the Italian community and the American police were forced by public opinion into an alliance which succeeded in abating the evil.

the United States, and American laws (with jury system, technicalities safeguarding the rights of the accused, etc.) are not adapted to dealing with the Sicilian character.

"The United States has become the refuge of all the delinquents and the bandits of Italy, of Sicily, Sardinia, and Calabria. About a year ago the authorities of Tunis decided to cleanse the Italian quarter of that city where there were a great number of crimes. The French government proceeded to make a rigorous inquest which resulted in the expulsion of 10,000 Italians from that country. Where did that flower of manhood go? They were welcomed with open arms by Uncle Sam. . . . Our Penal Code should be made more severe. The worst with immigrants who come here from Italy, Sicily, Sardinia, and Calabria is that they do not know how to use the liberty which is enjoyed in this country. . . ."—Statement of Lieutenant Petrosino, Head of the Italian Detective Bureau, New York City, *Bolletino della Sera*, January 7, 1908.

"To a certain type of Italian criminal, who in his native land lives in continual dread of the carabineers, the guards of public safety, the civic guards, and even the rural and forest guards, any one of whom may appear at his very bedside any hour of the night to make sure that he is at home from sunset until dawn, this country where such an abundance of guardians of the peace is replaced only by the policeman, often nothing but a creature of politics, cannot fail to appear as the promised land.

"To a certain type of Italian criminal, who, when mysterious crimes are committed, is liable to be locked up in jail as a suspect, sometimes even for months, simply because he is recognized as being capable of committing crime, this country, where hold-ups, thugs plying their trade in the most prominent streets, or in the elevated railroad stations and street cars, night riders and lynchers, so often escape justice, cannot fail to appear as a most fertile vineyard, easy of cultivation for one willing to take chances."—*La Mano Bianca*, p. 2.

OLD WORLD TRAITS TRANSPLANTED

We are unable to trace the whole history of this reform movement, but the following data, from one of the Italian newspapers published in New York, indicate the gradual modification of the attitude of the Italians:

157. In April, 1903, a murdered man was found in a barrel at Avenue A and Eleventh Street, New York. The Italian detectives arrested twelve Sicilians. The American newspapers had full accounts and articles abusive of the Italians and the Black Hand.[1] The Italian papers protested violently against the blackening of the Italian name. The *Bollettino* claimed that "the fear of the *mafia* is in great part a product of the reporter's fancy."[2]

During 1903 and 1904 the publicity given these crimes seemed merely to augment them. The *Bollettino* resented the fact that "that odious word '*mafia*' is continually thrown in our faces," quoted American newspaper accounts of American lawlessness—the feuds of the Kentucky mountains, etc.—and criticized the inefficiency of the American police.[3]

"Do the European newspapers say that the good Londoners are hyenas who suck the blood from the torn flesh of women, and that of all their sports the Americans prefer that of holding up trains, robbing the passengers, perhaps killing them, and dynamiting safes?"[4]

On October 18, 1905, the *Bollettino* published a statement of Lieutenant Petrosino that he needed more men, that there were 30,000 members of the Black Hand in America, and that the only way to

---
[1] *Bollettino della Sera*, April 16, 1903.
[2] *Ibid.*, April 17, 22, 27, May 11, 1903.
[3] *Ibid.*, July 24, December 23, 1903.   [4] *Ibid.*, May 7, 1903.

TYPES OF COMMUNITY INFLUENCE

deal with them was to deport their leaders. The municipal council of Scranton, Pennsylvania, offered $1,000 for information as to headquarters of the Black Hand in that city.[1]

July 10, 1905, the *Bollettino*, referring to the Black Hand, "which is said to have infiltrated itself among the workmen of the Croton aqueduct," advised Italians not to communicate details to the American reporters but to the Italian consul general. September 27, 1905, a Black Hand case appeared for the first time on the second page of the *Bollettino*. Heretofore these cases had appeared on the first page.

September 10, 1906, the *Bollettino* reprinted from the *Tribuna Italiana*, Chicago, an account of the outbreak of a vendetta during a religious procession in Chicago and "the dragging of the Italian name in the dirt." Both papers asked: "When will this end?" "Another Sunday like the past will see the proposal not of one plan, but of ten, to exclude Italian emigrants from America."

In 1907 the "activities" increased. "There is not a day that we are not compelled to record in increasing numbers deeds so horrible as to redden the faces of this puritanical people. To-day threatening letters, to-morrow murder, then kidnapping, following the explosion of bombs, and thus . . . we proceed upon the path of crime."[2] Judge Roberto Cortese, of Paterson, New Jersey, received an infernal machine through the mail and was blown to pieces. He had aided the police in connection with Black Hand cases. A protest meeting of 500 was led by Italians; $10,000 was raised to aid in the search for the criminals, and in addition the Municipal Council

---
[1] *Bollettino della Sera*, January 11, 1906.
[2] *Ibid.*, January 30, 1907.

of Paterson contributed $2,000, the Passaic Board of Freeholders, $1,000, the State Camp Woodmen, $2,500, etc.[1] The year 1908 shows the highest number of Black Hand activities. The *Bollettino* records 311 cases. Two columns in the *Bollettino* (January 25, 1908) call on Italians to rise up and put a stop to the crimes which are besmirching the Italian name, and call a mass meeting to effect an organization. An editorial headed "The Cry of Alarm," January 28th, warned that the doors of this country would be closed to Italians. At the meeting a society of over 300 was formed—"Association de Vigilanza e Protezione Italiana"—and Mr. Frugone, editor of the *Bollettino*, was made president.[2]

"In many places employers are beginning to refuse to take Italians."[3] The phrase, "It is about time to quit it," became current in Italian newspapers.[4] The *Bollettino*, commenting on a case where a man went to jail rather than disclose the name of a blackmailer, gave advice which proved very important later—to carry information to the police.[5] Commenting on a law proposed in West Virginia to exclude Italians from the state, the *Bollettino* said the Italians bade fair to be classed with the Chinese.[6] The *Bollettino* printed a letter from the King of Italy to an Italian policeman commending him for bravery in fighting the bad Italian element in Pittsburgh.[7] The *Bollettino* pointed out that Italians were afraid to inform the police of threatening letters, because the police were unable to protect them, cited the

---

[1] *Bollettino della Sera*, February 10–14, 1907.
[2] *Ibid.*, February 7, 1908.
[3] *Ibid.*, January 30, 1908.
[4] *Ibid.*, February 17, 1908.
[5] *Ibid.*, March 21, 1908.
[6] *Ibid.*, March 30, 1908.
[7] *Ibid.*, May 8, 1908.

TYPES OF COMMUNITY INFLUENCE

case of Mr. Spinella, and translated a communication sent by him to the *Times* in July, showing that he informed the police of threats, and his house was nevertheless dynamited six times.[1] The *Bollettino* printed a notice, "Against the Black Hand," advising all honest Italians to aid Commissioner Bingham by sending him, marked "personal," all threatening letters, and information about Black Handers and idle Italians, with a description of individuals.[2] Lieut. Giuseppe Petrosino was killed in Palermo. The *Bollettino* placed the blame on the chief of police for revealing the fact that Petrosino was in Italy.[3] A law was passed in Albany making punishment for kidnapping fifty years in prison.[4]

Rizzo, who killed three children in an attempt to extort money from their father, went to the electric chair.[5] Lupo, leader of a gang, was sentenced to thirty years, and members of that gang were given heavy sentences.[6] The Italian dailies attacked the Italian Civic League because it was collaborating too much with Americans—under the guise of defending the Italian name it called in Americans to discuss how to deal with Italian criminals.[7] Professor Pecorni of the Italian Civic League, admitted that the league could do nothing unless aided by the police. He blamed the police for not deporting the 700 criminals listed by Petrosino and Vaccarezza.[8] The *Bollettino* and many Italian societies protested against the use of the word "Italian" by the Amer-

---

[1] *Bollettino della Sera*, September 6, 1908.
[2] *Ibid.*, January 12, 1909. [7] *Ibid.*, December 17, 19, 27, etc., 1910.
[3] *Ibid.*, March 13, 1909. [8] *Ibid.*, December 17, 1910.
[4] *Ibid.*, April 6, 1909.
[5] *Ibid.*, November 22, 1909.
[6] *Ibid.* February 21, 1910.

ican press in describing a criminal. A coupon was run daily in the *Bollettino:* "We protest in the use of the word 'Italian' in the American press on any news item detrimental to our countrymen," to be signed and returned to the editor;[1] and in June, 1911, Mr. Frugone carried the protest to over 1,000 Italian lodges and 50 newspapers to the convention of newspaper managers in Chicago.[2]

The postoffice inspectors were instructed to watch the mails for Black Hand letters.[3] Italians protested against the action of the police commissioner in abolishing the Italian detective squad. The *Bollettino* printed an article in English, by Mr. Palmieri, in which he said in substance:

"Commissioner Waldo has injured the Italian colony by abolishing the detective squad, which sent back such dangerous criminals as Enrico Alfono, chief of the *camorra* in Italy. The Italian criminals find a haven here, with weak policing and immigration officials easily evaded. Lieutenant Petrosino died to perform the great duty of listing dangerous Italian criminals. Lieutenant Vaccarezza now has worthily succeeded him. There are in New York 600,000 Italians, and there were only 60 men to police them. Now Commissioner Waldo abolishes these. The Italian colony is sad. The Italian merchants once responded to the call for funds and will do so again; but a proper squad of Italian detectives is necessary, men who are familiar with the dialects, customs, habits, and methods of the criminals who prey on the Italian people by blackmailing, extortion, kidnapping, and other outrages. Let

---

[1] *Bollettino della Sera,* April 5, 1911.
[2] *Ibid.,* June 15, 1911.   [3] *Ibid.,* April 3, 1911.

TYPES OF COMMUNITY INFLUENCE

us not throw away valuable information. Let us not waste time, but restore the detective squad."[1]

"The Italian government is right in saying that the blame for the increase of the Black Hand is on the United States. Nowhere in the world does this organization flourish as here in America. Lieutenant Vaccarezza is right. The dissolution of his secret police department has increased the outrages. As long as the Black Hand is stronger than the police the mass of ignorant Italians will put their faith in settlements with the malefactors rather than rely on New York police. . . . The police cannot obtain the confidence of the people until they (1) re-establish the Italian detective bureau; (2) scrutinize passports; (3) agree with the Italian government as to precautions to keep criminals from the United States."[2]

". . . We cannot command respect unless we abolish this criminality among us. We often have to say we are French, or Spanish, or Turks, to hold a job. Think what a disgrace these Black Handers have brought upon us! The Americans are too good to us, too tolerant, but their limit is reached. They are passing laws to hit us directly. Why not quit it? We should appreciate this country. In Italy we could hardly dare to do what we do here. This tumor is of course produced by the corrupt New York police, but let us do our part to cut it out."[3]

In 1909 the Black Hand activities had begun to decline, owing to the efforts of the Italian press and organizations, severer laws,

---

[1] *Bollettino della Sera*, July 14, 1911.
[2] *Ibid.*, September 2, 1911.   [3] *Ibid.*, September 18, 1911.

extraordinary earnestness in the police department following the murder of Petrosino, and, above all, the disposition of the Italians to follow the advice of their newspapers and communicate information to Commissioner Bingham, "if not openly, then secretly or anonymously." In 1909 there were 205 activities as against 311 in 1908; in 1910, 128 activities. When the Italian squad was dispersed in 1911 (owing, as the Italians claimed, to corruption and vanity in the police department), the activities were renewed; but they were met with more resistance, because the Italian people had learned to have some confidence in the police and obey their leaders. Consequently the Black Handers were compelled to use more bombs than ever before in order to intimidate their victims. In 1908 only 20 bombs were exploded, because their victims settled readily. In 1909 and 1910 less than 20 bombs were used, but in 1911, while there were only 95 activities, 79 bombs were used. Between August 5 and September 25, 1911 (shortly after the abolition of the Italian detective bureau), 25 bombs were used. In 1912 there were 85 activities and 81 bombs; in 1913, 100 activities and 173 bombs. In the first twenty days of January, 1913, there were 17 bombs recorded. Fol-

TYPES OF COMMUNITY INFLUENCE

lowing the persistent protests of Italians, the Italian detective squad was restored, in July, 1913. In 1914 there were only 32 combined activities and bombs, and in 1915 Italian crime became "normal" in New York.

There is one particularly instructive feature in this record of Italian crime: while there was bad feeling between the Italian public and the American public, neither side could accomplish a reform without the participation of the other. A reading of the whole record impresses us with the fact that the Italian public responded as readily as was reasonable to their leaders' efforts to induce them to resist their tormentors. In the first place, one of the characteristic heritages of the southern Italian is a strong repugnance to any sort of co-operation with the state. Further, the Black-Handers always made good their threats. There are cases recorded where a man is killed at the hour and minute appointed;[1] where a man who betrayed his gang in Palermo is followed through the Transvaal, Australia, South America, and killed after ten years in a Brooklyn dance hall;[2] where a man who has testified in court asks for twenty years of the peniten-

[1] *Bollettino dela Sera*, April 15, 1912.
[2] *Ibid.*, May 19, 1913.

tiary because that means twenty years of life.[1] There is no such certitude in the operations of the law or of the police. The Italians held with the police as soon as they felt any degree of safety in doing so, and after they had taken this attitude they persisted in it even when the police disbanded for a time the organization in which the Italians had most confidence—the Italian detective squad.

---

[1] *Bollettino della Sera*, January 29, 1910.

IX

RECONCILIATION OF THE HERITAGES

IMMIGRATION in the form it has taken in America differs from all previous movements of population. Populous countries have planted colonies, states have been conquered and occupied, slaves have been imported. But when a single country is peacefully invaded by millions of men from scores of other countries, when there are added to one American city as many Jews as there are Danes in Denmark, and to the same city more Italians than there are Italians in Rome, we have something new in history.

Naturally the mass and quality of this immigration is important to us because it cannot fail to have an influence on our whole system of life. Every country must have an organization for securing order and efficiency, not only to insure the happiness and prosperity of its citizens within its boundaries, but also to protect it from foreign attack. The various nationalities and

OLD WORLD TRAITS TRANSPLANTED

civilizations of the world are in a state of rivalry, and a low efficiency in any country may lead to its destruction, actual or economic. Our wish to assimilate the immigrants who remain here means that we want to make them a practical part of our organization.

There is an interesting parallel between the influence which a country wishes to exercise over its members and the influence of what geographers and naturalists call an "area of characterization." In the natural world an area of characterization is a geographical region sufficiently marked in its physical features to put a characteristic imprint on its flora and fauna. In the same way, the human inhabitants of a country develop a body of characteristic values. A country is an area of cultural characterization.

REQUIRED IN A DEMOCRACY

Among the distinguishing features of the American "area of characterization" is the principle that no man is to be used as a tool and thus placed in the category of purely material values, and we have consequently repudiated the ancient conception of the state, in which by a system of "ordering and forbidding" great things were achieved, indeed, but only by keeping the masses permanently in the category of things.

Our state system is based on the participation of every member and assumes in all the wish and ability to participate; for in the last analysis we mean by democracy participation by all, both practically and imaginatively, in the common life of the community. Our democracy is not working perfectly at present because not even the native born are participating completely. Our old order was a territorial one. The autonomy of the political and social groups was based on size and geographical isolation. So long as the group remained small and isolated, individuals were able to act responsibly, because the situations they dealt with came easily within their understanding and capacity. But the free communication provided by the locomotive, the post, the telegraph, the press, has dissolved distances. As a result men find themselves in a system of relationships, political and economic, over which, in spite of their traditional liberties of speech and action, they no longer have control. The conditions of their daily living are vitally affected by events occurring without their knowledge, thousands of miles away.

It is similarly impossible for average

citizens to grasp all the elements of the political issues on which they give decisions. The economic nexus holds them in an inevitable interdependence; they are politically disfranchised while retaining the ceremony of a vote. No longer able to act intelligently or responsibly, they act upon vagrant impulses. They are directed by suggestion and advertising. This is the meaning of social unrest. It is the sign of a baffled wish to participate. It represents energy, and the problem is to use it constructively. While we are forming a new definition of the situation, we are subject to emotional states and random movements.

The founders of America defined the future state as a democracy characterized by the largest possible amount of individual freedom, but this ideal has not been fully realized. At best we can say that we are in the process of giving this country the cultural characterization of such a democracy.

While we have on our hands this problem we are importing large numbers of aliens, representing various types, in the main below our cultural level. Some of them bring a greater and more violent unrest than we know here: psychoses acquired under conditions where violence was the only means of political participation. Others belong

RECONCILIATION OF THE HERITAGES

to the nationalistic, opportunistic, or in fewer numbers to the radical elements, who not only do not regard this country as their country, but do not regard it as a country at all—do not recognize that we have a characteristic body of values and the right to preserve these values.

The immigrant usually brings a value which is very important to us—labor—and it would be possible to regard him in a narrowly practical way as a merely material value, just as the negro in slavery and Chinese labor in earlier days were regarded as material values, and as the Germans regarded the 600,000 laborers from Austria and Russia who crossed their borders annually and returned to their homes at the end of the harvest season. But we know from our experience with slavery and from the German experiences with the *Sachsengänger*, that this attitude has a bad effect both on the aliens and on the culture of the group which receives and uses them as mere things. If visitors are disorderly, unsanitary, or ignorant, the group which incorporates them, even temporarily, will not escape the bad effects of this.

Every country has a certain amount of culturally undeveloped material. We have it, for instance, in the Negroes and Indians, the Southern mountaineers, the Mexicans and Spanish-Americans, and the slums. There is a limit, however, to the amount of material of this kind that a country can incorporate without losing the character of its culture. For example, the "three R's" represent our minimum of cultural equipment, and we are able to transmit this much to practically everybody. With this equipment the individual is able to penetrate any sphere of life; without it, he cannot move upward at all. But if we should receive, say, a million Congo blacks and a million Chinese coolies annually, and if they should propagate faster than the white Americans, it is certain that our educational system would break down; we could not impart even the "three R's." We should then be in a state of chaos unless we abandoned the idea of democracy and secured efficiency by reverting to the "ordering and forbidding" type of state.

This is the general significance of immigration to our problem of democracy. We must make the immigrants a working part in our system of life, ideal and political, as well as economic, or lose the character of our culture. Self-preservation makes this necessary; the fact that they bring valuable additions to our culture makes it desirable.

RECONCILIATION OF THE HERITAGES

Now we can assimilate the immigrants only if their attitudes and values, their ideas on the conduct of life, are brought into harmony with our own. They cannot be intelligent citizens unless they "get the hang" of American ways of thinking as well as of doing. How fast and how well this is accomplished depends (1) on the degree of similarity between their attitudes and values and our own, giving them a certain preadaptation to our scheme of life and an ability to aid in their own Americanization; and (2) on how we treat them—our attitude toward their heritages. These are, roughly, the elements in our problem of assimilation.

SIMILARITY OF HERITAGES

It is one of the ordinary experiences of social intercourse that words and things do not have the same meanings with different people, in different periods of time, in different parts of a country—that is, in general, in different contexts. The same "thing" has a different meaning for the naïve person and the sophisticated person, for the child and the philosopher. The new experience derives its significance from the character and interpretation of previous experiences. To the peasant a comet, a plague, an epileptic person, may mean, respectively, a divine portent, a visitation of God, a possession by the devil; to the scientist they mean something quite different. The word slavery had a connotation in the ancient world very different from the one it bears to-day. It has a different significance to-day in the Southern and Northern states. "Socialism" has a very different significance to the immigrant from the Russian pale living on the "East Side" of New York City, to the citizen on Riverside Drive, and to the native American in the hills of Georgia.

The meaning any word has for an individual depends on his past experience, not only with the thing the word means, but with many other things associated with it in his mind. For example, the concept evoked in his mind by the word "food" is determined not only by the kinds of food he has eaten, but also by the normal state of his appetite and digestion, the ease or difficulty with which he secures his daily ration, whether he grows, hunts, or buys it, whether or not he prepares it, whether he has ever been near starvation, and so forth. No two people have exactly the same experience by which to define the same word, and sometimes the resulting difference in meaning is immeasurably great. This is

RECONCILIATION OF THE HERITAGES

the meaning of the saying of the logicians that persons who attach different meanings to the same words and the same things are in different "universes of discourse,"—that is, do not talk in the same world.

All the meanings of past experience retained in the memory of the individual form what is called by psychologists the "apperception mass." It is the body of memories with which every new item of experience comes in contact, to which it is related, and in connection with which it gets its meaning. The difference in the interpretation of words is merely an example of the fact that persons whose apperception masses are radically different give a different interpretation to all experience. The ecclesiastic, the artist; the mystic, the scientist; the Philistine, the Bohemian—are examples of classes not always mutually intelligible. Similarly, different races and nationalities, as wholes, represent different apperception masses and consequently different universes of discourse, and are not mutually intelligible. Even our forefathers are with difficulty intelligible to us, though always more intelligible than the eastern European immigrant, because of the continuity of our tradition.

The set of attitudes and values, which we call the immigrant's heritage, are the expression in ideas and action of his apperception mass. "Heritages" differ because the races and nationalities concerned have developed different apperception masses; and they have developed different apperception masses because, owing to historical circumstances, they have defined the situation in different ways. (See Chapter II.)

Certain prominent personalities, schools of thought, bodies of doctrine, historical events, have helped to define the situation and determine the attitudes and values of our various immigrant groups in characteristic ways in their home countries. To the Sicilian, for example, marital infidelity means conventionally the stiletto; to the American, the divorce court. These differences sometimes go so far that it is impossible for those concerned to talk to one another. The Western World, for example, appreciates learning, and we have signalized this in our schools. The Jews also show this appreciation (documents 1-3), and even the Polish peasant, in document 4, p. 7, appreciates learning, though not for his class. But in document 5, p. 8, we have a complete repudiation of learning; the situation is here defined in terms of piety, somewhat as we defined it before Darwin. We can imagine that if the Oriental who

RECONCILIATION OF THE HERITAGES

signs this document met a Western entomologist at dinner, and, interrogating him as to his interests, found that he spent his life in examining potato bugs, moving them from one temperature to another, from one degree of humidity to another, from one altitude to another, to see if their spots changed, and if they changed whether the change remained permanent under all conditions, or whether new generations reverted to the previous type if removed to the old conditions—in other words, that he was trying to create a new species—the Oriental would conclude that his interlocutor was not only impious, but insane.

If the immigrant possesses already an apperception mass corresponding in some degree to our own, his participation in our life will, of course, follow more easily. While we have given in Chapter I and elsewhere examples of heritages strange to us, the body of material presented shows that he does not differ from us profoundly. We can best appreciate the immigrants' mental kinship with ourselves negatively, by comparing them with what they are not. If the immigrants practiced and defended cannibalism and incest; if they burned their widows and killed their parents and broke the necks of their wayward daughters, customarily; if (as in a North African Arab tribe) a girl were not eligible for marriage until she had given her older brother a child born out of wedlock, to be reared as a slave; if immigrant families limited their children by law to one boy and one girl, killing the others (as in the Ellice Archipelago); or (as in the Solomon Islands) if they killed all, or nearly all, their children and bought others from their neighbors, as our farmers sell young calves to butchers and buy yearlings; if immigrant army recruits declined target practice because the bullet would go straight anyway if Allah willed it —then the problem of assimilation would be immensely complicated.

In comparison with these examples immigrant heritages usually differ but slightly from ours, probably not more than ours differ from those of our more conservative grandfathers. Slavery, dueling, burning of witches, contempt of soil analysis, condemnation of the view that plants and animals have been developed slowly, not suddenly created, are comparatively recent American values and attitudes.

PSYCHOLOGY OF ASSIMILATION

It is evidently necessary that the people who compose a community and participate

RECONCILIATION OF THE HERITAGES

in common enterprises shall have a body of common memories sufficient to enable them to understand one another. This is particularly true in a democracy, where it is intended that the public institution should be responsive to public opinion. There can be no public opinion unless the persons who compose the public are able to live and think in the same world. The process of assimilation involves the development in the immigrant and the native of similar apperception masses. To this end it is desirable that the immigrants should not only speak the language of the country, but also know something of the history of the people among whom they have chosen to dwell. For the same reason it is important that native Americans should know the history and social life of the countries from which the immigrants come.

It is important also that every individual should share as fully as possible a fund of knowledge, experience, sentiments, and ideals common to the whole community, and himself contribute to that fund. It is for this reason that we maintain and seek to maintain freedom of speech and free schools. The function of literature, including poetry, romance, and the newspaper, is to enable all to share vicariously the inner life of each.

The function of science is to gather up, classify, digest, and preserve, in a form in which they may be available to the community as a whole, the ideas, inventions, and technical experience of the individuals composing it. Not merely the possession of a common language, but the widest extension of the opportunities for education, is a condition of Americanization.

For the immigrant to achieve an apperception mass in common with the American community, involves the development of new attitudes on his part, and his old experiences are the only possible foundation for the new structure. If a person becomes interested in anything whatever, it is because there is already in him something to which it can appeal. Visitors to the Dresden Gallery are all affected by the Sistine Madonna in approximately the same way because they bring to it a similar body of socially created appreciations—the sanctity of motherhood, the sufferings of our Lord, the adoration of Mary, the æsthetic appreciation of female beauty, and so forth. No amount of explanation or persuasion would arouse the same feeling in an African black man. Livingstone relates that an African mother brought to him through the dust and heat a child pitiably misshapen

RECONCILIATION OF THE HERITAGES

through rupture. Two native men uncovered the basket and were moved, not to pity, but to laughter. These Africans evidently would not appreciate the painting of a Madonna because they have not developed our tenderness toward children, because white men and women impress them somewhat as cadavers and albinos impress us,[1] because they have not our tradition of chivalry and know nothing of the sufferings of our Lord.

A certain identity of experiences and memories between immigrants and Americans is of main importance for assimilation, because, in the process of learning, a new fact has a meaning and makes an appeal only if it is identified with some previous experience, something that is already known and felt. Thus, when we appealed to the patriotism of our immigrants during the war, we found a ready response, because they knew what patriotism is. The Bohemians in a Cleveland parade carried a banner with the inscription: "We are Americans through and through by the spirit of our nation," and interpreted this by another banner: "Americans, do not be discouraged. We have been fighting these tyrants for three

---

[1] Livingston states that after a long residence among black men, white men reminded him of celery and white mice.

hundred years." And in the following letter a Slovenian boy participates in American life on the basis of old-country attitudes:

158. DEAR BROTHER: . . . I received the civil clothes sent me from Cleveland, and at the same time a thought occurred to me which has never left me—that I should feel ashamed to leave the army and go back to civil life. I do, indeed, love my young healthy life, I long to be free again, going on my own ways, without hearing the command of another, but, alas! Am I justified in thinking of my own liberty and happy life when the moment is here that calls on every young man to bring liberty to others? Away, you selfish thoughts! On into the battle! I am a Slovene myself, and my fathers and grandfathers never had any opportunity to fight for liberty. Indeed, they fought for hundreds of years under the command of Hapsburgs to continue slavery and tyranny. . . . Goodbye, my beloved young life, I shall not return to my happy home until the day has come when I can proudly see the liberated Jugoslavia in a liberated world. Then I shall return, conscious that I have done my bit. If I shall perish— I am afraid I shall let it be so. The only thing I am sorry about is that I don't possess hundreds of lives, giving them all for liberty.

Dear brother, the suit of clothes you sent me, I sold to-day for thirty dollars, to a man who thinks less than I do.[1]

This process of making warm and personal something that would otherwise remain cold,

---

[1] Letter from a Slovene, eligible to release from military service on the declaration of war with Austria-Hungary (unpublished).

RECONCILIATION OF THE HERITAGES

extraneous, irrelevant, and foreign, by identifying it with a body of sentiments that is already intimate and warm, is illustrated in more detail by the case of the Italian boy whose first disillusionment in America is referred to in document 34, p. 46.

159. I go about the streets to find the great history, to feel the great emotion for all that is noble in America. I do not see how the people can think to compare the American city with the beauty of Rome, or Venice, or Naples. Even in big city like New York I do not find much monuments to the great deeds, to the great heroes, and the great artists. I was deeply surprised not to find the fountains. I do not find the great art to compare with the art of Italy. . . . But one day I see very, very big building. My mind is struck. With all I have seen in Italy, in Rome, in Venice, in Genoa, in Milano, in Florence, in Naples—I have never seen anything like that! I say, "There is the thing American. It is a giant!"

When I went to night school, I had a good impression to me. The teacher treat every one just the same. The Jew just the same the Chinaman, and the Chinaman just the same the Italian. This was a wonderful impression. When I saw the principal of the school, he look to me like Italian nobleman, the way he hold his eyeglasses. I went to this school just because I like the principal. He give it to me welcome like I was an American. I learn little English, and about the American government, and how the people can make change and progress by legislation without the force of revolution, and I like very much this idea. The teacher told me why not to become an American? . . .

I have good impression to become an American. But I do not become American because I think always of the grandeur of the Italy civilization of the past! . . . [Then I fall in love and] . . . I do not wish at all to go back to Italy. I think to take a wife. A man must situate himself. I think about many things, but I think especially about the future. Everything begin to look different. I have not think much about the future before, I have think about the past. Maybe I have a son, it is the future that is for him. America is to be his country. What is the past? It is gone. The future is to come, and I think that when my son shall live I wish it to be some great time. For the future I cannot see so much Italy as America. The grandeur of the Italian cities, Venice, Genoa, Florence, Naples, held Italy in the world's highest place for nearly one thousand years. But the world continue. It go on. Now comes the great day for America, the great financial, the great mercantile power, and I think with that the great science, the great art, the great letters. Why to live always in the memory of past grandeur? They were only men. I am a man, and my son will be a man. Why not live to be somebody ourselves, in a nation more great than any nation before, and my son perhaps the greatest of any great man?

And I see that big work to build the future. I see the necessity to learn the English, to become the citizen, to take part in the political life, to work to create the better understanding between the races that they come to love each another, to work for better conditions in industry, for health and safety and prosperity, to work for the progress in science,

RECONCILIATION OF THE HERITAGES

for the better government, and for the higher morality —and it become more pleasure to work than to take the leisure. Suddenly it looks to me like that is the American, that is what the American is always to do, always to work for the achievement. It come to me, like I am born—I am American![1]

In this case a new experience makes an appeal because it is identified with a wish. The Italian boy specifies that he wishes a wife, child, home, but more generally he wishes success, and he identifies this with the American principle of "achievement."

Most frequently the appreciation of America begins in connection with a wish or a general ideal which was not attainable in the old country, but is attainable here. In document 160 the writer realizes that America is a country where everybody can get an education:

160. The strongest reason for my preference of America to other countries is perhaps my appreciation of education and its opportunities. This is probably explained by my previous experience as a worker in the educational field in the old country— Russia. After graduating from a teachers' college at Petrograd I served as director of a pedegogical class in Esthonia during three years, from 1897 to 1900. As my views upon education conflicted with those of higher "Russianizing" authorities, I chose to leave the teaching field and entered a university to study law and political economy.

[1] Reference same as in document 10, p. 11.

OLD WORLD TRAITS TRANSPLANTED

The children in the public schools in Esthonia had to study everything except religion in Russian. They had to study Russian (Slavic) history instead of that of their own country and people. A good deal of time was given to lessons in religion and the singing of church hymns. But the saddest thing of all was that the children going through public school learned nothing or very little of the rudiments of the sciences. For adults there were no facilities for learning. The people forming private classes were pursued and in many instances arrested and fined.

Later I went to Germany and other West European countries and found that though public schools there gave some knowledge to the children, their individuality was suppressed by a system of discipline and punishment, and by being forced to learn rather by memorizing than by understanding, and rather by compulsion than by their own love for learning.

America is not only a "melting pot" for races but also a testing ground or laboratory for ideas, original American as well as imported European. Here they are compared in practical application, through which the degrees of their vitality can be determined. This makes America an interesting country in which to learn—to learn through observation and experience and through amply provided educational institutions and facilities, from the evening schools to the great universities, from various expositions to libraries. I know no other country where opportunities for learning by everybody are so rich as here.

The immigrants arriving on American shores soon find out that they need to learn, and first of all to learn the American methods of their prospective trades if they are going to make good in the New World. Formerly many of them were discouraged

RECONCILIATION OF THE HERITAGES

by not knowing or not finding opportunities for learning here. But nowadays they are, as it were, discovering these opportunities. For this reason I believe that the immigrants in the future will come here not only for higher earnings, but also for the sake of learning, desiring industrial training as well as general education.

The appreciation of America as a wonderful country in which to learn dawned upon me after years of wanderings, study, and observation here and in Europe, and as a result of comparing this country with the European countries, within the limitations of my personal experience.

My field study and observations led me to the conclusion that in the public school programs and methods in America and in Eueopean countries there is a still more pronounced difference than in the field of higher education. In Europe the main emphasis is laid upon form, authority, obedience, discipline, while in the American public schools freedom of action, imagination, initiative, and self-reliance are pursued as the main goal in the training of youth. The European public school suppresses individuality, while the American builds it up, or at least leaves it untrammeled.[1]

The identification of immigrant groups with America takes place on the psychological basis shown in the preceding documents. Points of contact are found in the respective apperception masses, where interests merge, and as a result of the increased community of interests other contacts are

[1] *Autobiography of an Intellectual Esthonian* (manuscript).

made progressively. Assimilation may be compared with skin grafting, where the new tissue is not applied to the whole surface, but spots are grafted, and from these the connecting tissues ramify.

TOLERANCE VS. SUPPRESSION

The apperception mass of the immigrant, expressed in the attitudes and values he brings with him from his old life, is the material from which he must build his Americanism. It is also the material we must work with, if we would aid this process. Our tools may be in part American customs and institutions, but the substance we seek to mold into new forms is the product of other centuries in other lands. In education it is valuable to let the child, as far as possible, make his own discoveries and follow his own interests. He should have the opportunity of seeking new experiences which have a meaning for him when connected with his old experiences. A wise policy of assimilation, like a wise educational policy, does not seek to destroy the attitudes and memories that are there, but to build on them.

There is a current opinion in America, of the "ordering and forbidding" type,

RECONCILIATION OF THE HERITAGES

demanding from the immigrant a quick and complete Americanization through the suppression and repudiation of all the signs that distinguish him from us.[1] Those who have this view wish the repudiation to be what the church fathers demanded of a confession of sin—"sudden, complete, and bitter."

It is notable that this destruction of memories is the plan of both those who demand a quick and complete Americanization and those who demand a quick and complete social revolution — the extreme Americanists and the extreme radicals. In the anarchist-communist manifesto (document 76, p. 100) we read: "We must mercilessly destroy. . . . We must take care that everything is wiped out from the earth that is a reminder." Both positions imply that there is nothing of value for the future in the whole of past experience; whereas we have shown, in speaking of the psychology of assimilation (particularly in the case of the Italian boy) that "reminders" are precisely what the individual uses in

---

[1] "Broadly speaking, we mean [by Americanization] an appreciation of the institutions of this country, absolute forgetfulness of all obligations or connections with other countries because of descent or birth."—Superintendent of the New York Public Schools, *N. Y. Evening Post*, August 9, 1918. Quoted by I. B. Berkson, *Americanization*, chapter ii (in press).

making constructive changes in his life; and in the chapter on demoralization we pointed out that the absence of reminders, forgetfulness of the standards of the community, failure to live in the light of the past, reduce a man to the basis of the instincts, with which humanity first began. How badly the mere instincts work is exemplified in document 56, p. 72.

There is an element of pure prejudice in this theory of Americanization. It appears as intolerance of the more obvious signs of unlikeness. Where color exists, it is the mark specially singled out by prejudice, but since our immigrants are mainly not colored, language becomes the most concrete sign of unlikeness and the foremost object of animosity. It is certainly true that a man cannot participate fully in our life without our language, and that its acquisition is rightly considered a sign and rough index of Americanization. But the American who does not know the details of the immigrant's life and problems cannot imagine how useful his language is here in the first stages. Take an actual case. The Danes are distinguished farmers, but here the soil, the demand, are unfamiliar and they have trouble. The American government could help them, but they do not know this. Even if they did

RECONCILIATION OF THE HERITAGES

they could not inquire in English; they would not know whether to address the President or the Senate; and they would not address either because they would not know with what honorific form to begin the letter. A certain Danish editor invites communications on specific plans and troubles of this kind. In each case (and the number is relatively large) he sends with his reply a letter in English, addressed to the Department of Agriculture, asking for the proper bulletin. The Dane is to copy the letter and send it. This much he will do, and the bulletin somehow gets read. Here again is the typical process of assimilation—the identification of the immigrant's success with America; here, too, is an example of what we mean when we say that the immigrants must assist in their own Americanization. Prejudice against language thus means bringing into disrepute one of the tools most useful in assimilation.

Again, the Yiddish language is a very useful heritage to the Jew, and this is a clear case of utility, without any obstinacy or sentimentality. The Jews associate their nationalism with Hebrew, the language of the Jews and the one that their national idealists are seeking to restore. Yiddish is a German dialect, with a mixture of

Hebrew, Polish, and so forth, developed originally by the Jews as a business expedient. It is an uncouth speech, with very limited power of literary expression, and nothing with which a man would seek to identify himself. The Jews in America drop it as soon as possible, and it is really difficult to induce a Jew to speak a few words of it in order to show you what it is like. And yet the Jewish community in New York City pays annually more than $2,000,000 for Yiddish newspapers. These newspapers and other Jewish institutions do thousands of particular and very personal services for Jews which American institutions could not do and which no one could undertake without the use of Yiddish. Language is a tool which its possessor cannot afford to throw away until he has another.

Quite aside from the question of utility, immigrants, especially the older ones, cherish the memories of their former home, and wish to preserve some signs identifying them with their past. This is a natural sentiment. It is frankly expressed in the following documents from groups which have no nationalistic psychoses and represent the settler type:

161. In a news item in *Skandinaven*, the editor of the *Lutheran Herald* . . . is quoted as saying . . . with reference to the Norwegian flag, that in this

RECONCILIATION OF THE HERITAGES

country it did not belong anywhere outside of the dictionary and the Norwegian legation headquarters in Washington. . . .

No flag except the American has a place as a national emblem in the heart of any good citizen. But how is it that we have here the flags of all the nations of the earth? During the war, when the country surely required the loyalty of every citizen as never before, there were foreign flags around us wherever we went. The English flag, the French, the Belgian, the Italian—they were to be seen everywhere. They were used at patriotic and other meetings; people displayed buttons with these flags on them, and it was very common to see automobiles decorated in this way. . . . No one feared enemy purposes from the nations these flags represent. The same can with even greater truth be said about Norway. In the first place, Norway's relatively small military strength makes this thought untenable. Also that country's pronounced peace policy puts the idea out of the question; also its later historical traditions. Norway is one of the few nations which have managed a decisive national crisis without resorting to war. . . .

When the Norwegian flag is seen here the object of its display is to celebrate the intellectual and spiritual values which Norway has achieved. In the same way we honor the important intellectual and spiritual revivals and achievements in all nations. If this had not been permitted, the Rev. Mr. Lee or any other American would not have a bible to teach from.

But when people of Norwegian extraction in this country hold fast to their Norwegian cultural heritages, then it is because a people who have lived together in the same country through centuries must have given birth to spiritual and intellectual values which are peculiar to such a people. . . .[1]

162. . . . The small Danish society of which I am the secretary has a membership of only twenty-eight, and while in regard to American ideas these men are as loyal as if they were born Americans—and this is the case with the immigrated Danes as a general rule—yet I cannot say that our society does much to Americanize its members. At their meetings they speak their mother tongue and sing their old country songs, looking upon one another almost as members of the same family, and their object is to help each other in case of necessity, especially, of course, in case of sickness. . . .

When the different Liberty loans were floated I found all of us personally deeply interested and buying to our capacity, and at my initiative our little society bought $500 worth of bonds, practically using all the cash money we had in the treasury; I, personally, managed out of my $35 per week job to buy bonds to the value of $600.[2]

Any fine fund of personal feeling is valuable in identifying the present with the past in the life of the immigrant, but aside from this these sentimental memories should command respect, and we should let them remain unmolested in the region of personal life. We should know by this time that under tolerance, peculiar group values—such as language and religion—are only means to

---
[1] Simon Johnson, *Skandinaven*, (Chicago) December 1, 1919.
[2] Communication from Mr. Fred Thomsen.

RECONCILIATION OF THE HERITAGES

a fuller life; under oppression, they become objects of life.

IMMIGRANT ORGANIZATIONS VALUABLE

Following the instinctive prejudice against strangeness, many Americans distrust immigrant organizations, as such, and consider them obstacles to assimilation. On the contrary, we have emphasized throughout this study the importance of these organizations. Indeed, the amount of immigration which we can continue to tolerate or encourage depends on their character.

Organizations, beginning in the family and community, are the means by which men regulate their lives. The healthy life of a society always depends more on the spontaneous organization of its members than on formal legal and political regulations. It is only in an organized group—in the home, the neighborhood, the trade union, the coöperative society—where he is a power and an influence, in some region where he has status and represents something, that man can maintain a stable personality. There is only one kind of neighborhood having no representative citizen—the slum; a world where men cease to be persons because they represent nothing. In the slum men live in an enforced intimacy, but they do not communicate. They suspect one another and keep away from one another. They cannot maintain a personality because there are no standards; if standards of decency, morality, and sanitation exist they are imposed from without. A slum is a place, composed at first of the poor, which has become inevitably a refuge for criminals and disorderly persons—a place of missions and lost souls.

If the face-to-face organization which made the immigrant moral at home is suddenly dissolved in this country, we have the general situation presented in the documents on demoralization in Chapter IV. We saw there that men, removed from the restraining influence of an organized community, tend to follow their immediate impulses and behave in monstrous ways. Ethnologists have shown that when the uncivilized races come into contact with the products of our civilization they appropriate the vices and ornaments, the whisky and beads, and leave the more substantial values. The same tendency appears among immigrants, especially the children. The term "Americanization" is not used popularly among the immigrants as we use it. They call a badly demoralized boy "completely

RECONCILIATION OF THE HERITAGES

Americanized." Thomas and Znaniecki have presented a large mass of materials on the demoralization of the Poles in America, and they conclude that the "wild" behavior found in this group is to be explained by the fact that "the individual does not feel himself backed in his dealings with the outside world by any strong social group of his own, and is not conscious of being a member of a steadily organized society. . . . This does not, of course, apply to the relatively intelligent and sociably responsible immigrants who take an active part in the construction of Polish institutions and have an economic ideal which gives stability to their lives. [It characterizes] that floating unorganized mass of the intellectually backward immigrant population which constitutes among the Poles from one-fourth to one-third of the total number."[1]

The organization of the immigrant community is necessary as a regulative measure. Any type of organization which succeeds in regulating the lives of its members is beneficial. If you can induce a man to belong to something, to co-operate with any group whatever, where something is expected of him, where he has responsibility, dignity, recognition, economic security, you have

[1] Thomas and Znaniecki, *The Polish Peasant*, vol. v (in press).

at least regulated his life. From this standpoint even the nationalistic societies do more to promote assimilation than to retard it. There is no doubt, for example, that the nationalistic newspapers do not want their readers to become Americanized, but they make them more intelligent, more prepared to be Americans, simply by printing the news of what is going on in America, and this they have to do in order to circulate at all. The nationalistic organizations are the means by which certain men make their living and get their distinction; they assist the home countries materially in their struggle for freedom, they stimulate some older people to return to Europe, but they have almost no effect in keeping the immigrant, especially the young generation, estranged from American life:

163. In spite of the continual use of patriotic Polish slogans by all local groups, Poland is for the great majority of the Poles mainly the object of an almost purely æsthetic interest, whose motive power is very small as compared with the many and complex practical interests connected with the immediate social environment. . . . Even before the great war Polish patriotism was not a vital matter with the great mass of American Poles.[1]

164. It is a very painful admission, but we cannot fail to recognize that our language has suffered and

---
[1] Thomas and Znaniecki, *The Polish Peasant*, vol. v (in press).

RECONCILIATION OF THE HERITAGES

is suffering constant and lamentable losses. . . . Children born in this country, and consequently American citizens by birth, have produced a third generation of a totally different mentality from the first. . . . [It is true that] some intelligent individuals who had in childhood no opportunity to secure a French education, and little opportunity to speak French, have applied themselves to the study of the French language, forcing themselves to practice it and to show themselves truly patriotic. But these are people of heart and character who appreciate all that is noble in the race from which they are issued and who were unwilling to be simply Americans.[1]

The propaganda of hate carried on notably by the Italian press, and described by an Italian in the note below,[2] is also partly

---

[1] J. G. Le Boutillier, *Preface* to Alexandre Belise, *Histoire de la Presse Franco-Américaine*.

[2] " I have seen a large number of articles from Italian newspapers, written by Italian professional men concerning America, which if translated and published, would open the eyes even of the blind. America is described in these articles as a ruthless, rapacious, hypocritical, puritanical country. American men are superficial weak, ridiculous; American women are vain and prefer to have a good time rather than to be good wives and mothers; churches in America are places of business; social and philanthropic work is established to furnish fat salaries to innumerable officeholders; the political life is incurably corrupt; and everything else is termed "Americanate," meaning the quintessence of foolishness. A sensational divorce case, a scandal at the City Hall, Dowie or Billy Sunday, anything and everything is used as a pretext for a long philippic against America. I have seen Italian newspapers with laudatory articles on America written in English, which no Italian would read, and with an article in Italian in the same issue, that the American would not understand, painting America in the blackest colors."—E. C. Sartorio, *Social and Religious Life of the Italians in America*, p. 50.

nationalistic in its aim. While not among the dependent nationalities, Italy has been particularly active in preserving the allegiance of her emigrated subjects, and her leaders have acted, so to speak, as representatives of a country that is trying to control a colony. They have used hate, because enmity is the motive through which men can be aroused and controlled most easily. But here also, if we recognize the fact that editors are playing on attitudes that are already there, not creating them, the propaganda has slight importance. Italians who returned to Sicily after the war, are now returning to America. They found that it was "too small" over there. They had entered their own country as immigrants, and suffered again the disillusionment of the immigrant. The fault to be found with the nationalistic organizations is not that they do the damage they imagine they are doing, but that they fail to do the constructive work of which, as organizations, they are capable; that they do not help their people to identify their success with America, in such ways as we have exemplified above in the case of the Danes and Jews.

We have not developed American institutions adapted to meeting the first needs of

RECONCILIATION OF THE HERITAGES

the immigrant and preserving in him the good qualities which he brings. Usually he reaches our institutions only after he has become a failure. The immigrant organizations are doing very positive services for their members by maintaining their sense of social responsibility, of responsibility to some type of community. We have seen examples of it in this chapter and in the chapter on "Types of Community Influence." But more than this, our experience has shown that, while it is possible for an individual immigrant, especially if he represents a relatively cultured type, to identify himself directly with American society without an intermediate connection with a group of his own nationality, in the main the immigrants are becoming Americanized *en masse*, by whole blocks, precisely through their own organizations. The organization as a whole is influenced, modified, Americanized by its efforts to adjust itself to American conditions. This happened, for example, when the immigrant athletic organizations recently joined the American Amateur Athletic Association; for this alliance implies acceptance by the immigrant of all the American athletic standards. Similarly, the immigrant who penetrates American society as a member of an immigrant group forms a bond between this group and American society. The Letts in New York City felt pride in a young violinist who had played at their weekly entertainments. For his further development the Lettish organization sent him to the American teacher, Damrosch. The individual thus forms a link between the immigrant society and American society. He will transmit the influence of his American contacts to the immigrant organization.

We illustrated in Chapter II the important fact that the immigrant is not a highly individualized person. He has been accustomed to live in a small, intimate, face-to-face group, and his conduct has been determined by this group. Naturally he needs the assistance of such a group for a time in America, and naturally this group is composed of his own people. This general condition explains the perfect success of our government in its appeal to the immigrant population for subscriptions to the Liberty loans. The appeal was not made to the immigrant individually, but through his organizations.

The type of organization which the immigrants bring with them from home (see Chapter II) is one which we ought to appreciate. It represents the individual's respon-

RECONCILIATION OF THE HERITAGES

sibility to society which we have in a measure lost, and are consciously attempting to restore by the reorganization of the local community. It is a type of organization which can be made the basis of all kinds of co-operative enterprise—the basis, in fact, on which the local community will again function. Co-operation is an attitude already present in immigrant consciousness, and co-operative economic enterprises are arising spontaneously among immigrant groups—the Finns, the Italians, the Poles, and others. This is especially true since younger men of immigrant parentage, who have gone through our schools, who are American in feeling, are beginning to assume the leadership in the immigrant groups and to employ constructively the traditional spirit of co-operation.

If we wish to help the immigrant to get a grip on American life, to understand its conditions, and find his own rôle in it, we must seize on everything in his old life which will serve either to interpret the new or to hold him steady while he is getting adjusted. The language through which his compatriots can give him their garnered experience, the "societies" which make him feel "at home," the symbols of his home land, reminding him of the moral standards under which he grew up. Common courtesy and kindness exact tolerance for these things, and common sense indicates that they are the foundation of the readjustment we seek.

PERPETUATION OF GROUPS IMPOSSIBLE

The evident value of these immigrant organizations during the period of adjustment raises another question. Is he to remain permanently in one of these racial organizations, and are they to continue as centers of cultures diverse from and competing with that of America? This question touches a larger aspect of the heritages, relating to the ideal character of our national life—whether we shall strive for a uniform or a diversified type of culture and whether the perpetuation of immigrant traits and organizations will accomplish this diversity.

We have recognized the importance of a resemblance between the members of a community which will enable them to understand and influence one another. In a peasant community, as in a herd or flock, great unanimity in following tested habits is sufficient, without any great intelligence, to enable all to live. But as communities progress the members behave more and more independently, use more freedom.

RECONCILIATION OF THE HERITAGES

Communities progress, indeed, because certain of their members insist on using more freedom.

The civilization we have is the product of an association of individuals who are widely unlike, and with the progress of civilization the divergence in individual human types has been and must continue to be constantly multiplied. Our progress in the arts and sciences and in the creation of values in general has been dependent on specialists whose distinctive worth was precisely their divergence from other individuals. It is even evident that we have been able to use productively persons who in a savage or peasant society would have been classed as insane—who were, perhaps, insane. Until recently our conception of insanity has been to some extent determined by the standards of the "primary group," which demands uniformity in its members. Many persons who had the qualities of genius have simply passed as queer in their local communities. Julius Robert Mayer, the discoverer of the law of the conservation of energy, was twice confined in insane asylums by the people of the provincial town of Heilbronn. Where else did a man belong who went about arguing that "heat was a mode of motion," that if a house burned down it was not destroyed? Indeed, he considered himself insane in his home town, and when the physicist Düring wished to visit him he declined to receive him in Heilbronn, but arranged to meet him in the neighboring village of Wildbad. "Since everybody here," he wrote, "considers me a fool, everybody considers himself justified in exercising a spiritual guardianship over me." [1] We have already pointed out that the Mohammedan could regard a modern scientist as insane. However, we have had so many profitable returns from the queer behavior of such men as Mayer, Darwin, and Langley (whose experiments with the flying machine were regarded by many as insane), that we have changed our definition of insanity and regard any man as sane the sum of whose activities is valuable to the community.[2]

The value of the principle of diversity has already been fully recognized in the scientific world and in the specialized occupations. Efficiency in these fields is based on far-going individualization of function. The astronomer or the physiological chemist

---

[1] The details are in Ostwald's *Grosse Männer*.
[2] "When we begin to acknowledge *many standards of normality* we take away the sting of a stigma."—Adolf Meyer, *Suggestions of Modern Science Concerning Education*, p. 143.

RECONCILIATION OF THE HERITAGES

awaits the result of the physicist or the chemist as condition of further steps in his own investigation. The more diversified the personalities, the more particularized the products of these personalities, the greater the likelihood that we shall find among them the elements for the realization of our own plans, the construction of our own values.

In the civilization having the highest efficiency all are not in the same "universe of discourse," but there tend to be smaller groups or circles who understand one another and co-operate. Although they are not understood by everybody, their products become useful to everybody. The physicists, for example, represent such a circle. The physicist demonstrates a law which the public cannot understand; but the engineer understands it and applies it in the invention of machines which become of general use.

Now representatives of the different immigrant groups claim a similar social value —that, on account of their racial peculiarities and the fact that they have developed by their past experiences different apperception masses, they are predisposed to individualized functions as groups, and that by permanently organizing along the lines of their aptitudes they will not only express their peculiar genius, but contribute unique values to America:

165. Democracy rejected the proposal of the superman who should rise through sacrifice of the many. It insists that the full development of each individual is not only a right, but a duty to society; and that our best hope for civilization lies not in uniformity, but in wide differentiation.

The movements of the last century have proved that whole peoples have individuality no less marked than that of the single person; that the individuality of a people is irrepressible and that the misnamed internationalism which seeks the obliteration of nationalities or peoples is unattainable. The new nationalism proclaims that each race or people, like each individual, has a right and duty to develop, and that only through such differentiated development will high civilization be attained. Not until these principles of nationalism, like those of democracy, are generally accepted, will liberty be fully attained, and minorities be secure in their rights.[1]

166. In contradistinction to fusion is the attitude which deals with the entire problem of Jewish life as the problem of a community, which wishes to preserve the integrity of its group life. Those who hold this attitude believe that the continued conservation of those values which are worth while in Jewish life can but work for the enrichment of the character of the American Jew, and must therefore redound to the benefit of America. They contend that America will accomplish its destiny to the fullest only if it will permit complete social expression on

---

[1] Louis D. Brandeis, *Jewish Rights and the* [Jewish] *Congress*, Address, Carnegie Hall, January 24, 1916.

RECONCILIATION OF THE HERITAGES

the part of all the people which come to its shores, provided, of course, such expression is co-operative and does not militate against the common good. . . . In his political and civic life, therefore, the individual must necessarily have a single affiliation. But it is possible for one individual to know many languages, to be acquainted with many literatures, and to be imbued with the ideals of many groups. Democracy not only permits such multiple spiritual affiliations, but encourages them to the utmost.[1]

167. The ethnic groups are justified in organizing among themselves for the perpetuation of what they consider to be of significance for their heritage, providing that by so doing they do not preclude the influence of what the state considers to be of significance to its own heritage. The adjustment of the individual born within an ethnic group to the total life must rightly be made through the co-operative work of the public and the ethnic schools.[2]

This position would seem very secure only if the groups represented in immigration were specialized by heredity, so that some of them could do certain things that others could not do, or do them better—if some of them were poetical, some philosophical, some born physicists. But it is not apparent that even the most distinct races, the black, white, and yellow, are characterized in this way. The anthropologists think that if

---
[1] Alexander M. Dushkin, *Jewish Education in New York City*, pp. 4 and 386.
[2] I. B. Berkson, *Americanization: A Critical Study* (in press).

such differences exist they are not very great. Certainly the Japanese have shown that in general they can do anything that we can do, and have not shown that they can do anything that we cannot do. It is easier to explain why the Jew is in the needle trades, is not a farmer, and is intelligent, on the ground of circumstances—that he has had a given racial history—than on the ground of inborn aptitudes.

In any case, so far as European immigration is concerned, we do not have to do with races at all in the proper sense. The "races" of Europe are all mongrel, and are classified on the basis of language and custom. The Magyars, for example, came in from Asia only a thousand years ago, but they are so interbred with Germans, Ruthenians, Slovaks Rumanians, Serbians, Croatians, that it is difficult to find an example of the original Magyar type. The Prussians were not originally Germans at all, but a Baltic tribe, akin to the Lithuanians. Even the Jews are greatly intermixed with both Asiatics and Europeans. Twenty per cent of the Jews are blond.[1]

We have referred in Chapter VI to the fact that the peasant does not greatly fear death for himself, but is terrified by a pest or war,

---

[1] Details are in Franz Boas' *The Mind of Primitive Man*.

RECONCILIATION OF THE HERITAGES

where the existence of his group is threatened. Men fear extinction, not only for themselves, but for their groups. We do not wish to have our families die out; we cannot think calmly of the white race as dying out; we do not wish to have even the birds and the flowers die out. We wish only our enemies to die out. The thought of a given group being swallowed up by another group leaves the apprehension of death in the minds of its members. The dread of the death of their communities is the instinctive basis of the wish of the immigrant groups to remain separate in America. The rational and practical basis of the wish is the claim that they will in that way have more security, recognition, and efficiency.

We see no objection to an immigrant group remaining perpetually in America as immigrant group or as racial element on the basis claimed by the Jews in documents 165-167, if it is able to do so. Certainly our opposition would fan the wish to a flame, as, on the contrary, laws compelling immigrants to remain in such groups would arouse their fanatical resistance. But since we must ascribe the peculiarities of these groups to a long train of common experiences, not to inborn and ineradicable traits, there are apparently only three grounds on the basis of one or more of which an immigrant group could remain culturally separate for an indefinite time: (1) the ability to perpetuate in the new generations the traditional memories of the group without loss; (2) the ability to create values superior to those of America, and the maintenance of separation in order not to sink to the cultural level of America; or (3) an ineradicable prejudice on one or both sides.

(1) Actually, individuals and groups cling to their memories only so long as they are practically or sentimentally useful. The efficiency of the newer immigrants depends on their not forgetting, and on contact with their own past, as is illustrated in the following document, which was sent from America to Norway, and advises against certain radical changes in the Norwegian language.

168. The Norwegians in America are and intend to remain Americans. They do not consider themselves colonists in a foreign land. They regard this country as their own. They have helped to build large sections of it. Here their children are born and here they will remain. But a supply of cultural values from the old country will strengthen them individually and collectively and make them even better citizens than they already are. . . .

Norwegian-Americans will continue for many years to need cultural supply from the mother country.

RECONCILIATION OF THE HERITAGES

The need will continue until our people have become so far assimilated that they can supply their own cultural requirements from American sources. But that will take a long time, because, while the pioneers, or those who are left of them, and their descendants are thoroughly Americanized, there are still hundreds of thousands of people of the first generation who are not yet in touch with American cultural sources and therefore depend upon Norway for their supply through the medium of their own language. . . . The continued cultural connection between Norway and the Norwegian-Americans ought, in my judgment, to be built up on a solid language foundation. If the language be lost we may be absolutely sure that cultural supply from Norway will cease.[1]

We know however, that the grandchildren of Norwegian immigrants have become practically indistinguishable from other Americans and that Norway has for them, at most, only a poetic value. All immigrant groups are losing, even too completely and rapidly, their languages, which would be the chief sign and instrument of their separate identity.

(2) There are frequent cases where a people of superior culture remains indefinitely separate in a culturally inferior group. The English in India and the Saxons in Transylvania have remained separate for centuries. But no immigrant group here can claim so great a diversity of values as

[1] H. Sundby-Hansen, in a communication from America to the Norwegian newspaper *Stavangeren*, October 4, 1919.

is produced by America as a whole, and to the degree that an immigrant group is separated from American life, voluntarily or by geographical isolation, it will be pauperized in even the culture which it brings. The document last quoted expresses this fear. No existing state or nation, and certainly no nation within a nation, can create alone the values necessary to a high degree of efficiency. In a world characterized by individualization of function, values must be secured from wherever they exist in the whole world.

(3) The question of prejudice and discrimination may be put aside as not serious enough in America to affect the persistence of immigrant groups. The Jews have felt it, but in general the Jew is losing the marks of his identity as fast as possible, and to the degree that he does this the prejudice disappears. "To the degree that racial minorities are not secure in their rights" (as Justice Brandeis puts it), the separateness will continue.

The present immigrant organizations represent a separateness of the immigrant groups from America, but these organizations exist precisely because they enable the immigrants to overcome this separateness. They are signs, not of the perpetuation of immigrant

RECONCILIATION OF THE HERITAGES

groups here, but of their assimilation. We know no type of immigrant organization which is able to live without some feature related to the needs of the immigrant in America. The success of the nationalistic societies is based on such features as insurance. In addition they provide entertainment and recognition, which represent universal needs. On the other hand, American organizations for the immigrant interest him only to the degree that they understand and supply his needs as immigrant.

We have recorded the wish of the Italian editor (document 147, p. 227) that the Italians would organize as do the Jews. From his standpoint this meant a gain to be made at the expense of the Americans, for the sake of "what constitutes a gain for our race over the Anglo-Saxon race." From our standpoint, the Jewish community is serving the Jew by enabling him to identify his interests with America. Because Jewish organizations make the Jew efficient they prepare him to use all the American institutions. If you open a school for immigrants it is filled with Jews; if you open a school for immigrant women it is filled with Jewish women. Some Americans are disquieted by the persistence of immigrant organizations even in groups of long-standing in this country. But they disregard the continual intake of recruits from the old country who need the support and schooling of their fellow countrymen, and the fact that these organizations are constantly graduating their members into general American life.

Assimilation is thus as inevitable as it is desirable; it is impossible for the immigrants we receive to remain permanently in separate groups. Through point after point of contact, as they find situations in America intelligible to them in the light of old knowledge and experience, they identify themselves with us. We can delay or hasten this development. We cannot stop it. If we give the immigrants a favorable milieu, if we tolerate their strangeness during their period of adjustment, if we give them freedom to make their own connections between old and new experiences, if we help them to find points of contact, then we hasten their assimilation. This is a process of growth as against the "ordering and forbidding" policy and the demand that the assimilation of the immigrant shall be "sudden, complete, and bitter." And this is the completely democratic process, for we cannot have a political democracy unless we have a social democracy also.

INDEX

Abbott, Grace, 121
Africans, 270, 272–273
Alfono, Enrico, 254
Aliens. *See* Immigrants
Alliance of Polish Socialists, 98, 137, 233
American Amateur Athletic Association, 293
Americanization, 62, 97, 98, 99, 110, 120, 264–265, 272, 281n, 282, 288–289, 290, 293. *See also* Assimilation
Anarchy, 99–101, 281
Apperception mass, 267, 268, 269, 271, 272, 279, 280, 299
Assimilation, 264–265, 270–271, 273, 280, 281, 283, 287, 307, 308. *See also* Americanization
Association de Vigilanza e Protezione Italiana, 252
Austin, Mary, 185, 186, 191, 194

Babcock, C. H., 224
Bagger, Eugene S., 95, 107, 118
Banks, 122–124
Bassi, Father, 239
Beck, F.O., 129
Beith, Major Ian Hay, 94
Benefit societies, 124–132, 160–163, 204, 207, 211, 217
 sick benefit fund, 126–127n
Berkson, I. B., 19, 281n, 301
Bernhard, Ludwig, 227
Bingham, Comm. Theodore A., 210, 253, 256

Bismarck, Prince Otto von, 227
Black Hand. *See* Italians, Black Hand
Bloch, Louis, 6
Boas, Franz, 302
Bohemian-Slavonian Benevolent Society, 220
 founded, 220
Bohemians, 149–150, 219–221
 freethinking organizations, 219–220
 illiteracy, 219
 labor, 219
 patriotism, 273
Bójnowski, Lucyan, 217, 219
Bollettino della Sera (N.Y. city), 22, 240, 249n, 250, 251, 252, 253, 254, 255, 257, 258
Brandeis, Louis D., 235n, 300, 306
Bridges, Horace E., 94
Bulletin, El (Taos, N.M.), 189

Canaan-complex, 116–117
Canadians. *See* French Canadians
Canado-Américan, 140
Capek, Thomas, 219n
Carniolian Slovenian Catholic Union, 128
Catholic church, 9–10
Chaves, Don Amado, 190
Chetlain, Judge H. N., 245
Chicago Tribune, 11n
Chinese, 159–167
 benefit companies, 131–132, 160
 arbitration, 131

309

Chinese *(cont'd)*
  benefit companies *(cont'd)*
    collection of debts, 132
    rules, 160–163
  clans, 36–37, 160
    murder prevented, 37
  criminals, 165
  nationalism, 139
  tongs, 164–167
    blackmail, 165
    highbinders, 165
    town councils, 37–38
    trade associations, 37
  traffic in women, 14, 20, 165
Clans, 35–37. *See also* Chinese, clans
Cleef, Eugene van, 14
Cohen, Rose, 45, 50, 51, 91, 128
Communism, 99–101, 281
Cooley, C. H., 30
Cortese, Judge Roberto, 251
Crime. *See* Immigrants, crime
Criminals, 164–165, 210, 241, 248–249n, 250, 255. *See also* Italians, Black Hand
Cultura Obrera (N.Y. city), 100
Cusumano, Gaspare, 96, 104, 151

Daluca, Alessandro, 12, 47
Danes, 282–283, 286. *See also* Scandinavians
Darmstadter, Renee, 198, 200, 204
Dembinski, Rev. Franciszek, 216
Democracy, 261, 264, 271, 300, 301, 308
Diritto, Il (N.Y. city), 101
Divorce, 70–71
Duels, 20
Dushkin, Alexander M., 18, 139, 197, 301

Education, 179, 224, 272, 277, 279, 280
Ellice Archipelago, 270
Emigrants' Protective Association of Warsaw, 10n
Engelgardt, A. N., 33

Englishmen, 94
  in India, 305
Estonia
  public schools, 278
Europe
  continental cafe, 114–115
  travel, 114

Federation of Oriental Jews, 200
Fedortchouk, Y., 98
Finns
  cooperative establishments, 13–14
  in Minnesota, 13
Forward (N.Y. city), 7, 18, 44, 53, 59, 64, 65, 78, 80, 100, 103, 200, 237
French Canadians, 140–142
French language, 291
Frugone, 252, 254

Gardner, J. Endicott, 166, 167
Gastello, Giovanni, 245
Gaynor, William Jay, 200
Gazeta Polska (Chicago), 137n
Gazeta Swiateczna (Warsaw), 8
Geringer, 220
Germans
  discipline, 278
Giardina, Joseph, 239
Giller, Agaton, 137
Goebel, J., 95
Golembianski, Dr., 230
Gorzynski, Franciszek, 216
Gulick, S. L., 41

Harper, H. L., 142
Hastings, Clinton, 164
Hebrew Free School, 17–18
Heritages
  defined, 2–4
Herzl, Theodore, 139
Hirschbein, P., 205
Horn Brothers, 230, 231
Hungarians, 95, 105–106, 150
Hungary, 84

Immigrants. *See also* specific nationalities

INDEX

Immigrants *(cont'd)*
  allegiance to home country, 93, 304, 305, 306
  attitudes, 3
  burying dead, 125, 127–128
  changes, 43–45
  crime, 61, 71–72
  decision to leave home, 83
  desires, 27–29
  disillusioned, 46
  frauds, 76–80
  gambling, 27
  intellectual, 104–107, 113
  labor, 263
  organizations, 56, 120, 289, 293, 294–295, 296, 307
    nationalistic societies, 290, 307
    primary group organizations, 38–39, 66, 119, 288
  patriotism, 273
  paupers, 61
  peasants, 28
  recognition, desire for, 29, 47, 95, 125
  self-respect, 48, 52
  traditions, 28
  values, 3
India
  burning widows, 3
Indians, American, 185, 186, 195
Industrialer Arbeiter, Der (Chicago), 101
Insanity, 42, 297–298
Irish, 149
Isaacs, Meir, 203
Italian Civic League, 253
Italian Industrial School (N.Y. city), 51n
Italians, 143, 146–159. 238–258, 275–277
  benefit societies, 129
  Black Hand, 21–22, 165, 241, 243, 247–258
    blackmail, 241, 243–247
    bombs, 256–257
    murder, 247–248
  brotherhoods, 154

Italians *(cont'd)*
  Caffone, 103–104, 143
  Camorra, 241, 254
  communities, 146
  criminals, 241, 248–249n, 255. *See also* Italians, Black Hand
  detectives, 250, 254, 255, 256, 257, 258
  family loyalty, 153
  laborers, 182
  mafia, 241, 250. *See also* Italians, Black Hand
  organizations, 239, 307
    nationalistic societies, 292
    primary group, 241
  police, 252
  population, 225
  Sicilians, 123, 143, 268
    Chicago, 11
    heritages, 158–159
    moral code, 10
    murders, 10–11
    New Orleans, 95
    New York (city), 147–158
    Santa Fara festival, 151
  Sons of Italy, 132–133, 239
  talent, 51
  vendetta, 19, 241, 247, 251
  White Hand Society, 243, 244, 246, 249n
  women, 155–157
Italy, 11
  consul general, 251
  government, 255
  king, 252
  Sicily, 104, 292

Jackowski, Maximilian, 226
Japan
  government, 169
  Imperial University, 41
  sovereign, 40–41
Japanese, 167–180, 302
  camps, 170–171
  commercial relations, 176–177
  education, 179
  laborers, 171, 177–178
  marriages, 179

OLD WORLD TRAITS TRANSPLANTED

Japanese *(cont'd)*
  patriotism, 41
  organizations, 171–173, 238
  prefectoral societies, 130
  Japanese Association of America, 130, 139, 167, 169–170, 178, 179, 180
    branches, 169
    objects, 169–170
  Japanese Benevolent Society, 130
Jewish Communal Register, 210
Jewish Protective Association, 59
Jews, 143, 195–211, 234–238, 239–240, 268, 300–301, 302, 303, 306
  "allrightnick," 52, 101–102, 204
  benefit organizations, 126–127n, 204, 207
  Bureau of Industry, 236
    purpose, 236
  Bureau of Jewish Education, 236
    purpose, 236
  Chassidic sect, 198
  countries of origin, 198–200
  criminals, 210
  customs, 203–204
  "day eating" system, 4
  demoralization, 237
  expenses, 197
  fraternal orders, 129–130
  ghettos, 202–203
  Haskallah movement, 138
  Hebrew religion, 126n
  intellectual, 82
  Kehillah, 202, 210, 236
    aim, 236
    districts, 207
  labor union, 127n
  learning, devotion to, 17, 18
  New York (city), 195–197, 234, 236
  organizations, 210, 307
    expenses, 210
    primary group, 30n
  population, 195–198, 207–209, 225

Jews *(cont'd)*
  separatists, 202
  synagogues, 202, 203, 204, 205–207, 209
  Verbands, 199–200
  Vilna, 4–5
  Yiddish, 198, 283–284
    newspapers, 284
  Zionism, 138
John Worthy School, 68, 69
Johnson, Simon, 286
Jury system, 249n

Kaplan, M. M., 206, 209
Kato, H., 41
Kaupas, A., 98
Khlieb i Volva (N.Y. city), 101
Kidnapping law, 253
Kovacs, Janos, 84
Kozakiewicz, 137
Krauss, Friedrich S., 31, 32

Laborers, 171, 177–178, 181–182, 219, 263
Laukas, Menas, 146
Layard, Sir Austen Henry, 9n
Leavitt, Marie, 11, 158, 241, 248
Le Boutillier, J.G., 291
Ledbetter, E. E., 128
Lee, Rev. 285
Legal Aid Society, Chicago, 70, 230, 231, 232
Lettish organization, 294
Liebau, Reinhold, 91
Lithuanians, 98
Livingstone, David, 272–273
Lodges. *See* Benefit societies
Loomis, A. W., 132
Lummis, Charles, 186
Lutheran Herald, 284

Magyar chauvinism, 106
Magyars, 302
Margoshes, S., 200
Mayer, Julius Robert, 297
Mexicans, 180–195
  civil cases, 194
  craftsman, 187

INDEX

Mexicans *(cont'd)*
  Hermanos Penitentes, Los, 191–194
    aid, 193
    object, 192
    practices, 192–193
    ignorance, 186
    laborers, 177–178, 181
    literacy, 188–189
  New Mexico, 180–181, 184–195
    nationalism, 195
    population, 180
    schools, 186, 188
Meyer, Adolf, 298n
Miller, Herbert A., 221
Millis, H. A., 175
Millkan, 69
Misicki, Dr., 217
Murdoch, James, 176
Mutual aid societies. *See* Benefit societies

Nationalistic organizations, 132–142, 290, 292, 307
Negroes, 182
New Mexico
  Mexicans, 180–181, 184–195
  sheepherders, 42
New York (city), 46–47, 147–158, 195–197, 234, 236
New York, College of the City of, 18
Newspapers. *See also* specific newspapers
  American, 248, 250, 254
  foreign language, 21
  Italian, 248, 253, 291
Norway, 84, 285
Norwegian language, 305
Norwegians. *See* Scandinavians
Novomirsky: Manifesto of Anarchists - Communists, 100

O'Neil, R. N., 52
Opalski, Joseph, 75
Opium War, 38
Order of Francis Joseph, 95

Order of Loretto, 186
Ostrowski, Tomasz, 217
Ostwald, Wilhelm, 298

Padrone system 121
Palafox de Pina, Marie Teresa, 184
Palmieri, 254
Passaic (N.J.) Board of Freeholders, 252
Paterson (N.J.) Municipal Council, 251–252
Patriotism, 41, 273, 290
Pavlov, N. M., 41
Pecorni, Prof., 253
Peddling, 53–54
Pelissier, Jean, 98
Penal code, 249n
Petrosino, Lieut. Giuseppe, 249n, 250, 253, 254, 256
Philblad, E. F., 13
Poland, 225–227
  arson, 9
  cooperatives, 226
  Prussian defeat, 226–227
  Russian Poland, 227
Poles, 98, 99, 136, 211–219, 225–234
  charitable institutions, 228, 229
  church, 217
  cooperative organizations, 218
    assets, 218
    founded, 218
    New Britain (Conn.)
      Clothing Corporation, 218
    People's Savings Bank, 218
    Polish Army Fund, 218
    Polish Investment and Loan Corporation, 218
    Polish Loan and Industrial Corporation, 218
    Polish Relief Fund, 218
    White Eagle Factory, 218
  demoralization, 228–229, 289
  intellectual, 82, 96, 107
  mutual aid society, 211, 217
  nationalists, 97
  organizations, 213–215

OLD WORLD TRAITS TRANSPLANTED

Poles *(cont'd)*
  orphanage, 218
  parish, 211–212
  patriotism, 290
  peasants, 33–35, 135, 145, 268
  population, 212, 218, 225
  school, 217–218
  Zuaves of St. Stanislaus Kostka, 216
    organized, 216
Police, 248, 249n, 250, 252, 253, 255, 256, 258
Polish National Alliance, 133, 137, 229, 230, 232
  founded, 133
  branches, 134
Prejudice, 24, 282, 283, 289, 304, 306
Press. *See* Newspapers
Presse, La (Montreal), 140
Prussians, 302

Ravage, M. E., 48, 49
Revista, La (Taos, N.M.), 189
Rihbany, A. M., 36, 46, 54
Robbins, Emily F., 12
Robotnik (N.Y. city), 100
Rubinow, I. M., 127n
Russia
  Bielostok, 5
  Bund Central Committee, 5–6
  censorship, 108
  revolutionary movement, 6
  sovereign, 40
Russians
  attitude toward Americans, 22–24
Russkoye Slovo (N.Y. city), 24, 92
Ruthenians, 98

St. Jean de Bapiste d'Amerique, 140, 142
Sartorio, E. C., 291n
Saxons
  in Transylvania, 305
Scandinavians, 221–224. *See also* Danes; Swedish

Scandinavians *(cont'd)*
  education, 224
  Lutheran Brotherhood, 222
  National Lutheran Commission, 222
  religious literature, 221
  Synod, 222
Schiro, Antonio, 245
Skandinaven (Chicago), 284
Slavery, 263, 266
Slavs, 31–32
Slovaks, 98
Slovenian, 274
  fraternal organizations
    assets, 128
    branches, 128
    founded, 128
  Slovenian National Benefit Society, 128
  Slovenian Workingmen's Benefit Association, 128
Slums, 21, 287–288
Society
  American society, 108–109
  attitude toward foreigners, 108
  individualism, 41
  organizations, 26
  primary group, 30, 33, 41–42
Smith, Adam, 240n
Solomon Islands, 270
Speer, Robert Elliott, 38, 163
State Camp Woodmen (N.J.), 252
Stecki, Sigmund, 229, 231
Steiner, Prof., 220
Stern, E. C., 46
Stock, F., 66
Sturges, Vera L., 183, 184
Sundby-Hansen, H., 305
Sweden, 84, 86
Swedish. *See also* Scandinavians
  colony, 12–13
Swedish Emigration Commission, 86n
Syrian clan, 35–36

Thomas, William I., 9, 10, 27,

INDEX

Thomas, William I *(cont'd)*
  35, 40, 68, 71, 124, 125,
  229, 233, 289, 290
Thomsen, Fred, 286
Tribuna Italiana (Chicago), 251

Unione Siciliana (Chicago), 129
United States, Bureau of Labor
  Bulletin, 180, 181, 182
United States, Department of
  Agriculture, 283
United States, Immigration
  Commission Report, 21,
  122, 123, 124, 130, 170,
  171, 175, 177, 178
United States, Industrial Commission Report, 14, 132,
  164, 166, 167

Vaccarezza, Lt., 253, 254, 255

Waldo, Comm., 254
Wawrzyniak, 226
Wermert, G., 10
Westermarck, Edward, 20
Wiech, Frank, 49
Wilson, Woodrow, 180n
Wolfson, Leo, 130

Yamagata, Isoh, 176
Y.W.C.A. Southwestern Field
  Committee, 184

Zadi, Imaum Ali, 9
Zaleski, 99
Zedalicia, Joseph, 200
Znaniecki, Florian, 9, 10, 27,
  35, 40, 68, 71, 96, 99,
  124, 125, 138, 212, 219n,
  229, 233, 289, 290
Zunser, Eliakum, 5

PATTERSON SMITH REPRINT SERIES IN
CRIMINOLOGY, LAW ENFORCEMENT, AND SOCIAL PROBLEMS

1. Lewis: *The Development of American Prisons and Prison Customs, 1776-1845*
2. Carpenter: *Reformatory Prison Discipline*
3. Brace: *The Dangerous Classes of New York*
4. Dix: *Remarks on Prisons and Prison Discipline in the United States*
5. Bruce et al: *The Workings of the Indeterminate-Sentence Law and the Parole System in Illinois*
6. Wickersham Commission: *Complete Reports, Including the Mooney-Billings Report*. 14 Vols.
7. Livingston: *Complete Works on Criminal Jurisprudence*. 2 Vols.
8. Cleveland Foundation: *Criminal Justice in Cleveland*
9. Illinois Association for Criminal Justice: *The Illinois Crime Survey*
10. Missouri Association for Criminal Justice: *The Missouri Crime Survey*
11. Aschaffenburg: *Crime and Its Repression*
12. Garofalo: *Criminology*
13. Gross: *Criminal Psychology*
14. Lombroso: *Crime, Its Causes and Remedies*
15. Saleilles: *The Individualization of Punishment*
16. Tarde: *Penal Philosophy*
17. McKelvey: *American Prisons*
18. Sanders: *Negro Child Welfare in North Carolina*
19. Pike: *A History of Crime in England*. 2 Vols.
20. Herring: *Welfare Work in Mill Villages*
21. Barnes: *The Evolution of Penology in Pennsylvania*
22. Puckett: *Folk Beliefs of the Southern Negro*
23. Fernald et al: *A Study of Women Delinquents in New York State*
24. Wines: *The State of the Prisons and of Child-Saving Institutions*
25. Raper: *The Tragedy of Lynching*
26. Thomas: *The Unadjusted Girl*
27. Jorns: *The Quakers as Pioneers in Social Work*
28. Owings: *Women Police*
29. Woolston: *Prostitution in the United States*
30. Flexner: *Prostitution in Europe*
31. Kelso: *The History of Public Poor Relief in Massachusetts: 1820-1920*
32. Spivak: *Georgia Nigger*
33. Earle: *Curious Punishments of Bygone Days*
34. Bonger: *Race and Crime*
35. Fishman: *Crucibles of Crime*
36. Brearley: *Homicide in the United States*
37. Graper: *American Police Administration*
38. Hichborn: *"The System"*
39. Steiner & Brown: *The North Carolina Chain Gang*
40. Cherrington: *The Evolution of Prohibition in the United States of America*
41. Colquhoun: *A Treatise on the Commerce and Police of the River Thames*
42. Colquhoun: *A Treatise on the Police of the Metropolis*
43. Abrahamsen: *Crime and the Human Mind*
44. Schneider: *The History of Public Welfare in New York State: 1609-1866*
45. Schneider & Deutsch: *The History of Public Welfare in New York State: 1867-1940*
46. Crapsey: *The Nether Side of New York*
47. Young: *Social Treatment in Probation and Delinquency*
48. Quinn: *Gambling and Gambling Devices*
49. McCord & McCord: *Origins of Crime*
50. Worthington & Topping: *Specialized Courts Dealing with Sex Delinquency*

PATTERSON SMITH REPRINT SERIES IN
CRIMINOLOGY, LAW ENFORCEMENT, AND SOCIAL PROBLEMS

51. Asbury: *Sucker's Progress*
52. Kneeland: *Commercialized Prostitution in New York City*
53. Fosdick: *American Police Systems*
54. Fosdick: *European Police Systems*
55. Shay: *Judge Lynch: His First Hundred Years*
56. Barnes: *The Repression of Crime*
57. Cable: *The Silent South*
58. Kammerer: *The Unmarried Mother*
59. Doshay: *The Boy Sex Offender and His Later Career*
60. Spaulding: *An Experimental Study of Psychopathic Delinquent Women*
61. Brockway: *Fifty Years of Prison Service*
62. Lawes: *Man's Judgment of Death*
63. Healy & Healy: *Pathological Lying, Accusation, and Swindling*
64. Smith: *The State Police*
65. Adams: *Interracial Marriage in Hawaii*
66. Halpern: *A Decade of Probation*
67. Tappan: *Delinquent Girls in Court*
68. Alexander & Healy: *Roots of Crime*
69. Healy & Bronner: *Delinquents and Criminals*
70. Cutler: *Lynch-Law*
71. Gillin: *Taming the Criminal*
72. Osborne: *Within Prison Walls*
73. Ashton: *The History of Gambling in England*
74. Whitlock: *On the Enforcement of Law in Cities*
75. Goldberg: *Child Offenders*
76. Cressey: *The Taxi-Dance Hall*
77. Riis: *The Battle with the Slum*
78. Larson et al: *Lying and Its Detection*
79. Comstock: *Frauds Exposed*
80. Carpenter: *Our Convicts*. 2 Vols. in 1
81. Horn: *Invisible Empire: The Story of the Ku Klux Klan, 1866-1871*
82. Faris et al: *Intelligent Philanthropy*
83. Robinson: *History and Organization of Criminal Statistics in the United States*
84. Reckless: *Vice in Chicago*
85. Healy: *The Individual Delinquent*
86. Bogen: *Jewish Philanthropy*
87. Clinard: *The Black Market: A Study of White Collar Crime*
88. Healy: *Mental Conflicts and Misconduct*
89. Citizens' Police Committee: *Chicago Police Problems*
90. Clay: *The Prison Chaplain*
91. Peirce: *A Half Century with Juvenile Delinquents*
92. Richmond: *Friendly Visiting Among the Poor*
93. Brasol: *Elements of Crime*
94. Strong: *Public Welfare Administration in Canada*
95. Beard: *Juvenile Probation*
96. Steinmetz: *The Gaming Table*. 2 Vols.
97. Crawford: *Report on the Penitentiaries of the United States*
98. Kuhlman: *A Guide to Material on Crime and Criminal Justice*
99. Culver: *Bibliography of Crime and Criminal Justice: 1927-1931*
100. Culver: *Bibliography of Crime and Criminal Justice: 1932-1937*

PATTERSON SMITH REPRINT SERIES IN
CRIMINOLOGY, LAW ENFORCEMENT, AND SOCIAL PROBLEMS

101. Tompkins: *Administration of Criminal Justice, 1938-1948*
102. Tompkins: *Administration of Criminal Justice, 1949-1956*
103. Cumming: *Bibliography Dealing with Crime and Cognate Subjects*
104. Addams et al: *Philanthropy and Social Progress*
105. Powell: *The American Siberia*
106. Carpenter: *Reformatory Schools*
107. Carpenter: *Juvenile Delinquents*
108. Montague: *Sixty Years in Waifdom*
109. Mannheim: *Juvenile Delinquency in an English Middletown*
110. Semmes: *Crime and Punishment in Early Maryland*
111. National Conference of Charities and Correction: *History of Child Saving in the United States*
112. Barnes: *The Story of Punishment.* 2d ed.
113. Phillipson: *Three Criminal Law Reformers*
114. Drähms: *The Criminal*
115. Terry & Pellens: *The Opium Problem*
116. Ewing: *The Morality of Punishment*
117. Mannheim: *Group Problems in Crime and Punishment*
118. Michael & Adler: *Crime, Law and Social Science*
119. Lee: *A History of Police in England*
120. Schafer: *Compensation and Restitution to Victims of Crime.* 2d ed.
121. Mannheim: *Pioneers in Criminology.* 2d ed.
122. Goebel & Naughton: *Law Enforcement in Colonial New York*
123. Savage: *Police Records and Recollections*
124. Ives: *A History of Penal Methods*
125. Bernard (Ed.): *The Americanization Studies*
    Thompson: *The Schooling of the Immigrant*
    Daniels: *America via the Neighborhood*
    Thomas et al: *Old World Traits Transplanted*
    Speek: *A Stake in the Land*
    Davis: *Immigrant Health and the Community*
    Breckinridge: *New Homes for Old*
    Park: *The Immigrant Press and Its Control*
    Gavit: *Americans by Choice*
    Claghorn: *The Immigrant's Day in Court*
    Leiserson: *Adjusting Immigrant and Industry*
126. Dai: *Opium Addiction in Chicago*
127. Costello: *Our Police Protectors*
128. Wade: *A Treatise on the Police and Crimes of the Metropolis*
129. Robison: *Can Delinquency Be Measured?*
130. Augustus: *A Report of the Labors of John Augustus*
131. Vollmer: *The Police and Modern Society*
132. Jessel: *A Bibliography of Works in English on Playing Cards and Gaming.* Enlarged
133. Walling: *Recollections of a New York Chief of Police*
134. Lombroso: *Criminal Man*
135. Howard: *Prisons and Lazarettos.* 2 vols.
136. Fitzgerald: *Chronicles of Bow Street Police-Office.* 2 vols. in 1
137. Goring: *The English Convict*
138. Ribton-Turner: *A History of Vagrants and Vagrancy*
139. Smith: *Justice and the Poor*
140. Willard: *Tramping with Tramps*